Truth in the Late Foucault

Bloomsbury Studies in Classical Reception

Bloomsbury Studies in Classical Reception presents scholarly monographs offering new and innovative research and debate to students and scholars in the reception of Classical Studies. Each volume will explore the appropriation, reconceptualization, and recontextualization of various aspects of the Greco-Roman world and its culture, looking at the impact of the ancient world on modernity. Research will also cover reception within antiquity, the theory and practice of translation, and reception theory.

Also available in the series

Alexander the Great in the Early Christian Tradition: Classical Reception and Patristic Literature, Christian Thrue Djurslev

Ancient Magic and the Supernatural in the Modern Visual and Performing Arts, edited by Filippo Carlà and Irene Berti

Ancient Greek Myth in World Fiction since 1989, edited by Justine McConnell and Edith Hall

Anne Carson/Antiquity, edited by Laura Jansen

Antipodean Antiquities, edited by Marguerite Johnson

Classical Antiquity and Medieval Ireland: An Anthology of Medieval Irish Texts and Interpretations, edited by Michael James Clark, Erich Poppe and Isabelle Torrance

Classics in Extremis, edited by Edmund Richardson

Faulkner's Reception of Apuleius' The Golden Ass in The Reivers, Vernon L. Provencal

Frankenstein and Its Classics, edited by Jesse Weiner, Benjamin Eldon Stevens and Brett M. Rogers

Gender, Creation Myths and their Reception in Western Civilization: Prometheus, Pandora, Adam and Eve, edited by Lisa Maurice and Tovi Bibring

Greek and Roman Classics in the British Struggle for Social Reform, edited by Henry Stead and Edith Hall

Greeks and Romans on the Latin American Stage, edited by Rosa Andújar and Konstantinos P. Nikoloutsos

Homer's Iliad and the Trojan War: Dialogues on Tradition, Jan Haywood and Naoíse Mac Sweeney

Imagining Xerxes, Emma Bridges

Julius Caesar's Self-Created Image and Its Dramatic Afterlife, Miryana Dimitrova
Kinaesthesia and Classical Antiquity 1750–1820: Moved by Stone, Helen Slaney
Once and Future Antiquities in Science Fiction and Fantasy,
edited by Brett M. Rogers and Benjamin Eldon Stevens
Ovid's Myth of Pygmalion on Screen, Paula James
Performing Gods in Classical Antiquity and the Age of Shakespeare,
Dustin W. Dixon and John S. Garrison
Reading Poetry, Writing Genre, edited by Silvio Bär and Emily Hauser
Sex, Symbolists and the Greek Body, Richard Warren
The Classics in Modernist Translation, edited by Miranda Hickman
and Lynn Kozak
The Classics in South America: Five Case Studies, Germán Campos Muñoz
The Codex Fori Mussolini, Han Lamers and Bettina Reitz-Joosse
The Gentle, Jealous God, Simon Perris
*The Thucydidean Turn: (Re)Interpreting Thucydides' Political Thought Before,
During and After the Great War*, Benjamin Earley
Translations of Greek Tragedy in the Work of Ezra Pound, Peter Liebregts
Victorian Classical Burlesques, Laura Monrós-Gaspar
Victorian Epic Burlesques, Rachel Bryant Davies
Virgil's Map: Geography, Empire, and the Georgics, Charlie Kerrigan

Truth in the Late Foucault

Antiquity, Sexuality, and Psychoanalysis

Edited by Paul Allen Miller

BLOOMSBURY ACADEMIC
LONDON • NEW YORK • OXFORD • NEW DELHI • SYDNEY

BLOOMSBURY ACADEMIC
Bloomsbury Publishing Plc, 50 Bedford Square, London, WC1B 3DP, UK
Bloomsbury Publishing Inc, 1359 Broadway, 12th Floor, New York, NY 10018, USA
Bloomsbury Publishing Ireland, 29 Earlsfort Terrace, Dublin 2, D02 AY28, Ireland

BLOOMSBURY, BLOOMSBURY ACADEMIC and the Diana logo
are trademarks of Bloomsbury Publishing Plc

First published in Great Britain 2024
This paperback edition published 2026

Copyright © Paul Allen Miller, 2024

Paul Allen Miller and Contributors have asserted their right under the Copyright, Designs and Patents Act, 1988, to be identified as Authors of this work.

For legal purposes the Acknowledgments on p. xiv constitute an extension of this copyright page.

Cover design: Terry Woodley
Cover image: Pan fleeing having detected the bisexual nature of Hermaphrodite. Pompeian wall painting. Pompeii VI, 9, 6, house of the Dioskuroi, atrium (37). Napoli, Museo Archeologico Nazionale 27700

All rights reserved. No part of this publication may be: i) reproduced or transmitted in any form, electronic or mechanical, including photocopying, recording or by means of any information storage or retrieval system without prior permission in writing from the publishers; or ii) used or reproduced in any way for the training, development or operation of artificial intelligence (AI) technologies, including generative AI technologies. The rights holders expressly reserve this publication from the text and data mining exception as per Article 4(3) of the Digital Single Market Directive (EU) 2019/790.

Bloomsbury Publishing Inc does not have any control over, or responsibility for, any third-party websites referred to or in this book. All internet addresses given in this book were correct at the time of going to press. The author and publisher regret any inconvenience caused if addresses have changed or sites have ceased to exist, but can accept no responsibility for any such changes.

A catalogue record for this book is available from the British Library.

Library of Congress Cataloging-in-Publication Data
Names: Miller, Paul Allen, 1959– editor.
Title: Truth in the late Foucault: antiquity, sexuality and psychoanalysis / edited by Paul Allen Miller.
Description: London; New York, NY: Bloomsbury Academic, 2024. | Series: Bloomsbury studies in classical reception | Includes bibliographical references and index.
Identifiers: LCCN 2023054080 (print) | LCCN 2023054081 (ebook) | ISBN 9781350357266 (hardback) | ISBN 9781350357303 (paperback) | ISBN 9781350357273 (pdf) | ISBN 9781350357280 (ebook)
Subjects: LCSH: Foucault, Michel, 1926-1984–Criticism and interpretation. | Philosophy, French–20th century. | Truth (Aesthetics)
Classification: LCC B2430.F724 A68 2024 (print) | LCC B2430.F724 (ebook) | DDC 194—dc23/eng/20240208
LC record available at https://lccn.loc.gov/2023054080
LC ebook record available at https://lccn.loc.gov/2023054081

ISBN: HB: 978-1-3503-5726-6
PB: 978-1-3503-5730-3
ePDF: 978-1-3503-5727-3
eBook: 978-1-3503-5728-0

Typeset by RefineCatch Limited, Bungay, Suffolk

For product safety related questions contact productsafety@bloomsbury.com.

To find out more about our authors and books visit www.bloomsbury.com and sign up for our newsletters.

For those who love the truth, in all its many forms.

Contents

List of Illustrations		x
List of Contributors		xi
Acknowledgments		xiv
	Introduction: Truth, Dreams, and Psychoanalysis in the Late Foucault *Paul Allen Miller*	1
1	On Dreams, Truth, and the Aesthetics of Existence *Edward McGushin*	11
2	Foucault in the Cave with Gadamer: On Truth, Understanding, and Experience *Arash Shokrisaravi*	29
3	Nothing to Do with the Truth? New Reflections on Foucault's Reading of Artemidorus *Sandra Boehringer*	49
4	To Dream the Impossible Dream: *Parrhēsia* and Rhetoric (*De Oratore* 3) *Paul Allen Miller*	67
5	From True-Confessions to True-Discourse in Late Foucault *Niki Kasumi Clements*	85
6	Confessing in Communities: The Genealogical Exclusion of Joy from Late Antique Christianity *Alex Dressler*	103
7	Artemidorus as Symptom: Freud and Foucault *Richard H. Armstrong*	121
8	The Desiring Subject Seeks Pleasure in History: Li Yinhe's Sadomasochistic Fictions and the Cultural Revolution *Leihua Weng*	141
9	Foucault's Herculine Barbin: A Step in the Genealogy of Psychoanalysis *Laurie Laufer*	157
10	The Foucault Effect: Queer Theory and Its Discontents *David Greven*	171
Notes		193
References		208
Index		226

Illustrations

The facsimiles are reproduced with the kind authorization of Henri-Paul Fruchaud.

Figure 3.1	*Tu connais déjà (cependant, le bas de la page 52 t'amusera peut-être). Amicalement, Veyne.* "You already know about this! but maybe you'll enjoy the bottom of page 52. Warmly, Veyne." From an off-print of "La famille et l'amour sous le Haut-Empire romain" (1978), with a manuscript inscription from Paul Veyne to Michel Foucault. BNF, Fonds Foucault, NAF 28730, Box 28, f. 843	55
Figure 3.2 A and 2 B	Annotated photocopies from the 1963 Roger Pack edition of the Greek text of Artemidorus' *Interpretation of Dreams*. BNF, Fonds Foucault, NAF 28730, Box 28 "Ultimes papiers 'sur le bureau," Folder 5, ff. 727–728	63

Contributors

Richard H. Armstrong teaches at the University of Houston. His research focuses on classical reception in early psychoanalysis and translation studies. He is author of *A Compulsion for Antiquity: Freud and the Ancient World* (2005), co-editor with Alexandra Lianeri of *A Companion to the Translation of Classical Epic* (forthcoming 2024) and *Classical Translation Studies: Transfigurations in Reception and Cultural History* (forthcoming 2025), and with Paul Allen Miller, Daniel Orrells, and Vanda Zajko of *The Bloomsbury Handbook to Psychoanalysis and Classical Reception* (forthcoming 2025). He was co-curator of the recent exhibition at the Freud Museum London, *Freud's Antiquity: Object, Idea, Desire*.

Sandra Boehringer is Associate Professor of Greek History at the University of Strasbourg. Her work focuses on questions of gender and sexuality in classical antiquity and Foucault's influence on our understanding of ancient worlds. She is the author of *Female Homosexuality in Ancient Greece and Rome* (2021). Boehringer has edited *Après Les Aveux de la chair: Généalogie du sujet chez Michel Foucault* (2020) with Laurie Laufer and *Foucault, la sexualité, l'Antiquité* (2020) with Daniele Lorenzini. For several years she ran a seminar at the EHESS (Paris, Centre Gernet) with Claude Calame, on how anthropological comparison with distant societies enables us to perceive the processes at play and to rethink today's world.

Niki Kasumi Clements is Watt J. and Lilly G. Jackson Associate Professor of Religion and courtesy faculty in the Department of Philosophy, at Rice University. Clements specializes in Foucault's work on Christianity and ethics in the *History of Sexuality* series. She is currently writing two books based on Foucault's extensive archives: *Foucault's Histories of Sexuality* and *Foucault the Confessor*. The author of *Sites of the Ascetic Self: John Cassian and Christian Ethical Formation* (2020), Clements is also the co-editor with James Faubion and Daniel Wyche of *Foucault's Confessions* (under contract).

Alex Dressler, Professor of Classics at the University of Wisconsin-Madison, studies the Greek and Roman Classics as an evolving canon of texts and methods rooted in Euro-American traditions but aimed at redefining the modern reader's practical sense of art and life, past and present, and politics and personal flourishing. Dressler's current book project, *Marx's Plautus: Knowledge, Labor, and Feeling in Pre-Capitalist Cultural Production*, extends to pre-Classical/pre-modern cultures the analysis of poverty and aesthetics first developed for Late Antique/post-Classical culture in his introduction, translation, and commentary, *Selections from the Poems of Paulinus of Nola, including the Correspondence with Ausonius* (2023).

David Greven is Professor of English at the University of South Carolina and publishes in the fields of nineteenth-century American literature and film studies. His books include *All the Devils Are Here: American Romanticism and Literary Influence* (2024) and *Intimate Violence: Hitchcock, Sex, and Queer Theory* (2017).

Laurie Laufer is a psychoanalyst and Professor in the Psychoanalytic Studies Department of the Institut des Humanités, Sciences et Sociétés (IHSS) at Université Paris Cité, where she is also Director of the UFR IHSS. Author of numerous articles on questions of norms, psychoanalysis and gender, and psychoanalysis and literature, she has co-edited *Foucault et la psychanalyse* (2015) with Amos Squverer and *Après Les Aveux de la chair: Généalogie du sujet chez Michel Foucault* (2020) with Sandra Boehringer. Laufer is the author of *Murmures de l'art à la psychanalyse* (2021), *Vers une psychanalyse émancipée: Renouer avec la subversion* (2022) and *Questions de genre* (2022) with Serge Hefez.

Edward McGushin is Professor of Philosophy and Director of the Moreau Honors Program at Stonehill College in Easton, MA. He is the author of *Foucault's Askésis: An Introduction to the Philosophical Life* (2007). He has edited and co-edited several volumes and written articles and book chapters on topics in contemporary Continental philosophy. He is Coordinator of the Foucault Circle and an Affiliate Scholar Member of the Boston Psychoanalytic Society and Institute.

Paul Allen Miller is Carolina Distinguished Professor of Classics and Comparative Literature at the University of South Carolina and Distinguished Guest Professor of English at Ewha Womans University. He has held visiting appointments in Bochum, Paris, and Beijing. He is the author of ten books, has edited fifteen volumes, and published over 100 articles on theory, poetry, and philosophy. His latest book is *Foucault's Seminars on Antiquity: Learning to Speak the Truth*. He is at work on a book entitled *Truth and Enjoyment in Cicero: Rhetoric and Philosophy Beyond the Pleasure Principle*, which reflects on Cicero in the post-truth age.

Arash Shokrisaravi is a PhD student of Comparative Literature at Cornell University. He works on theory and the history of metaphysics. His research interests also include ancient Greek philosophy and literature, Iranian studies, and gender studies.

Dr. Leihua Weng teaches as the Chinese Endowed Assistant Professor of Chinese Language and Literature in the East Asian Studies Department at Kalamazoo College. Her publications encompass hermeneutics, authorship, and gender studies. Dr. Weng earned her PhD in Comparative Literature from the University of South Carolina, an MA in English Language and Literature from Peking University, and a BA from Zhejiang University.

Acknowledgments

Many of these papers were first given at the twenty-fourth annual University of South Carolina Comparative Literature Conference in 2022. I would like first to thank my fellow organizers, Jie Guo and Alexander Beecroft, as well as all the many presenters from across the globe. This was originally to be an in-person conference, but due to the last gasps of the Covid 19 pandemic it became a virtual conference. In addition, I need to thank the Office of Research at the University of South Carolina, the College of Arts and Sciences, the Program in Comparative Literature, the Women's and Gender Studies Program, the Department of Anthropology, the Department English Literature and Culture, the Department of Languages, Literatures and Cultures, and the Department of Philosophy for their sponsorship and support. Lastly, none of this could have happened without the support of our graduate assistants, Dan Luo, Grace Alger, and Caroline Driscol.

INTRODUCTION

Truth, Dreams, and Psychoanalysis in the Late Foucault

Paul Allen Miller
University of South Carolina and Ewha Womans University

One often hears that we live in a "post-truth culture." Alternative facts, disinformation, fake news, social media bots, and the rise of conspiracy theories have led many to despair of the continued saliency of scientific, historical, or philosophical truth in public discourse. While few doubt the contributions of electoral politics, concentrated media ownership, transnational capital, or the rise of authoritarian and populist nationalism to the current epistemic crisis, analysts also point to another culprit: postmodern French thought (Wight 2018). A Google search for post-truth and postmodernism received "about 2,960,000 results" as of this writing (April 13, 2023). Indeed, the causal relationship between the two is widely assumed, and while Michel Foucault would probably have objected to being categorized as a postmodernist, for many his work is "exhibit A" (Lorenzini 2023: 1–2).

Typical of this intellectual laxity is a 2016 post in *The Conversation*, whose masthead promises, "Academic Rigor, Journalistic Flair." The title of the article by Andrew Calcutt, a lecturer in "Journalism, Humanities, and Creative Industries" at the University of East London, says it all, "The Surprising Origins of 'Post-Truth'—and How It Was Spawned by the Liberal Left." Calcutt's piece does not directly name Foucault. He focuses instead on Lyotard's *Postmodern Condition*. Sean Iling, a former political theorist who wrote a dissertation on Camus, however, makes the anti-Foucauldian subtext explicit. His 2019 article for *Vox* features an opening photo montage that frames symmetrical pictures of Foucault and Derrida within a triangular frame of Donald Trump photos. Pushback has begun in some quarters, with a recent article on the site *EUvsDisinfo*, which is devoted to challenging disinformation coming from Russia, posing the question, "Foucault, Did He Blaze the Trail for the Post-Truth Era?" (2021). There can be little doubt that the question of truth in the late Foucault is not just of interest to scholars of French philosophy but is central to the political and ethical debates roiling politics and culture in the contemporary world. We need, however, to move beyond sweeping generalizations and caricature if we wish to come to a useful understanding of what truth is, Foucault's understanding of it, and how this understanding illuminates his late work. In what follows, I will survey at a high level three specific topics Foucault engages—truth, the dream, and psychoanalysis—before offering a brief overview of the essays in this volume, which engage these topics in more depth. As we will see, these three topics are not only important, but they are also profoundly interrelated.

Recently, at the urging of Niki Clements, one the contributors to this volume, I had the good fortune to spend ten days in the Fonds Michel Foucault at the Bibliothèque nationale de France examining notes, sketches, and drafts for a book that Foucault did not live to publish, *The Government of the Self and Others*. The manuscript was primarily occupied with questions in ancient philosophy of how one forms and cares for oneself in order to be able to exercise power over oneself and others in both the polity and household. It occupied what we might term the intersection of ethics and politics. No serious person who read the multiple drafts, the numerous corrections, the vast quantity of primary sources Foucault consulted, both those explicitly cited in the drafts and those merely in his notes, could conflate the care and rigor with which Foucault pursued his object with Donald Trump's alternative facts, the fantasies of the QANON possessed, or state sponsored disinformation, be it on Covid 19, climate denial, or the deep state. It is certainly possible to disagree with Foucault on many things or to fault his research methods, but the claim that he did not care about or was cavalier with the truth is not supported by the evidence. Whence came these calumnies?

Foucault's thoughts about truth are complex and sophisticated. They cannot simply be briefly summed up in a short introduction. But there are two passages from the late lectures that can stand as indicia of what is at stake in Foucauldian truth. They make clear that neither does he claim the truth does not exist, nor can it simply be whatever anyone says it is, but he also rejects the naive view that there is a world to which one can simply point where the facts speak for themselves, and that the truth is waiting to be discovered, like some hidden Platonic essence (Lorenzini 2023: 3). Truth, for Foucault, is both infinitely more powerful and infinitely more complex. Truth is a human project; it is not the secret of the world.

The first passage comes from a lecture Foucault gave at the Collège de France, March 18, 1981. During a discussion of marriage practices among the Roman elite and the discourse surrounding them, he says, "[We should wonder] about the fact that in addition to things, there are discourses; [we should pose] this problem: why, in addition to reality, is there truth?" (Foucault 2017a: 237). This question is simple to the point of innocence and yet devastating in its implications: for, we are accustomed to conflating truth with reality. "The true is the real." But philosophically we know that this cannot be the case. Truth is a property of discourse. Only statements are true or false not things in themselves—we speak of a "true" or "false" rock or table or cloud in only the most metaphorical sense. Thus, our discourses and the things that serve as their referents are logically never identical (cf. Lorenzini 2023: 6). This is not a denial of science. Indeed, the truth is only *discoverable*, as opposed to being ever present, to the extent that our statements and their referents are not identical. Thus, Foucault states very clearly that truth *is* a construction, one subject always to forms of qualification and verification, but a thing that comes into existence through human action and so can pass out of existence or be superseded. He says this not in a perverse attempt to claim all statements are equally true, nor that all truths are purely relative, but in the recognition of an ontological reality that has been acknowledged at least since Cicero: *res* and *verba* are not one.

Yet if this is the case, then what lies at the "root of the truth"? What "is the truth of the truth" (Foucault 2017a: 48)? Can we imagine a purified truth? A transparent truth with no alien admixture of mechanism, institution, or interest, a truth in itself, a truth devoid of, beyond appearance? Or is there always a foreign element at its heart, an unassimilable remainder? For insofar as the perceiving subject remains at the center of truth, the question that preoccupied Descartes, and later Foucault and Derrida remains, "Could I be dreaming?" What appears before me, or is staged before me, may not be there or may refer to something radically other, a literal untruth. "At the root of truth there is something other than truth itself" (Foucault 2017a: 48). This foreign object, this moment of illusion or opacity, must have its own truth produced, which in turn must be interpreted if the truth of the truth is to be true. What is the truth of the dreaming subject?

Foucault poses these questions during his discussion of Artemidorus, Freud, and Descartes at the beginning of the same 1980/1 course, appropriately entitled *Subjectivity and Truth*. Each of these topics will be discussed from a variety of angles in this book. Edward McGushin directly engages Foucault's interest in dreams from his earliest work on Binswanger until the final Foucault. Sandra Boehringer examines more closely his reading of Artemidorus' *Oneirocriticon* in the context of the *History of Sexuality*, where it opens the beginning of Volume 3. Richard Armstrong compares Freud's Artemidorus in turn with Foucault's by way of Binswanger. Likewise, Arash Shokrisaravi asks us to consider more profoundly the "appearance" of truth in Plato's "Myth of the Cave" and the relation of this truth to Gadamer's *Erlebnis*, often translated "experience," but more literally and more profoundly "living with." What is the truth of living with the things of this world, including our dreams; what is the truth of the subject?

If the truth is something that is both constructed in discourse and something that appears to someone, who is the subject of veridiction, and if that subject might indeed be "dreaming," or put another way, if the veridical subject might be subjected to a variety of institutional, bodily, and rhetorical forces that determine what appears to them and how it appears to them, with the dream as the most extreme version of these determinations—as in Descartes's *First Meditation*—then the truth of the truth may ultimately only be accessible through the interpretation of illusions, parapraxes, and dreams, that is to say through a kind of rhetoric we term psychoanalysis.

> And then you find again [this theme of the relationship between] subjectivity-truth and dream with Freud, when the question raised was: how can one know the truth of the subject, what is the situation of the truth of the subject, and might it not be that the subject's most secret truth is expressed through what is most manifestly illusory in the subject.
>
> (Foucault 2017a: 48–9)

Now Foucault is not a Freudian, and he has a critique of psychoanalysis as it was commonly practiced. He scoffs at the notion that by speaking the truth of our unconscious we would somehow be miraculously liberated from the power of our sexual secrets. But the later Freud does as well, as does Lacan. Foucault's position was never a simple rejection of the Freudian tradition, even if some in the psychoanalytic and the Foucauldian community have received it as such, what he did ask was precisely, "what was the truth of the psychoanalytic subject?" What were its conditions of possibility? What is the unthought in its history that make psychoanalysis and the larger therapeutic enterprise possible, for they are not simply givens? They have a history, and, like all institutions of knowledge and practice, they have power. What is the truth of their truth?

Nonetheless, Freud's fundamental question of why Oedipus has continued to speak to us for over two thousand years—why has this tale of incest, murder, and unknowing constituted an undying topic of fascination—continues to resonate.

Foucault himself lectured on the *Oedipus Tyrannus* multiple times between 1971 and 1981. But equally pertinent for Foucault is the fact that there was no psychoanalysis for Oedipus or for Sophocles, for Hamlet or for Shakespeare. The analytic situation and the analytic subject are specific historical constructions, which require their own truth to be produced, their own genealogy to be given, and hence their own opacities, distortions, and imbrications with power to be revealed. To deny this is to deny perhaps the most basic lesson of Freud at all: "the subject's most secret truth" might well be "expressed through what is most manifestly illusory." The current volume is unique, then, in that it will not so much take sides in a tired and often fruitless debate between Foucault and Freud, but rather it will stage their encounter through the fabric of the dream, its rhetoric, its truth, and our own.

We begin with an overview of Foucault's views on truth, dreams, and the possibility of thinking differently, in McGushin's "On Dreams, Truth, and the Aesthetics of Existence." McGushin argues that the problem of dreams in Foucault is more central to the philosopher's core concerns than has been realized. Indeed, McGushin shows that there is a clear continuity from Foucault's earliest published work, his introduction to the Heideggerian psychoanalyst, Ludwig Binswanger's book on the interpretation of dreams, to his final work on the problem of truth and the subject. McGushin opens our argument, by showing that the theme of an essential relation between truth, ethics, and dreaming runs throughout Foucault's work from the *History of Madness* to the genealogy of neoliberalism, to Artemidorus and oneirocriticism in *Subjectivity and Truth*. The dream, on this reading, becomes a site of resistance, an alternative scene from that produced by hegemonic structures of discourse and power.

Arash Shokrisaravi continues our interrogation of the sites of truth by probing Foucault's relation to Heidegger, Gadamer, and the hermeneutic tradition, in "Foucault in the Cave with Gadamer: On Truth, Understanding, and Experience." The question of truth is central to Plato's reading of the cave, but what kind of truth is it and is there only one? The Myth of the Cave is crucial to Heidegger's understanding of the transformation of *alētheia* from the Presocratics to the dawn of Platonism and metaphysics. The importance of Heidegger for Foucault is, of course, well known. Shokrisaravi investigates Heidegger's understanding of the cave, compares this understanding to Foucault's concept of truth, and then explores their relation to *Erlebnis* or "experience" as derived from Gadamer. The central questions this chapter poses are: can the genealogist have access to a truth beyond shadows and does allegory as a device provide the possibility of a hermeneutic encounter with the occupants of the cave and its own externality? Moreover, where then does the genealogist sit and what is his experience?

The late Foucault is, of course, best known for the *History of Sexuality*, and within that for his contention that in the west the subject is constituted in its relation between itself and the games of truth operative within the culture at the time. In the modern world, this truth is most intimately determined by what he terms a *scientia sexualis*, a form of knowledge that tells us who we are by soliciting from us the confession of our sexual identities. Sandra Boehringer in "Nothing to Do with the Truth? New Reflections on Foucault's Reading of Artemidorus" asks what is the status of Artemidorus' *Oneirocriticon*, an ancient manual on dream interpretation? Artemidorus' understanding of the message the dream sends to the subject is fundamentally different from that of psychoanalysis: far from harboring a sexual secret, the truth of dreams for Artemidorus is to be found in their relation to everyday acts that are either in conformity with custom, not in conformity with custom, or unintelligible and hence not natural. Intellectual exchanges between Foucault and Paul Veyne, the posthumous publication of *Aveux de la Chair*, and newly available archives at the Bibliothèque nationale de France enable us to better understand the path Foucault's thinking took: Boehringer shows that while studying a document from the culture of the *aphrodisia* ("pleasures"), his interpretation was nonetheless marked by the Christian problematic of postulating a truth of the subject both in sex and in dreams.

In chapter four, Paul Allen Miller turns to the vexed problem of truth and rhetoric in "To Dream the Impossible Dream: *Parrhēsia* and Rhetoric (*De Oratore* 3)." In the *Government of the Self and Others* (2010), Foucault makes a strict distinction between *parrhēsia* and rhetoric. Returning to the classic text in which philosophy and rhetoric are first distinguished, Plato's *Gorgias*, he places philosophy on the side of truth and *parrhēsia* on the side of philosophy. If the practice of philosophy is focused on determining what is the truth, as in Plato's cave, and the parrhesiast is the truth-teller who has the courage to risk their life on speaking the truth, then the true philosopher, someone who lives a philosophical life, will be a parrhesiast. The *rhētor*, on the other hand, is concerned not with the truth of their statements but with their effect. He is the opposite of the parrhesiast. But Cicero, an author largely neglected by Foucault, casts *De Oratore* as an answer to the *Gorgias*. In his model the perfect orator and the perfect philosopher are one. Not only is this unity of rhetoric and philosophy posited as the telos of Ciceronian practice, but Crassus in Book 3 argues that the split between *parrhēsia* and rhetoric was effected by no less than Socrates himself.

This essay rereads Cicero to imagine what it would mean for truth and persuasion to be one and how would Foucault understand that possibility within the opposition he posits between *parrhēsia* and rhetoric.

With Niki Kasumi Clements' essay, "From True-Confessions to True Discourse in Late Foucault" we move from understanding the implications and limitations of Foucault's concepts of truth and their consequences for rhetoric, politics, and philosophy, to a specific focus on how he became interested in the problem of *parrhēsia* as central to his conception of the role of the philosopher, the constitution of ethics, and their relation to confession. Confession had a been a central concern of Foucault's since the mid-seventies. The disciplinary subject is one who recognizes their own truth, can articulate it to another, and thus as a consequence and effect of power forms themselves to realize it, in an endless circle of observation, confession, and reinscription. *Parrhēsia*, however, is a form of truth, articulated by the subject to the other, in which the subject stakes its being on that truth. It is the possibility of a true relationship of the self through the other. How Foucault moves from a focus on true confession as a reinscription of the self to itself within the bonds of discipline, to *parrhēsia* as the possibility of a *bios alēthēs* is the central focus of Clements' detailed work within the Foucauldian archive from his first encounter with Philodemus' *peri parrhēsias* to Cassian's confessional truth.

If Foucault begins by understanding confession as a technique for inscribing the disciplinary subject within the structures of power, his archeology of that subject led him eventually to reconceptualize what truth could mean to the subject, how the subject relates to himself in the articulation of that truth, and how he relates to others. Whether in Stoic practices of self-monitoring, early Christian practices of public *exomologesis*, or monastic *exagoreusis* with a director of conscience, confession is something that happens with another, in a community. Alex Dressler in "Confessing in Communities: The Genealogical Exclusion of Joy from Late Antique Christianity" argues that the site of that other is also a site of enjoyment. The public that views the spectacle of repentance is a subject that enjoys the spectacle even in the moment of their own pro/confession of faith. The coming together of communities of believers in confessions of faith is not only an individualizing and disciplinary moment, but it can also be a communal or festive one as well, producing in the works of writers like Paulinus of Nola a true "communism of the senses."

If the subject has a certain set of forms and those forms have a history, then what is the human? More precisely, what is the inhuman? In a real sense, this is the Freudian question. What is this other that speaks within us? How does it reveal our truth? One place this truth is revealed is in our dreams. Dreams are a site where the other speaks, but it is always an other that is uniquely our own. No one else can have my dream. Foucault's challenge to Freud and the reason he must ultimately return to antiquity is to say that this other is historicizeable. The unconscious or the unthought has a history. Artemidorus tells us that men who dream of sex are really dreaming about their political and economic lives. Freud tells us that men who dream about business are really (most of the time) dreaming about the sexual. Something fundamental has changed. As Richard Armstrong demonstrates in "Artemidorus as Symptom: Freud and Foucault," an essay that in many ways serves as a pendant to McGushin's and Boehringer's, where Freud finds in Artemidorus an uncomfortable *Döppelganger* of his own interpretive desire and its repression, for Foucault Artemidorus serves in turn as the symptom of his ambivalence toward Freud himself.

If Foucault asks us to imagine different possible relations between the subject and truth, and then forces us to pose the question of whether the psychoanalytic subject is the cause or the effect of a certain historically specific discourse, the sadomasochistic fictions of Li Yinhe, an avid reader of Foucault's *History of Sexuality*, ask us to imagine what it means to perform a genealogy of the Western sexual subject in China. These texts by Li, who was a translator of Foucault, with settings in the Cultural Revolution or with rich references to Mao's era, ask us to experience the Cultural Revolution as a series of sadomasochistic games played out for physical pleasure. Leihua Weng in "The Desiring Subject Seeks Pleasure in History: Li Yinhe's Sadomasochistic Fictions and the Cultural Revolution," argues that the enjoyment is not only that of the viewer but also that of the viewed: the performance of loyalty, the receiving of punishment, the public confession of one's ideological crimes become eroticized as sadomasochistic rituals. The erotic ritualization of politically charged moments in these fictions forces us to inquire further into the relationship between the subject and truth. How does Foucault's theory help us to understand the subject's desire in experiencing physical pleasure by repeating and revisiting these political moments as sadomasochistic games?

From Volume 1 of the *History of Sexuality* to *The Confessions of the Flesh*, Foucault concentrated on a series of phenomena at the intersection of three terms: truth, subjectivity, and sexuality. He posed certain fundamental questions. In *Lectures on the Will to Know*, Foucault (2013) asked "What is the invention of the truth? What turn of events made it possible?". He later asked, why have the veridiction regimes of sexuality been so rarely interrogated? In "Foucault's Herculine Barbin: A Step in the Genealogy of Psychoanalysis," Laurie Laufer, a practicing analyst, uses Foucault's reading of the diary of Herculine Barbin to take a fresh look at the triad of truth, subjectivity, and sexuality that he attributes to psychoanalysis and that he considered the inheritance of a Western *scientia sexualis* seeking the truth at the core of sex. For Foucault, the genealogy of the practice of confession confirms the connection between psychoanalysis and the *scientia sexualis* that binds truth with sexuality.

The volume finishes by looking at the reception of the *History of Sexuality* in David Greven's "The Foucault Effect: Queer Theory and Its Discontents" What did Foucault mean to young gay men in the eighties, nineties, and early two-thousands? One story has been told many times. Following David Halperin and D. A. Miller, Volume 1 of the *History* was the equivalent of the *Communist Manifesto* for a generation of gay men coming to consciousness in the middle of the AIDS epidemic. Foucault was "a fucking saint." His disciples told us *How to be Gay*. If one read Freud, if one did not go to the right kind of gym, if one did not pursue the right kinds of limit experiences, then one was not really gay, one was not properly queer. In this way, Greven argues, a discourse that was supposed to be liberatory became normalizing and oppressive. Greven begins by recounting his and others' experience of a more celebratory and more performative queer experience that has it roots in an earlier tradition of queer icons. Finally, in light of the previous essays in this volume, he asks was this the way Foucault had to be received or is it a specifically American phenomenon, one shaped in the crucible of reaction during the Reagan years and the AIDS epidemic? Can we not adopt a more open, less disciplinary model of what it might mean to be queer, one that celebrates what we have been and could be?

In sum this volume makes at least three salient contributions to our evolving understanding of Foucault. First, Foucault's understanding of truth was never dismissive or merely "postmodern" in the trivializing sense, but always deeply historically informed and philosophically challenging. Far from launching us into a post-truth society, he asks us to understand truth as something central to human existence. As such, it is complex, imbricated in structures of power and within institutions. Truth takes multiple forms in different scientific, social, and existential situations. The truths of myself, whether dreaming or awake, of Newtonian physics, and of rhetorical and political struggle can never be identical with one another or naively superimposable. This observation does not make these truths any less real and effective.

Second, Foucault's critique of psychoanalysis can never be reduced to a simple rejection or refutation. His ongoing dialogue and argument with Freud must constantly posit psychoanalysis as a necessary interlocutor, as a locus of truth that is at once historically constructed, often normalizing, and, to use a French term that English never really translates "incontournable." The question is not Freud *or* Foucault, but how Foucault changes our reading of Freud *and* how Freud makes possible Foucault.

Third, Foucault's work remains fundamental to how we understand the erotic and the sexual from Artemidorus to the Church fathers to the present, and not only in the West. This understanding is never totalizing or complete, let alone prescriptive. It does not tell us what our truth is or must be. Instead, Foucault's work offers us a series of tools that allow us to do things, to think differently, to posit new forms of truth and understanding, and so to reimagine love, pleasure, joy, and friendship in ways that fundamentally look beyond the discourse of sexuality and its demand to say who we are.

1

On Dreams, Truth, and the Aesthetics of Existence[1]

Edward McGushin
Stonehill College

Foucault's late works are full of dreams. In *Subjectivity and Truth*, he claims that "the dream is obviously a strategic point, a privileged test for the question of relations between truth and subjectivity" (Foucault 2017a: 47). In most cultures for most of history, Foucault states, the dream is "a surface of emergence for the truth." It reveals who one is, has been, and will be. And dream analysis—oneirocriticism—is "a way of living inasmuch as, for at least a part of one's nights, one is a dreamer subject" (Foucault 2017a: 50). In *The Care of the Self*, Foucault writes that in classical antiquity, "the analysis of dreams was one of the techniques of existence ... a reasonable life could scarcely dispense with the task" (Foucault 1986: 5). The dream and oneirocriticism are fundamental to the arts (techniques) of living and to finding the truth of oneself. These statements recall Foucault's early fascination with dreams and dream interpretation. In his first published work, Foucault argued that the dream is a privileged disclosure of the "radical freedom" and "ethical content" of human existence, "the heart laid bare" (Foucault 1984c: 51 and 52). For the subject seeking the truth, the dream is indeed a privileged experience.

In *On the Government of the Living*, Foucault (2012a: 49) suggests that "a whole study could be made of the dream as alethurgy, in what way and why [it] speaks the truth." The following draws selectively and speculatively on Foucault's early and late writings to imagine one chapter of such a study. It seems to me that such a project has much to offer Foucault's critical diagnosis of modern power as well as his search for a contemporary "ethics of the self" or "aesthetics of existence," which he describes in *The Hermeneutics of the Subject*, as "an urgent, fundamental, and politically indispensable task" (Foucault 2005: 252). What precisely is an ethics or aesthetics of the self? Why might such a contemporary ethics and aesthetics of the self be a "politically indispensable task"? And what role might the dream play in this task?

Getting our present situation into view, and sketching Foucault's genealogy of how we become who we are, will allow us to better specify the importance of the dream for an ethical resistance to modern relations of power. Foucault's genealogies trace two trajectories in the history of relations of power, truth, and subjection that have given birth to our present.[2] First, in the 1960s and 1970s Foucault's works show that since the middle of the seventeenth century there has been a relentless multiplication, extension, and intensification of productive, positive power relations—that is to say, forms of power that *produce* individual subjects and populations, that *produce* the objective reality of the modern world. On the other hand, in the 1980s Foucault traced another trajectory with an older history that reveals how this modern deployment of productive power was prepared by the displacement and disqualification of the ethical experience of subjectivity and truth exemplified in ancient Greek and Hellenistic philosophy. The link between the modern invention and deployment of productive power and the modern disqualification of the ancient philosophical ethics of the self is the Christianization of the ancient philosophical practices of care of the self, first in the lives and thought of the early ascetics and monastics, and eventually in the form of an increasingly hierarchical, intensive, and extensive new form of power, the Church. Thus two trajectories: the modern proliferation of productive power relations and the prior disqualification and elimination of the philosophical arts of life and care of the self that paved the way for it.

First let us look at the modern deployment of positive power and the production of subjectivity. Beginning with *The History of Madness* and through all his major works up until his final lectures, Foucault charted a counter narrative to our more familiar line that beginning in the seventeenth century, and especially with the period of the Enlightenment, history has been a story of humanistic, scientific, technological, political, economic, and moral progress defined by the steady realization of reason and freedom in the world. Foucault's works trouble that story.

"Since the classical age," Foucault (1990: 136) writes in *The History of Sexuality 1*, "the West has undergone a very profound transformation" in its "mechanisms of power." Up until the modern era, the power of the sovereign was realized in the right to "take life or let live." This classical form of power, Foucault says, was defined in terms of subtraction, a power to *negate*—it was defined by its capacity to eliminate, to kill, those who threaten the sovereign. But a defining characteristic of the modern era is the spread of new modes of *positive, productive* power through society (Foucault 1990: 138). The modern world is increasingly invested by forms of power "working to incite reinforce, control, monitor, optimize, and organize the forces under it: a power bent on generating forces, making them grow, and ordering them" (Foucault 1990: 136).

The rise of liberalism, then, does not simply reflect the increasing limitation of sovereign power in the name of individual rights, but also the positive deployment of new productive relations of power: what Foucault calls discipline and bio-power. The modern period sees the multiplication of sites of "disciplinary power," a "political technology of the body" (Foucault 1997a: 26). The function of this "micro-physics of power" was to decompose the body into its various forces in order to reconstruct it as economically productive and politically docile. *Discipline and Punish* goes into great detail examining the methods by which the body was broken down analytically—each movement, each capacity analyzed into its components—so that it could be built back up from its basic components, more efficiently, to maximize its capacities to function in the social roles it was assigned to. Schools, hospitals, military barracks, prisons, factories, are all technologies for training, organizing, observing, documenting, comparing and judging, measuring, calculating human behavior, personality, and mood, in order to optimize these for functioning in defined socio-economic roles.³ Discipline, then, is a *normalizing* power—it trains individuals *en masse* to play the defined roles that are called for in society, to be productive workers or obedient, capable soldiers, for example. We are geared by the disciplines to be normal, well-adjusted, productive citizens. The normalized, well-trained individual expresses discipline in the very form of their body and mind, their health and strength, their seamless functioning, appropriate comportment, in their normal moods and thoughts.

Foucault (1997a) turns to Jeremy Bentham's notorious prison design—*The Panopticon*—to exemplify this modern power of disciplinary normalization. The Panopticon is a prison designed in such a way as to make the prisoners in their cells available to observation at all times from a central tower. But the tower is designed so that the prisoners can never know who, if anyone, is watching them. It is an architecture of power as asymmetrical relations of visibility-invisibility. The awareness that I might be under observation at any given instant, or at all times, infects my consciousness of myself, in fact *produces* and *intensifies* a consciousness of oneself as an object of knowledge and judgment. Control is automated by a construction of space that affects the subjectivity of those who inhabit it. The very objectivity of the world calls into being a certain form of subjectivity and this subjectivity sustains and empowers that objectivity. The

Panopticon, Foucault argues, is exemplary of disciplinary normalization and of modern relations of power in general. Modernity is not then simply a movement by which the naturally free, rational, self-interested individual is liberated from irrational domination under despotic power. Rather, the "individual is ... a reality fabricated by this specific technology of power ... power produces; it produces reality; it produces domains of objects and rituals of truth" (Foucault 1997a: 194).

Along with the disciplinary normalization of individuals *en masse*, the classical age ushers in the deployment of modern bio-politics, the political management of biological life at the level of the population.[4] This form of political power involved "an entire series of interventions and *regulatory controls: a bio-politics of the population*" to know and govern the population as a biological entity in order to foster its health, happiness, and productivity (Foucault 1990: 139). These two forms of power came together in the modern science of sexuality where the discipline of the body's forces and the regulation of the health of the population intersect (Foucault 1990: 145–59). The human comes to be constituted in terms of the truth of desire that must be revealed through constant confession to doctors and therapists: "Western man has become a singularly confessing animal."[5] This is one way that Foucault explains the significance of Freud for modernity and of sexuality for Freud. In a sense, Freud is the key figure who brings these threads together in his configuration of the human subject as an inner text that must be confessed and submitted to interpretation, the hermeneutics of the subject. The truth of the subject is the hidden source of this inner text: the libido and the Oedipal triangle.[6]

The much later deployment of neo-liberal governmentality takes place against the background of this disciplinary, bio-political liberalism. In *The Birth of Biopolitics*, Foucault provides a sketch of American neo-liberal theory, which takes the individual to be "an entrepreneur of himself ... being for himself his own capital" (Foucault 2008a: 226). For Foucault, neo-liberalism is much more than a program for political and economic policy. It is a new configuration of what it means to be human, of practical reason, and the proper conduct of life. Neo-liberalism constitutes the individual person as human capital and life as the individual's enterprise. Neo-liberal *homo oeconomicus* "is someone who accepts reality" and sees himself, his life, and the world as opportunities to invest and maximize his human capital (Foucault 2008a: 269). Because the entrepreneur of the self "accepts reality" and seeks to economize her human capital, this individual "appears precisely as someone manageable, someone who responds systematically to modifications artificially introduced into the environment. *Homo oeconomicus* is eminently governable" (Foucault 2008a: 270). This entrepreneur of the self, this docile yet productive individual, focused on health, productivity, personal success and happiness, accepts this system of actuality—the reality constituted by the operations of discipline and bio-power—simply as *reality*, as the necessary, natural, inevitable conditions for the realization of freedom and truth. In other words, modernity is a particular deployment of power-knowledge-subjectivity, a particular interpretation of life, that presents itself as the objective nature of things, as human nature, as rationality as such.

Here I would like to draw on Jonathan Crary's book, *24/7*, which makes clear the critical value and stakes of a genealogy of the dream and which seems in many important respects to be a theoretical extension of Foucault's insights. For Crary the catchphrase, 24/7, strikes at the heart of our present era. He writes that, "24/7 markets and a global infrastructure for continuous work and consumption have been in place for some time, but now a human subject is in the making to coincide with these more intensively" (Crary 2014: 3–4). What Foucault, in the 1970s, began to diagnose as the productive and affirmative function of modern power, Crary presents in its contemporary, hyperbolic form as ceaseless production and consumption, ceaseless activity and self-activation. We have become transfixed by the image of full and constant awakeness, total self-control and economization, constant activity—jittery, over-caffeinated versions of *homo oeconomicus*, who think: "Would not less sleep allow more chance for 'living life to the fullest'?" (Crary 2014: 14). The result however is that we are all busy all of the time, occupied with tasks that more and more are designed to produce measurable, if meaningless, outcomes that can be constantly assessed, managed, and improved for greater efficiency, despite their utter uselessness.

Crary highlights the cruel irony of this situation where the promise of 24/7 bears a disquieting resemblance to both torture (sleep deprivation) and to a state of emergency, "when a bank of floodlights are suddenly switched on in the middle of the night, seemingly as a response to some extreme circumstances, but which never get turned off and become domesticated into a permanent condition" (Crary 2014: 17). Crary's thought reinforces Foucault's insight that it is precisely when we set out to increase our powers to act, to maximize our own human capital, that we are most subject to modern governmental forces.

Crary's analysis, as an extension of Foucault's, helps bring into focus the need for a contemporary political ethics to reactivate the powers of sleep and the dream. It shows how 24/7 governmentality takes aim at all forms of "sleep" and consequently "dreaming." Disqualified and progressively displaced by all the demands to "do," is the time of reflection, contemplation, reverie, distraction.

24/7 aims at the maximization of time as an economic resource and hence, "[b]illions of dollars are spent every year researching how to reduce decision-making time, how to eliminate the useless time of reflection and contemplation" (Crary 2014: 40). Time spent sleeping, dreaming, daydreaming, or in silent, solitary contemplation is characterized as time lost or wasted: "[t]here is a profound incompatibility of anything resembling reverie with the priorities of efficiency, functionality, and speed" (Crary 2014: 88). The dream, and the sleep which enables and protects it, represent an obstacle and threat to the deployment and intensification of discipline, bio-power, and neo-liberalism, to the construction of 24/7 subjectivity. Clearly, 24/7 is a direct assault on "the examined life."

In a configuration in which our agency, our will itself, is an effect and a conduit of power relations, the non-voluntary or involuntary, and the "useless," take on a heightened ethical and political value. Here is where I think we can situate the dream as a site of resistance—the dream spontaneously disables the modern, frenetically self-mastering subject. It is the spontaneous emergence of times and spaces beyond the reach of an imperialistic cogito. The thoughts, visions, voices, moods that occur over and against the will and control of the subject need not be defined exclusively as irrational failures, meaningless lapses, or even as symptoms of our repressed anti-social wishes—they are also spontaneous resistances to the intensification of power in our lives.[7]

So far, we have looked at the formation of our present through the proliferation of productive forms of power and I have suggested that in this configuration the dream appears as a spontaneous form of resistance. But Foucault's late work shows that another historical trajectory is equally essential to constituting our present: the disqualification of the ancient philosophical ethics of care of the self and the arts of living or aesthetics of existence. In this period Foucault continues his critical genealogy of our present. But he also more explicitly articulates resources and possibilities for an ethical resistance to power. I agree with Todd May when he says that Foucault's thought is driven by two questions: Who are we? What might we become? (May 2006: 306). The later Foucault responds to this second question more directly. In ancient Greek and Hellenistic philosophy, Foucault sees a framework for an ethics of the self and aesthetics of existence for our own situation.[8] It is within this framework that we might understand the ethical power of the dream.

The transformation of life that began in the middle of the seventeenth century was accompanied by a reconfiguration of subjectivity that Foucault (2005: 1419) calls in *The Hermeneutics of the Subject*, "within a lot of inverted commas," the "Cartesian Moment." This event in the history of thought is the dividing point between the ancient relationship of the self to itself and to the truth, and the emergence of the modern subject of objective, scientific knowledge and modern forms of power.

Beginning with *Subjectivity and Truth* and up until his final works, Foucault argued that philosophy in the ancient world was a reflection on and practice of care of the self (*epimeleia heautou, souci de soi*); that is, philosophy was conceived of as the "art of living" (*techné tou biou*).[9] The care of the self was the very stuff of ethics for Foucault. Care involved not just an affective state of concern or anxiety about the condition of the self, but also an attention to specific domains that constituted the concerning dimension of who one is. For the ancient Greeks, for example, the concern was our pursuit and enjoyment of pleasure. To give in to pleasure too much or in the wrong ways strengthened the appetites to the point of making us slaves to them, a condition that is both desperate and shameful. This condition results from forgetting oneself, neglecting oneself. This concern gave rise to a need for practices of controlling the appetites, satisfying them in the right way and within the proper limits so that one could remain master of oneself. Care, then, entailed various techniques for forming one's relation to the self, for mastering oneself. These included, for example, meditative exercises, journal writing, tests of endurance, fasts, and speaking frankly with someone who could serve as a spiritual director or guide. Ethics, for Foucault, following this reading of ancient philosophical practices, focuses on the work one does to establish and sustain the right relationship of the self to itself. This work is a process of subjectivation, of transforming and forming our subjectivity, who we are. The self works on itself, develops and makes use of various arts of self-fashioning, the techniques (*tekhnē*, technology) of the self. Ethical subjectivity in the care of the self is a work of art, produced through our fashioning a relationship of the self to itself, through what the Greeks called a *poiesis*, a making. We can see then that ethics and poetics are connected, and that "what we might become" is really what Foucault calls, borrowing from the ancients, an ethopoetic project.[10] I take the term aesthetics, then, in this context, to refer primarily to the notion of a *poiesis*, an art of the self and of life.

The ethopoetics of the self was premised on a specific form of relationship between subjectivity and truth, what Foucault called in *The Hermeneutics of the Subject*, "spirituality" (Foucault 2005: 14–19). Spirituality, Foucault holds, entails three basic postulates. First, the subject does not have a natural right or capacity to know the truth. The very being or subjectivity of the subject—its initial and everyday, ordinary mode of being or way of living—cuts it off from the truth. In order to gain access to the truth, then, the subject must undergo a conversion, a transformation of its very being as subject—it must become *Other* than it is. The second postulate of spirituality is that this conversion is brought about either through *eros* or *askésis*. The subject brings about a conversion through working on itself, through the labor of spiritual exercises. This work transforms the subject in its subjectivity giving it access to truth. Finally, the third postulate of spirituality is that truth is not experienced as a quality of propositions, it is not the correspondence between a proposition and a state-of-affairs. Rather, truth is experienced in existential terms as a transfigured and fully realized state of being—beatitude, tranquility, peace, joy, fulfillment, or self-mastery, for example. Truth is realized in the true life (*aléthés, bios*) and the true speech (*parrhésia*) of the one who takes care of the self.

From Ancient Greece to the time of the Reformation, Counter-Reformation, and Renaissance, the effort to discover and deploy an art of the "government of the self and others" was a fundamental feature of Western civilization and had important political functions. Only someone who first took care of his soul and of the truth would be ready to take care of the city and have the good sense (knowledge, truth) to properly care for, govern, the polis. But recognizing who practiced the true art of living and care of the self and who was truly qualified to speak the truth and lead the city was a matter of enormous contention. As a result, the care of the self and others was continuously problematized.

The problematization of care of the self and the true life gave rise then to a long history of various philosophical schools, techniques of the self, relations of spiritual direction, arts of living, and theoretical systems from the ancient Greek through the Hellenistic period. This problematization was taken up by the early Christian ascetics, mystics, and monastics and formed the basis of Christian care of the self, spiritual direction, and arts of living. Over the course of a long slow series of struggles and transformations, Christian care of the self and arts of living were increasingly institutionalized as the Church: a complex hierarchical set of relationships of spiritual direction, of the government of life and of the soul, of forms of obedience among monks but also between lay people and priests. Over the course of centuries, then, the practices of the self were transformed into a radically new form of power relation (Foucault 1994h: 332–3). This was the power of the pastor to care for, to govern or conduct, each and every member of his flock. The pastor controlled by serving, governed by guiding to salvation. In this pastoral power, as Foucault called it, the concern was the state of the soul, its deep inner workings, secret desires, and thoughts. Each member of the flock had to be shepherded to its salvation and this required knowing the truth of that soul, knowing whether the individual was pure of heart, not just in action.[11] The danger, temptation, the vulnerability to being led astray came primarily from within, from the sensations, thoughts, and desires in one's soul. Were these pure or did they have a hidden, evil source? Spiritual direction and confession required a new kind of truth telling—the one who confessed had to speak everything, especially the most shameful. And the confessor had to know the proper art of interpretation to discern both the sources and dangers, and also the proper penance to purify the soul.

The investment of power in the inner life of the soul and the body—as the very truth of the self—generated strong forms of resistance. The increasing intensity and extension of pastoral power in the Church was a source of constant struggle, resistance, and counter-resistance. In Foucault's account, the major upheavals of the Reformation, Renaissance, and Scientific Revolution that so radically transformed Western civilization were essentially tied to struggles over the arts of living, of governing oneself and others, over the institutionalization of processes of subjectivation and subjection, and of the relationship of subjectivity to the truth (Foucault 2007: 227–30). Who governs who, how, and upon what basis of knowledge and truth?

It is against this background that Foucault situates the thought of Descartes and what he calls the "Cartesian Moment." Descartes' thought exemplifies a major historical rupture in which the relation between the subject and the truth undergoes a fundamental change. On the one hand, Descartes' search to get free from error and discover the "proper conduct (government) of the mind" was a struggle to get free of pastoral power, of the mode of government of self and others, that defined a whole system of actuality, a whole form of knowledge and experience rooted in relations of pastoral government (Foucault 2007: 230, for example). The constitution of the subject in this system of government, knowledge, and subjectivity was precisely what Descartes needed to break with in order to establish a new mode of self-government, a new conduct of life and of thought, a new foundation for truth: the subject itself, the cogito, as the truth of the truth. Descartes gets free of pastoral power by founding the true conduct of the mind and of life upon a subject who by nature has access to the truth and therefore is not tied to a spiritual director, a confession and penance, an ethopoetics.

Descartes' thought helps bring about the displacement and disqualification of spirituality and care of the self to make room for the modern subject of scientific objectivity. In the wake of the Cartesian moment, the relation to the truth no longer depends on the ethical and ontological modification of the subject and is not tied to the way the subject lives (Foucault 2005: 17–19, for example). Access to truth is no longer gained through an etho-poietics, but rather, in the mode of scientific objectivity, through evidence and the correct application of method. The truth that one discovers no longer takes the form of a true life that is Other or the ethical truth of *parrhēsia*, but rather is the truth of objective knowledge—truth becomes the quality of propositions insofar as they are adequate to the facts.

But, in freeing the cogito from pastoral power, from spirituality and care of the self, Descartes not only established a new foundation for truth, the cogito, he also helped clear the space for new and more intensive modes of control. The government of life, released from the ethical, philosophical work of care of the self and the arts of living, could now be colonized by modern disciplinary normalization, bio-political regulation, and neo-liberalism.

This brings us to the point where we can return to the dream and its place in the care of the self and the arts of living. Our way into this is through another look at the Cartesian moment and the modern subject that Descartes helps establish. In the ancient world and right up to the Cartesian moment, it was within the context of spirituality, care of the self, and the arts of living, that the dream and dream analysis, found their singular importance. The interpretation of dreams concerns, Foucault writes,

> what to do with one's dream, what to do when awake, what to make of that obscure part of ourselves that is illuminated in the night.... how can I insert the dreamer subject that I was, how can I integrate it, give it meaning and value in my waking life? Ancient oneirocriticism is this: ... a way of living inasmuch as, for at least a part of one's nights, one is a dreamer subject.
>
> (Foucault 2017a: 49–50)[12]

The waking self had to confront, understand, and live with the truth of the dream: the analysis of the dream was a way of forming the relationship of the self to itself, of the waking self to the dreaming self. The dream, then, plays a crucial role in this spiritualized mode of subjectivity–truth relation: "the problem, the theme of the dream reappears when it is a matter of founding the subject's access to truth, of wondering about the truth of the truth, or again of searching for what is the truth of the subject" (Foucault 2017a: 49). The subject who seeks their own truth must listen to the dream and make a proper interpretation of it.

But the problem of the dream takes on a new meaning and intensity in modernity, evident in Descartes' *Meditations*. In order to discover and fix the cogito as foundation of truth Descartes must confront and dispel the threat of skepticism posed by the dream. Foucault writes:

> When the question had to be posed of how the subject can be certain of having access to the true truth, how he can possess the truth of the truth, this question, contemporary with the foundation of classical science, could be answered only by way of the *problem*, the *obstacle*, and the *threat* of the dream.
>
> (Foucault 2017a: 48, *my emphasis*)

For most of history and in most cultures the dream is the privileged site for the emergence of the truth of the self. But for Descartes the dream is no longer the surface of emergence for the truth of the self. It is, on the contrary, an obstacle and threat, mere illusion and error. Why does the dream appear in the form of an obstacle or threat that must be overcome at the beginning of the modern era? And what might this tell us about the relation between dreaming and that deployment?

Perhap, we come right to the heart of the problem in a line from Binswanger's *Dream and Existence*: "To dream means: I don't know what is happening to me" (Binswanger 1984: 102). The dream is the experience I have when I am no longer the sovereign subject of my own experience. The dream occurs when the waking, rational subject goes to sleep—it is a form of experience, a way of thinking, contingent upon the displacement and disqualification of the waking subject. In *On The Government of the Living*, Foucault says: "dreams speak the truth ... precisely because I am not the master of the dream and something else happens in me in the dream, someone else emerges, someone else who speaks, who gives signs ... if it speaks the truth, it is precisely because it is not me who speaks in my dream" (Foucault 2012a: 49).

Traditionally the dream is valorized as a voice of truth and meaning *because* it displaces the sovereignty of the waking self. This reflects the spiritual model of subjectivity–truth relations in which the subject does not have a natural capacity for, or access to, the truth. But this is precisely what makes it an obstacle and threat to modern subjectivity. To establish the modern subject as sovereign over itself and over the truth, Descartes must defeat and disqualify the dream as revelation of truth and meaning. For Descartes the dream is not a source of truth but rather it is inherently deceptive, showing us nothing but all too life-like illusions. The cogito does not look to the dream for its truth but rather disarms the dream by claiming to gain truth *despite* the dream's deceptions. But this means, then, that the dream as such is a mode of experience, a way of thinking, seeing, and speaking that runs counter to modern subjectivity and to the powers that coalesce in, around, and through it.[13]

The alterity of the dream stands over and against the sovereign subject of modern reason and objectivity, self-same and responsible for itself. This other, the dream, has the power to overtake the individual. At night, in the dark, it commandeers one's thoughts, shows one visions, fills one's head with voices. In times past it was believed that in sleep the dreamer traveled to another realm or that a god or a demon came to them. Either way, the dream was capable of delivering a message from elsewhere. But as Crary observes, since the seventeenth century the "imaginative capability of the dreaming sleeper underwent a relentless erosion, and the vitiated identity of a visionary was left over for a tolerated minority of poets, artists, and mad people. Modernization could not proceed in a world populated with large numbers of individuals who believed in the value or potency of their own internal visons or voices" (Crary 2014: 126). The all too captivating and compelling dreamworld offers itself as an alternate source of truth and power, coming from somewhere Other than the reasoning and volition of the cogito. The dream's insistence unsettles the waking self, it conjures the de-centering specter of ancient spirituality.

Given our current disciplinary, bio-political, neo-liberal situation—in which our experience is increasingly captured and invested by relations of power that keep us active and productive, *awake*, tied to mechanisms of surveillance, training, efficiency, and individuation—sleeping and dreaming become increasingly important as a space of spontaneous problematization, resistance, and counter-subjectivity, counter-conduct.

What might the dream offer a contemporary aesthetics of existence and care for the self as a practice of freedom? Reading Foucault's early essay on the dream through his later work on care of the self we can imagine the outlines of an ethopoetics of the dream. In 1954, Foucault was intrigued by the possibility that phenomenological psychology might pave the way to a philosophical anthropology—an understanding of the basic structures of the embodied, lived modes of human being as "presence to Being."[14] While Foucault moved away from the idea of anything like a transcendental subject or human nature as the condition of possible experience, much of what he says in this early work—about the dream in relation to waking experience, freedom, truth, imagination, art, and ethics—anticipates his later concerns. We can disengage these insights from their phenomenological approach and re-think them within a genealogical approach shifting them from a psychological-therapeutic context to the context of care of the self and aesthetics of existence. What happens then is we can see the dream as not so much a disclosure of the fundamental structures of "presence-to-being," but rather as the disclosure of the agonistic play of forces that bring into being and sustain our waking subjectivity.

Let us begin with a dense passage that articulates a number of ideas Foucault reiterates and develops as central themes of his early essay. Foucault writes: "By breaking with the objectivity which fascinates waking consciousness and by reinstating the human subject in its radical freedom, the dream discloses paradoxically the movement of freedom toward the world, the point of origin from which freedom makes itself world. The cosmogony of the dream is the origination itself of existence" (Foucault 1984c: 51).

First of all, Foucault characterizes the dream as a "break" from the "objectivity which fascinates waking subjectivity." This notion of a break has at least two senses. On the one hand, the break can be understood negatively, so to speak, as a refusal and a departure. We dream, in the most literal sense, when we fall asleep, when we turn away from and lose direct consciousness and active engagement with our environment. When awake we attend to our surroundings, deal with them, are absorbed by them. The dream then stands in a relation of refusal of, or resistance to, an objectivity which "fascinates" the waking subject. Within the genealogical framework, we take both objectivity, *and* our fascination with it, to be the concrete deployment of relations of power, knowledge, and subjection—the field of experience set up by disciplinary normalization, bio-political regulation, the hermeneutics of desire, and neo-liberal governmentality. The waking subject who we are in the world is a node in and key agent of this deployment, both an effect of power and also the primary conduit channeling, maintaining, intensifying the dispositif. From this perspective then the dream is a refusal of and resistance to power–knowledge–subjectivity relations.

But there is a second, "positive," sense to this "break." The dream does not just refuse to attend directly to the objectivity of the surrounding world. It "reinstates the human subject in its radical freedom, the dream discloses paradoxically the movement of freedom toward the world, the point of origin from which freedom makes itself world." The dream tears the subject away from an objectivity that captures, holds, and colonizes its forces—body and soul—and "reinstates" the subject in its radical freedom. This freedom is clearly not the same as our waking experience of freedom. The sovereign subject of waking experience presupposes a freedom to choose and to act, to think and do as it pleases. This freedom of the will, to choose, to do as one pleases, is taken to be an essential and defining characteristic of the human subject. But this waking sense of freedom as my possession and my essence is itself inscribed in and invested by the deployment of discipline, bio-power, hermeneutics, and neo-liberal governmentality. This freedom, whether it is understood juridically in terms of rights, economically in terms of maximizing preferences, psychologically as satisfying drives or desires, depends on the sovereign, disciplinary, bio-political, and neo-liberal deployments of power and knowledge. These freedoms can only exist in a world organized by these relations of power–knowledge and such a world only exists insofar as individuals subject themselves and each other to it. The radical freedom of the dream is neither the juridical, economic, nor psychological freedom of the sovereign subject of waking experience. The dream is freedom from this subject.

When dreaming the subject, typically, does not control its actions, thoughts, words, but is swept along by the flow of the dream itself. Another subject speaks in the dream: "The subject of the dream, the first person of the dream, is the dream itself, the whole dream. In the dream, everything says, 'I', even the things and the animals, even the empty space, even the objects distant and strange which populate the phantasmagoria" (Foucault 1984c: 59). The dream then, for Foucault, is the spontaneous constitution of a world of experience in which the subject who I am is dispersed and where I find myself not *acting* my role but *being acted*, not taking my seat in the audience but rather *being posited as* a view from nowhere.

But this "is not another way of experiencing another world, it is for the dreaming subject the radical way of experiencing its own world" (Foucault 1984c: 59). The dream offers us the experience of the world *and* the subject coming to be, the movement of a becoming. For Foucault this movement is the play of multiple, heterogeneous force relations in the environment, the body, and the soul that create constant tensions, upheavals, ruptures, and that spontaneously organize themselves into forms, objects, and relations.[15] The radical freedom of the dream is not an escape from reality to some utopian, or dystopian, fiction. Rather, we experience the conflictual movement at the root of our waking experience of objectivity and subjectivity. *Radical* freedom then is not *absolute* freedom. It discloses the constituting movement that originates and sustains our waking experience of ourselves as subjects operating in an objective system of actuality.

This is why Foucault can write that the dream "restores the movement of freedom in its authentic meaning ... The dream is that absolute disclosure of the ethical content, the heart shown naked" (Foucault 1984c: 52). The dream frees us from the *constituted* selves we are in the *constituted* world of our waking experience and situates us in the *constituting* movement that makes possible, but subsequently gets captured, held, and colonized by, the objective forms of waking life. In the dream, the plasticity, the movement, the problematic nature of the objective world comes to life for us. This space where the relation of the self to itself, to others, and to the world is not fixed in the form of objectivity, is the condition of possibility for an ethical and aesthetic work of the self on itself. In a late interview, Foucault says that, freedom "is the ontological condition of ethics.

But ethics is the considered form that freedom takes when it is informed by reflection" (Foucault 1997d: 284). The dream makes that space of freedom available, opening us up to the ontological condition of ethics, reminding us that life is not completely captured by the operation and calculations of power.

For Foucault the movement of becoming that we experience in the dream takes on a "dramatic essence in theatrical form" (Foucault 1984c: 56). It stages, puts on display, directs our gaze. Foucault develops this point most clearly in his discussion of the constitution of dream space—anticipating his later work which so famously captures the spatiality of power/knowledge relations, the way these relations deploy themselves in the objective shaping of spaces of control, conduct, observation, documentation, organization, etc. The cellular, functional, panoptic space of the disciplines, the security spaces of bio-politics, are displaced in the dream, where space is no longer fixed by power but is still in play and exhibits forms that Foucault describes in terms of aesthetics and ethics (Foucault 1984c: 60–1). For example, Foucault describes the space of the dream world in dramatic, poetic terms: the *epic* space of near and far, of journey and return; the *lyrical* space of light and dark, of blindness and revelation; and the *tragic* space of high and low, the space of soaring and of the fall (Foucault 1984c: 60–3). "This set of oppositions defines the essential dimensions of existence. They form the primitive coordinates of the dream and, as it were, the mythic space of its cosmogony" (Foucault 1984c: 62).

The waking subject is increasingly fixed by disciplinary, bio-political, panoptic, neo-liberal coordinates where space itself is ordered toward surveillance, economization, data collection, documentation, control of behavior, feelings, desires, thoughts, in order to amplify and direct productive forces and consumption. The dream breaks from the objectivity of these spaces and the pressure they exert on us. It brings to light, stages or frames, their complex struggles and interconnections with other modes of spatiality, spaces that open up modes of feeling, thinking, desiring that have not been completely captured by power-knowledge, that run counter to its demands and develop other dimensions of life, relationships, thoughts and feelings that, for that reason, feel more free, more alive. The dream opens up the possibility of inhabiting a world shaped aesthetically and ethically around subjectivities that are not saturated by normalizing processes, bio-political concerns and regulations, or neo-liberal calculations.

In the dream the stuff of experience becomes the matter of a profound contemplation, a vision to behold, a movement to be swept up in. It brings to life a world where every element becomes uncanny, mysterious. In the dream, this play of strange, unexpected, mysterious and meaningful spaces is open to poetic and ethical possibilities. Every object is alive with irony, beauty, desire, terror, dignity, in fact, with a limitless, ever-shifting array of uncanny forces, like a work of art or like the sublime, like Marcel duChamp's *Fountain* or Warhol's *Campbell's Soup Cans*, or like the world itself when we pause for a moment our relentless effort to master it and merely behold it.

The dream, Foucault writes, was traditionally experienced as a call from beyond or from the core of one's existence (Foucault 2017a: 54). Certain dreams leave us shaken upon waking and stay with us in the form of an affectively charged memory. Such dreams are calls to interpretation *par excellence*, questions or challenges posed to the waking self. For the subject who wishes to interpret their dream the first steps are always to remember it, to describe it for oneself or another, to speak it or write it out. When we take this stance toward the dream we inevitably transform it into an object submitted to the sovereignty of the waking subject—to be known and mastered. But at the same time, as we strive to recall the details of the dream so often they begin to flow back to us, emerging out of our sleep, as if now the dream strives to speak for itself and is not merely content to remain an object under the power of the waking self. Dream analysis then is not merely a process of objectifying the dream for the waking subject, it also has the capacity to revive the dream as subject, to continue the dream while awake.

Foucault captures this power of the dream in his early essay in his claim that the dream is the condition of possibility of imagination itself. Through the imagination "I undertake to adopt once more that mode of presence in which the movement of my freedom was not yet caught up in this world toward which it moves, where everything still denoted the constitutive possession of the world of my existence" (Foucault 1984c: 67–8). The imagination is the attempt by the waking subject to lose itself in an imaginary experience where the "I" is dispersed in a movement of becoming more fundamental than itself, the constituting movement out of which a constituted, waking self emerges as its effect. Imagining is a modification of our presence by which "consciousness aims at the original movement which discloses itself in dreams" (Foucault 1984c: 68). To imagine is to continue to dream when we are awake.

To be awake means to take things as they are—facts, objects, evidence. And the waking self takes itself as itself. But in the dream and imagination nothing simply is what it is, or what it appears to be, and no one is who they appear to be. Things are both more and less than what they are, they are other than themselves. Likewise, in the dream and the imagination, "I is another." Foucault writes: "To imagine . . . is first of all to derealize myself, to absent myself" (Foucault 1984c: 67). The imagination like the dream is a break from objectivity, a "derealization" or "absenting" of the self. It is not first of all the power to conjure an image of an object that is not actually present. It is rather a way in which the subject refuses to be absorbed in the "system of actuality" where they find themself. At the same time, it is "through the imaginary that the original meaning of reality is disclosed ... At the very heart of perception it can throw into bright light the secret power at work in the most manifest forms of presence" (Foucault 1984c: 69). The imagination brings the "system of actuality" to life by awakening us to the movement of becoming that constitutes "the original meaning of reality."

The imagination problematizes our inscription in relations of power, discourse, and subjection, loosens the hold of these relations, and makes possible a freer, more spontaneous encounter with ourselves, others, and the world. But the imagination maintains a precarious relation to the image. The image all too often represents a failure of imagination, a parodic sense of closure or completion that mimics the objectivity of waking perception and the satisfaction of a desire: we fixate on images of happiness and misery, goodness and evil, health and illness, success and failure, love and indifference. This temptation of the image is intensified by the fascination with objectivity that captures us in waking life and shapes our subjectivity (Foucault 1984c: 71). It is through the image, then, that objectivity takes hold of the imagination and turns it towards itself.[16] The *dispositif* colonizes and makes use of the imagination by fixing it on images that reinforce the grip of its objectivity.

For this reason, Foucault writes that the imagination "is in essence iconoclastic." With respect to the role of the imagination in aesthetic production, he argues that the "true poet denies himself the accomplishment of desire in the image because the freedom of imagination imposes itself on him as a task of refusal ... The value of poetic imagination is to be measured by the inner destructive power of the image" (Foucault 1984c: 72). The same would hold true for the arts of the self and the aesthetics of existence. The function of the imagination in the aesthetics of existence, just as in the "*ars poetica*" has no meaning unless it teaches us to break with the fascination of images and to reopen, for imagination its path of freedom toward the dream that offers it, as its absolute truth, the 'unshatterable kernel of night'" (Foucault 1984c: 73–4). Foucault wrote in 1954 that the "aim of psychotherapy should be to free the imaginary that is trapped in the image" (Foucault 1984c: 72). Perhaps now we must turn to genealogy and archaeology to free the problematizations, the dreams, trapped in the objective deployments of power, knowledge, and subjectivity.

I have argued that given the particular configurations of power, truth, and subjection that shape our world, the dream might be more important than ever. The forces gathering and intensifying today aim toward ever increasing productivity and consumption, ever increasing activity, efficiency, speed, endurance, like an asymptotic curve rising toward some impossible ideal of constant, full wakefulness, a limitless power over self, others, and world. Sleep and the dream for which it makes space stand in the way of this "progress."

The dream and the imagination teach us that the aesthetics of existence is not first of all a transformation of what I *do* or how I *look*—stylizing my physical appearance or comportment—but rather of who I *am* and how I *see*. It is a transformation not of my *objective appearance* in the world, but of my *subjective way of disclosing* the world, my *being* as *subject*. Life as dreamed becomes an aesthetics and the subject becomes a "visionary" rather than an agent of normalization, bio-political regulation, or neo-liberal capitalization (Deleuze 1989: xi, 19–21). In the dream—whether during our sleep or in daydreams, reveries, fantasy, contemplation, meditation, or other modes—we find ourselves swept along by the current of all the thoughts, sensations, visions, sounds, feelings, urges, that come and go, form patterns or make connections, only to disperse again and reappear otherwise than before. We bear witness to a spectacle that displaces the waking sense of reality and rationality and immerses us in a limit experience, where thought struggles with, inverts, distorts, and parodies the operations of power. In the dream, we experience that region where who we are remains a profound mystery, a question problematizing itself and where affect, vision, voice, matter, movement are no longer bound captive to the objectivity that fascinates waking subjectivity. Rather our present appears obliquely in the light of "what we might become," open to the ethopoetic work of the imagination informed by the critical diagnosis of power, truth, and subjectivity.

2

Foucault in the Cave with Gadamer

On Truth, Understanding, and Experience

Arash Shokrisaravi
Cornell University

Introduction

In *On the Government of the Living*, Foucault tries to illuminate the relationship between the exercise of power and the *manifestation* of truth or alethurgy through a reading of *Oedipus*. In his interpretation of *Oedipus Tyrannus*, he attracts our attention to the reasons for Oedipus' failure to master the truth of the plague and so retain his position. Foucault then moves on to a comparison of the different alethurgies or *truth-tellings* found in this tragedy. For the purposes of this chapter, I will focus on the divine alethurgy and the alethurgy of slaves. As can be seen in this categorization, Foucault argues that certain types of truth can only be practiced by certain types of subjects. We are not all priests, prophets, or gods. The chorus too is unable to settle the debate between Oedipus and Tiresias because it was not equipped with the vision required to see the divine or oracular truth. Foucault makes a further distinction, this time based on the procedure (*procédure*) of truth: "with the seer and the god, we have the divine, prophetic, oracular, divinatory half of this procedure of truth. Obviously, the second half of the procedure of the truth will be the human half" (Foucault 2016: 28). Thus only certain types of subjects can practice certain kinds of veridiction and have certain kinds of experiences, and those various kinds of veridiction operate using different procedures.

In addition to the divine and the oracular modes, we should add the dream as well to this first group of procedures of truth: "dreams speak the truth...precisely because I am not the master of the dream and something else happens to me in the dream, someone else emerges, someone who speaks, who gives signs... and if it speaks the truth, it is precisely because it is not me who speaks in my dream" (Foucault 2016: 49). In other words, in the dream, just as in the other modes of experiencing the truth in the first group, the subject does not require a testimonial language in his relationship with the truth. The subject does not speak the truth, the truth speaks through him.

Foucault returned to dream in *Subjectivity and Truth*. There he explained the relationship between the subject and dream: the dream here is more private than in the case of Tiresias' vision or Apollo's oracle. The dream is supposed "to *tell* a truth that, most often, concerns [the dreamer]" (Foucault 2019: 47). In this set of lectures, however, Foucault is less concerned with the subject's actual experience of the dream per se than with *oneirocriticism* (the interpretation of dreams). In other words, the primary relationship between the subject and dream is replaced by the secondary one of understanding and explanation. The main reason for this approach is that what is essential regarding truth for Foucault at this point in his teaching is not the experience of truth itself, but truth-telling, the articulation and dissemination of the truth, and so its connection with power. Furthermore, what is told here and in Foucault's interpretation of *Oedipus Tyrannus* is always truth "in terms of knowledge (*savoir*)" (Foucault 2016: 33). Therefore, Foucault investigates the relationship between the subject and truth-telling as it related to sharing the knowledge extracted in the interpretation of dreams, instead of what the subject can experience in those dreams.

His interpretation of oracular Truth in *The Courage of the Truth* is another example of this approach. He makes a distinction between the different faculties and methods that are required to experience oracular truth in his study of Socrates' approach toward the oracle's response to his friend, Chaerephon. Here Socrates is the subject who receives a prophecy from the oracle. Socrates as a man of his period never denies the authenticity and the power of oracle and Apollo. In fact, he emphasizes that he accepts and honors the oracle's response and the mission he is assigned by the god via it to the extent that he is even willing to risk his life to fulfill that mission. Therefore, on the experiential level, he accepts prophecy and oracles. On the discursive level, however, he tries to examine (ζητεύω) the oracle's response. Socrates knows that the knowledge hidden in the prophecy of the oracle is not a subject-matter of interpretation but of a validity check. Foucault explains that "the investigation Socrates undertakes aims to find out if the oracle *told* the truth" (Foucault 2012: 81). But while the subject's relationship to the oralce could be investigated as an experience of the oracle's truth, we can see that here again Foucault is more focused on truth-*telling* and the subject's relationship to truth as knowledge.

What is discussed above is not a critique of Foucault's works on truth, but quite the opposite. It offers a preparatory analysis of what he can add to our study of truth. But before elaborating that contribution more fully, we need first to discuss truth in the *Apology*; look more closely at the various types of truths, their modes and required faculties, and the subject's relationship with each of these truths. Following that, I utilize these modes and conditions of truth in the second section to read the allegory of the cave. There I reject Heidegger's interpretation of the allegory. Heidegger only examines the subject from the perspective of making judgments of quiddity or ontology, as a subject of understanding, but he neglects the subject of experience.

Essential to the second section of this chapter comparing the different theories of truth is how each theory differs in what it calls truth. In the face of this multiplicity of signifieds, in order to have a dialogue, we need first to bracket our ordinary concept of truth and point to these signifieds directly. I use Plato's allegory of the cave as a medium that can provide us with such an option. The allegory itself acts as a system parallel to our world. It models (1) us, (2) what we cannot understand and encounter, (3) the regimes of truths, (4) their manifestations of truths, and (5) what we experience. In addition, it provides us with an opportunity to go beyond the horizon and dimension of its characters' time. It accepts us as outsiders who do not have a standpoint in the cave. Due to this lack of a standpoint, we succeed in understanding the truth more comprehensively. Furthermore, the allegory resolves our problem of the multiplicity of the signifieds of truth by allowing us to bracket *the truth*, and point to what corresponds to it in the allegory.

My interpretation of the first two stages of the allegory investigates human beings' conditions and horizon of understanding truth (modeled as shackled prisoners in the allegory of the cave). I use Hans-Georg Gadamer's theory of the fusion of horizons to illuminate the conditions of understanding truth to explain why the prisoner's *experience* of seeing the beings at the second stage fails to produce knowledge.

In the third section, I discuss the connection between Foucault's truth and alethurgy, and explain how Foucault's genealogy can detect a neglected gap, a regime of truth operative in the cave. Furthermore, I investigate the genealogist's standpoint inside the cave and the reliability of genealogy in exploring the regimes of truth. What we achieve in the end is an integral understanding of the truth.

On ἀλήθεια and ἄλλη θεία in *Apology*

καὶ ἐπειδάν τις αὐτοὺς ἐρωτᾷ ὅτι ποιῶν καὶ ὅτι διδάσκων, ἔχουσι μὲν οὐδὲν εἰπεῖν ἀλλ' ἀγνοοῦσιν, ἵνα δὲ μὴ δοκῶσιν ἀπορεῖν, τὰ κατὰ πάντων τῶν φιλοσοφούντων πρόχειρα ταῦτα λέγουσιν, ὅτι "τὰ μετέωρα καὶ τὰ ὑπὸ γῆς" καὶ "θεοὺς μὴ νομίζειν" καὶ "τὸν ἥττω λόγον κρείττω ποιεῖν." τὰ γὰρ *ἀληθῆ* οἴομαι οὐκ ἂν ἐθέλοιεν λέγειν, ὅτι κατάδηλοι γίγνονται προσποιούμενοι μὲν *εἰδέναι*, *εἰδότες* δὲ οὐδέν.

(23-d)

(And if someone asks them what he (Socrates) does and teaches (to corrupt the youngsters), they remain silent as they are ignorant. But to not appear at a loss, they mention those accusations against all philosophers, about "things in the sky and the ones below the earth" and "not believing in Gods" as well as "making the worse argument, the stronger one." They would not want to tell *truth* for sure, and that they have been proven to claim *perceiving* when they *examine/investigate/see* nothing.)

The first point to notice is the translation of *εἰδέναι* and *εἰδότες* in this passage. While G. M. A. Grube translates them as knowledge and to know, which confuses them with *οἶδα*, I insist on translating them as to *see/perceive/understand/examine/investigate/experience* (as used in *Phaedo* 70d). While the former is a *cognitive* concept, the latter is not a faculty for the cognition of an object but instead, extends it over the whole sphere of those who understand, in a pure subjectiveness, and this is precisely the mode of understanding. Accordingly, Socrates' critique of the accusers is not their lack of knowledge or not knowing the subject and details of his debates, but their persistence in not examining this method, avoiding any investigation, refusing to see, resisting understanding, or bracketing the *logos*. Therefore, Socrates warns that the ones who avoid the logos and refuse to experience understanding will not have access to truth. This is truth indebted to understanding and *logos* as its instrument. In addition, it is not just Socrates who is being accused by them, but all philosophers. Therefore, what is being blamed and resisted is philosophy, the philosophical method, or logos itself.

Now let us take a closer look at the accusations:

Σωκράτη φησὶν ἀδικεῖν τούς τε νέους διαφθείροντα καὶ θεοὺς οὓς ἡ πόλις νομίζει οὐ νομίζοντα, ἕτερα δὲ δαιμόνια καινά.

(24-b-c)

(They say Socrates is guilty of corrupting the youngsters and of not believing in the gods in whom the city believes, but instead, in other spiritual things.)

I want to focus on believing in *other spiritual things*. The key question is what these other spiritual things are and how they are connected to our discourse of truth. But before that, Socrates makes an essential claim in the trial regarding truth, or in particular, the twofold nature of the truth. This is the key moment of what I term the truth-Truth debate in Socrates' discourse:

> οὕτω γὰρ ἔχει, ὦ ἄνδρες Ἀθηναῖοι, τῇ ἀληθείᾳ· οὗ ἄν τις ἑαυτὸν τάξῃ ἡγησάμενος βέλτιστον εἶναι ἢ ὑπ' ἄρχοντος ταχθῇ, ἐνταῦθα δεῖ, ὡς ἐμοὶ δοκεῖ, μένοντα κινδυνεύειν, μηδὲν ὑπολογιζόμενον μήτε θάνατον μήτε ἄλλο μηδὲν πρὸ τοῦ αἰσχροῦ.
>
> (28-d)
>
> (For this is the truth, Athenian gentlemen, whenever a man has taken a position that he thinks to be the best or has been stationed by his commander, I think he must remain (at that position) and face danger, without considering death or anything else, before disgrace.)

The truth itself here is divided into two major subgroups; it is either the direct order of the commander—who is the god as he affirms directly (ταῦτα γὰρ κελεύει ὁ θεός, εὖ ἴστε, καὶ ἐγὼ οἴομαι οὐδέν πω ὑμῖν μεῖζον ἀγαθὸν γενέσθαι ἐν τῇ πόλει ἢ τὴν ἐμὴν τῷ θεῷ ὑπηρεσίαν (30a)) and you experience directly, or it is the result of thinking (discourse) and investigation. Socrates' accusers do not have access to the truth as they refuse to understand, to examine, to participate in discourse, not for their lack of factual knowledge, but for their refusal to participate in the logos; nor are they guided by Socrates' experience of divinity. Therefore, they cannot have access to the truth of Socrates

> ἐμοὶ δὲ τοῦτο, ὡς ἐγώ φημι, προστέτακται ὑπὸ τοῦ θεοῦ πράττειν καὶ ἐκ μαντείων καὶ ἐξ ἐνυπνίων καὶ παντὶ τρόπῳ ᾧπέρ τίς ποτε καὶ <u>ἄλλη θεία</u> μοῖρα ἀνθρώπῳ καὶ ὁτιοῦν προσέταξε πράττειν.
>
> (33-c)
>
> (Accordingly, doing so [Socratic philosophical discourse], has been assigned to me by God, as I say, and by oracles and dreams, and also in every other way that *another divine* fate has ever ordered anyone to do anything.)

Our last quote posits a relationship between ἀλήθεια and ἄλλη θεία that illuminates the accusation against Socrates. He was blamed for believing in other spiritual matters instead of the gods of the city, and here he openly discusses that his philosophical discourse, that understanding and discourse have not only been assigned to him by the gods and spirituality but also by the other force that he earlier emphasized that is worthy of trust and taking risks, namely his *logos* and understanding. Therefore, ἀλήθεια (what we call *the truth* generally) comports to two distinct notions of (1) discourse or ἄλλη θεία (I call this *truth*), and (2) the divine matter itself directed by the God and oracles, and dreams (I call it *Truth*), and unlike ἄλλη θεία, its instrument is not *logos* but dreams and spiritual experiences. This distinction will become clearer as we progress.

One may ask are not both Truth and truth divine matters based on Socrates' claim? What causes a distinction between them then? Essential to the Truth and truth is that the former is the subject-matter of experience, and the latter is only the subject-matter of understanding. We bracket the notion of divinity in investigating the conditions and modes of truth and Truth, as what relates divinity to ἀλήθεία in Socrates' theory of the truth is searching for the origin of the truth through mythology; however, what I will prove in the next sections is the irrelevance of the questions of what-being and origin in understanding truth or experiencing Truth. Therefore, what is the most essential in regard to truth and Truth, the divine matter and another divine matter for us in *Apology* is this *distinction* (ἄλλη) between θεία and ἄλλη θεία, between the experience of oracular truth, divine connection and dream on the one hand, and the experience of logos in form of understanding on the other hand.

The Politics of the Cave

"We wish to consider the essence of truth," writes Heidegger (2013: 1). He begins his lecture on Plato's allegory of the cave with a specific purpose; to search for the essence of the truth in Plato's philosophy. He discusses that the general definition indicates that the truth is the thing that contains something true. Thus, the truth should be *correspondence*. As the concept of essence refers to a *universal picture* of it, correspondence can be known as the essence of the truth. But then he asks: is not the truth always derived from a perspective about its object? His answer to this question is that whenever there is a claim of the truth of a subject-matter, there is also a prior piece of knowledge (it must be true, otherwise it cannot be knowledge) about the subject-matter that fulfills the possibility of the truth. The necessity of this pre-knowledge reshapes the truth as "correspondence with another correspondence" (Heidegger 2013: 3). The problem then is the new correspondence will be predicated on another correspondence and this chain will be unlimited. Therefore, correspondence, in Heidegger's opinion, is not self-evident and intelligible as the essence of truth.

I have several disagreements with his argument. The truth in the general sense is *experience* (*Erlebnis*). That is to say, truth is not simply a correspondence between a state of things and a proposition, it must always be also an experience, even if it is only our experience of the proposition and its relation to its objects.

It is on this level that we can speak of the truth of a dream, a prophecy, or even of an illusion. Gadamer attracts our attention to the history of the word '*Erlebnis*' when he points out that this word first appeared in one of Hegel's letters and became more common much later (in the 1870s) than the verb '*erleben*', which was widely used in the age of Goethe. *Erleben*, as one of the roots of *Erlebnis*, means "to be still alive when something happens." Therefore, as Gadamer explains, the word suggests a certain immediacy at work in grasping something, *from one's own experience*. Accordingly, what *erleben* illuminates about *Erlebnis* is "what is experienced is always what one has experienced oneself" (Gadamer 2013: 56).

In addition to *erleben*, we have '*das Erlebte*' which means "the permanent content of what is experienced" (Gadamer 2013: 56). Similar to *erleben*, *das Erlebte* too indicates the primacy and the immediacy of experience over interpretation and content. Studying the history of *Erlebnis* shows us that this word is also rooted in biographical literature, which engages *Erlebnis* with the concept of life. This connection illuminates the mode of *Erlebnis* as experience, that "something becomes an experience not only in so far as it is experienced but in so far as it is being experienced makes a special impression that gives it lasting importance" (Gadamer 2013: 56). To be an *Erlebnis* means to be circulated in a significant whole (the subject's life) as a distinguished part (an experience) from what was experienced before, and also from the rest of life, in which nothing is experienced yet. Experience then belongs to the unity of self; the unity of *the life of* oneself that experienced it.

Essential to this experience is that it "has a definite immediacy which eludes every opinion about its meaning" (Gadamer 2013: 61). Experience is not interpretive, but only experienceable by oneself, constantly in relation to the wholeness of one's life. *Erlebnis* singularly is free of the exhaustion of the search for its meaning, as its mode is to be experienced. In the case of experience, we do not face the main failure that Heidegger detected in the concept of correspondence. The singularity of experience is that its mode is to be experienced, and *there is nothing beyond the experience of experience*. In other words, there is no experience of experience of experience. Experience cannot perform an independent signification on the experience of experience. Every form of this new signification is to be experienced by the act of the exterior experience in experience of experience. Therefore, experience remains in two levels. The question then is how experience itself can be experienced.

We already discussed that the truth (ἀλnθεία) is the totality of truth (ἄλλη θεία, the *logos*) and Truth (θεία and dreams). The form of the truth and Truth is experience and the form of truth (ἄλλη θεία) is *to be understood*. This understanding is an experience in the general sense; an experience whose its instrument or procedure is only *logos*. When the experience is in the form of understanding, it can be communicated and shared with others who understand the same system of *logos*. Unlike truth, the experience of Truth is not sharable or a subject-matter of understanding, but it is only to be experienced by oneself. We do not understand our dreams in the moment of dreaming, but we allow ourselves to experience them. What is experienced then can only be experienced in its original form. Therefore, it is not possible to share it with others. As the concept of experience suggests, experience is always only the experience of the one who is experiencing it. Furthermore, unlike truth, Truth is not intentional. While one can decide and intend to understand, experience as Truth is not in the hands of the subject. The one who experiences Truth is always *chosen* to experience it or finds himself in the experience (in the case of dreaming). Therefore, what we want to discuss in this chapter is the conditions and the possibility of *understanding* the truth. Understanding the truth for us is experiencing the experience but we also want to be able to share and discuss this experience with others and this is an intentional investigation. Therefore, we aim to experience the experience (understand truth). Thus, in our logical experience of our subject (truth), we have to bracket the *inexponible* Truth, which is only a subject-matter of experience, not understanding.

In addition, we need a medium to allow us to discuss the conditions and the limits of understanding truth. While I understand truth as what is understood by the subject of understanding, the whole horizon of truth, our horizon of understanding, and what can be outside the border of this horizon remain key questions. Accordingly, in order to demonstrate this system, the horizon of understandables and what belongs outside this horizon, we require a medium, designed to model the relationship between what is beyond our horizon of understanding or cannot be encountered in our world on the one hand, and our own horizon of understanding on the other hand, all corresponding to our understanding; a medium capable of providing us with a different standpoint in the demonstration of what we are not supposed to encounter in our world due to its mode of conception (non-understandability), which is modeled as a being we are able to encounter in this avatar. This medium is *allegory*. Through understanding the allegories of the truth we come to experience this experience.

By the same token, in the plethora of signifieds for truth, we need a medium to help us bracket the concepts and point to them without the necessity of simultaneously using these concepts (calling them). This is another characteristic of allegory; providing the reader/writer with a medium to *show* the relationships between the elements, demonstrating what is called truth for each thinker, and comparing them instead of relying on a single name (truth) when the name actually refers to various signifieds. What remains a question then is the conditions and the horizon of understanding. But before following our discussion, I need to discuss the difference between Heidegger's metaphysical notions of truth and understanding.

For Heidegger, the problem of the essence of truth seems to be the ambiguity of essence-hood, the *what-being* that is necessary to be known in advance, in order to recognize all things that we encounter, including the truth itself. Heidegger continues his discussion of the essence of the truth, concentrating on the conditions of encounter and understanding. He aims to answer the question: What makes our understanding of an object possible when we encounter it? How do we recognize it? His answer is the knowledge of a *universal understanding* of that object as a category. Therefore, the *essence-hood* of the truth for Heidegger is the what-being of the truth required to be known in advance to make understanding the truth possible. What I discuss regarding the truth in this essay is that the mode of truth is *to be understood*, and the mode of both Truth and the truth is *to be experienced*. I use *the mode* instead of *the mode of being* on purpose. One may raise the question of how this understanding essentially differs from the judgment of existence or from the judgment predicated on being-non-being. What Kant discusses in response to this question in the third critique then is that the concept of "What sort of thing it is supposed to be" (Kant 2007: 112) belongs to the *representation* of an *objective purposiveness*; however, essential to understanding is that it is not "a faculty for the cognition of an object" (Kant 2007: 113), which is the main difference between understanding and knowing, that we addressed at the beginning of the chapter. Accordingly, what should be reconsidered regarding truth is its different mode, its lack of presence as being and existence, but only to be understood. What is to be understood is not knowledge to be present or accessible or even inaccessible. Therefore, truth is not the subject of being-non-being but is always to be understood. Truth is not an object or objective to be understood, it is not the ultimate knowledge, but truth is always understood by the subject who experiences it. The significance of truth then is that it *is* not. It is essentially a ὑποτύπωσις (hypotyposis); one should not explore it as what *is*, but only in us and in the structure of our understanding and logos.

Stage one: Situation of man in the cave (514a to 515c)

This stage of the allegory illuminates what people take as the unhidden or true. The significance of this situation is, as Heidegger (2013: 22) explains, "Plato does not say *an* unhidden[1], but *the*[2] unhidden"; where Heidegger interprets this as *the* truth, as the specific object, I want to ask about the truth experienced (or experienceable for him) by the caveman, about his being set before *the* unhidden *to him*. Even in this specific situation, there is something immediate to be grasped, something prior to any question or difficulty; an irreducible thing that belongs to him.

For Heidegger, the unhidden to the caveman is nothing but the shadows in front of him. For him, this means that the caveman is not capable of raising the question of what the being of the shadows is, as he is too close to the horizon of shadows to be able to question it. Thus, the caveman takes the shadows as the unhidden. He cannot see the fire and other beings that Heidegger and we can distinguish as the readers of this allegory, as the ones whose horizons allow them to understand truth through the medium specific to human beings and their understanding. Heidegger concludes that for cave-dwellers, the shadows are not shadows of beings, but the very beings; "man straightforwardly takes whatever presents itself before him as unhidden" (Heidegger 2013: 24).

But Heidegger fails to recognize that there is no universal truth. Every evaluation and understanding is *from the perspective of a viewer*. Thus, truth is always the subject matter of the one who is understanding it. It is the allegory, however, that provides us with the possibility of comparing the horizon of the experiences of the characters and our own. The prisoners do not consider themselves in a situation, they do not consider what is in front of them as shadows but experience what is experienceable for them in the form of understanding; however, Heidegger sees them in *misapprehension* and he forgets his own stance.

Stage two: The moment of distraction (515c to 515e)

What happens if one of the prisoners gets unshackled and is free to turn his head and look behind him? Socrates believes that the prisoner will think that the things he saw earlier were truer than the ones he is now being shown (R 515d). Within his experience, it is the shadows that remain unhidden. The gradation of unhiddenness is a new characteristic of the truth that Plato discusses here. These *more* and *less* are not by means of a numerical measure; Plato does not discuss that more things are unhidden now, that there are things unhidden in addition to the shadows which were unhidden before. His point is that the truth does not have the same strength for everyone and regarding every being. In this case, the shadows will be more truthful, more unhidden (more understandable) to the prisoner than the unknown fire and the beings that he faces when he turns; however, that is not all the argument. The form of the question that Plato utilizes is important: "What do you think he'd say, if we told him that what he'd seen before was nonsense, but now that he is closer to the things and is turned towards things that are more (μᾶλλον)—he sees straighter?" (R 515d).

Heidegger himself makes the most of the ambiguity of Plato's text here as it is not mentioned in the text to what μᾶλλον refers. Heidegger (2013: 27) relates it to the beingfulness of things and translated the second part as *"more beingful beings."* Heidegger does not deny that *for the prisoner*, the shadows will be still more truthful after he sees the fire and the beings, but he argues for an understanding of truth as *correctness* and traces its relationship to *beingfulness*. Heidegger claims that "the things themselves are more unhidden, the things which the now unshackled prisoner, as he turns around, is supposed to see" (Heidegger 2013: 28). But if Heidegger agrees that unhiddenness and truthfulness are related to the subject who experiences them (as to the prisoner, the shadows remain more truthful, but to Socrates, Heidegger, and the readers, the things are more truthful), he should be able to see that this "more truthful" is only related to Socrates' *stance* and the standpoint of the readers of the allegory, as we all share the same *position* and horizon of understanding that allows us to experience both shadows and the beings. Heidegger in the second stage of the allegory neglects the stance of the subjects of the truth (the prisoners, the jailors, the beings outside the cave, and himself as the reader of the allegory), their distinct worlds and truths. Heidegger focuses on our stance and neglects what is more unhidden *to the prisoner*. Heidegger emphasizes Plato's point, that *beings* are more truthful than their shadows, and concludes that this greater truthfulness is actually greater beingfulness. As a result, the closer you get to beings, the more unhidden they will be in your access to them; the more unhidden the object, the more correct the perception. Therefore, truth as correctness is in debt to proximity and to the increased unhiddenness of the beings. Heidegger explains that Plato shows us here a method to solve the problem of the ambiguous relationship between the two concepts of truth (correctness and *alētheia*), and a way to access the origin.

But the so-called process of accessing the more beingful, or as Heidegger addresses it, the "process of liberation" fails. The prisoner decides to return to his former position, toward the shadows. The prisoner wants to return to what *he* sees as more truthful. Heidegger believes that "the main standard for his estimation of higher or lower unhidden is the preservation of the undisturbedness of his ordinary activities, without being set out to any kind of demand or command" (Heidegger 2013: 30). Heidegger tries to explain why liberation fails and for what reason the prisoner decides to turn back again, he believes that the shadowy life of the prisoner in the cave only brings confusion. He goes even further: "He is sick, and healing is necessary" (Heidegger 2013: 31). Heidegger finishes his interpretation of this stage by explaining that "In the second stage what happens is a failure, namely that he who has been unshackled fails to encounter unhiddenness as such" (Heidegger 2013: 32). We can either understand or experience what we encounter. What we cannot understand is either a subject-matter of only experiencing or that non-accessibility would be its mode of conception. When incomprehensibility is the subject-matter's mode of conception, in our failure in encountering the subject-matter of understanding, we accomplish our understanding of it. In writing and understanding an allegory of truth and modeling a being as the avatar of what we cannot encounter in our world, we make a detour into the possibility of the incomprehensible. Therefore, this lack of encounter in the cave is not a failure. Quite opposite to defeat, the caveman in his lack of recognition, and we all, sharing the similar faculties of experiencing the truth with Socrates who spoke the allegory, turn our so-called failure (the existence of incomprehensible subject-matter in our world) into victory; as the readers and listeners to the allegory, we all can have an understanding of the incomprehensible in our world which is modeled as the beings inside the cave. In this way we overcome the incomprehensible in our world, postpone our hypothesis of existence of the incomprehensible, and fulfill our understanding of it by means of the allegory.

Seeing and the conditions of understanding

One of the main questions regarding this allegory is why the prisoner cannot look at the fire and see the beings clearly. Is this only a physical seeing? I want now to discuss the meaning of this seeing as the possibility of an *encounter*, as the condition of understanding truth, and the way it can be interpreted in this allegory.

What distinguishes seeing with the bodily eye, and seeing as such discussed in the allegory is that at the second stage, the prisoner can see the beings with his bodily eye, he has the physical image of the being in front of him, he has time to get adapted to the light of the fire, to the light in the cave, but his seeing as such does not take place. This specific seeing, different from seeing with the eyes, is an *encounter*. Encounter is the precondition of understanding and what sabotages the seeing here is the impossibility of the prisoner's encountering the beings.

What is not experienceable for the prisoner inside the cave, when he turns his face is not some aspects of the beings in the cave, which are not experienceable to his senses, but the aspects that "make it possible to see an object as an object" (Vessey 2009: 534). These are what the hermeneutic tradition refers to as the horizons "above and beyond what is given directly to our senses" (Vessey 2009: 534), that frame and hence make perceptible the objects in cognition. Such a horizon is both enabling and necessarily marks a limit. Gadamer explains that "Every finite present has its limitations. We define the concept of *situation* by saying that it represents a standpoint that limits the possibility of vision. Hence essential to the concept of situation is the concept of *horizon*. The horizon is the range of vision that includes everything that can be seen from a particular vantage point" (Gadamer 2013: 313). Everything we see is seen from *a particular standpoint* in time.

Every standpoint then is a historical horizon. The present is not isolated from the horizons of the past, and none of these are constant, but they are constantly changing as the one who wants to understand encounters the past, while moving forward in the horizon of history and changing the position of the present. In order to understand, the person who wants understanding must encounter other historically extant horizons. As Gadamer explains, "understanding is the fusion of these horizons supposedly existing by themselves" (Gadamer 2013: 317). Therefore, the one who wants to understand must: (1) foreground the past from the perspective of the present, and consider history as the integration of whole and parts; (2) understand the limits of his own horizon; and (3) recognize the existence of alternative horizons, which can touch his own. The existence of these conditions makes the encounter, as a moment of understanding, possible: the touching of two horizons.

The prisoner sees the beings with his eyes, but he does not have an *encounter* with them. This means that his horizon of history cannot touch the horizon of the history of the beings next to the fire. Therefore, the prisoner cannot form a broader horizon, his horizon cannot accept the horizon of the other beings in it. There can be two different hypotheses. The first one is that the prisoner does not see far enough; however, we know that he is able to see the shadows. The second theory is that the separation of the horizon of the history of the prisoner and the horizon of the history of the other beings inside the cave blocks the possibility of the fusion of the horizons of history. The prisoner understands (ἄλλη θεία) in his own horizon of history, while his horizon cannot touch the horizon of the other beings next to the fire, and consequently, there can never be an encounter or understanding of the beings inside the cave for the prisoner. This is the impossibility of experiencing the incomprehensible which does not belong to the world of the prisoner due to its mode of conception (the very hypothesis and significance of allegory) for the prisoner at the second stage, not the impossibility of accessing the truth. This is the time that I want to return to Foucault and address what he can add to our study of truth in the cave.

The Foucauldian Truth

The problem of the impossibility of a dialogue between hermeneutics and Foucault can be traced in the multiplicity of signifieds of truth, a problematic naming, the consequential confusion in the dialogue, in addition to neglecting the specific aspect of truth that each one of these theories tries to illuminate. Foucault recognizes an unnoticed problem regarding the *manifestation* of truth in our cave, that the shadows may be manipulated, and this can affect our access to ἄλλη θεία. Our history of interpretations then will be the history of interpretation of the corrupted shadows, which requires, as he diagnosed, a further investigation. The investigation that he addresses is in history. Foucault diagnoses the necessity of an investigation to clarify the *formation of the shadows* or the manifestation of truth.

What is Foucauldian truth? "Truth is essentially conceived as a system of obligations, independently of the fact that it may or may not be considered true from this or that point of view. Truth is above all a system of obligations" (Foucault 2019: 12). This is where the line between the manifestation of truth and truth itself disappears for him and the signifier (truth) signifies both of these signifieds in his theory after that. I called this a problematic naming that causes some confusion in the dialogue on truth with his theory. What specific aspect of truth is the subject of his work and the most important to him? "What is important in this question (truth as a universal knowledge) is that a certain number of things actually pass for true, and that the subject must produce them himself, or accept them, or submit to them. So, what has been and will be at issue is the truth as bond, as obligation, and also as politics" (Foucault 2019: 13). Therefore, what is discussed by our sets of both verbal and non-verbal procedures, what takes the form of recorded information, knowledge, note, rituals, ceremonies, magical operations or oracular consultation is different manifestations of truth.

Foucault is interested in identifying the ritual manifestations of truth (alethurgies) and "the relations between the exercise of power and manifestation of truth" (Foucault 2016: 22). He explains power's reliance on the manifestation of truth as "power in general, could not be exercised if truth were not manifested" (Foucault 2016: 73). Foucault realized that behind the forces that oblige individuals, there are processes and institutions that exercise "a right of sovereignty". The subject's relationship with the procedures of (manifestation of) truth for Foucault is the obligations that are forced on individuals by the regimes of truth. A regime of truth in Foucault's theory of truth *constrains* the subject to certain truth acts and also defines their conditions and effects. Although the subject knows that what is manifested as truth may be false and finds it impossible to be manifested independently, he submits to what is manifested and posits it as truth. That is how truth creates obligations in a regime of truth.

What Foucault adds to our study of truth and the allegory of the cave is detecting a regime of truth in our system that escaped the notice of hermeneutics and metaphysics; a judicial alethurgy. The caveman, the shackled prisoner inside the cave accepts what he sees, what he understands, namely the shadows shown on the wall in front of him as truth. He knows that it is he who is using his faculty of understanding and making his connection with the shadows; that he was there and this understanding took place in front of his eyes. But he, in his own identity, authenticates the jailors' institution of the manifestation of truth (shadow play). He does not question the authenticity of the manifestation of truth as he finds himself *witnessing* the manifestations of truth, understanding, and speaking them; even though this powerless man, this *slave* is nothing but a powerless spectator who summons himself as it is common in judicial alethurgy to testify the truth, and as he does not need any torture to confess the truth, he remembers and testifies what he saw (shadows) in his conscience, and as the confession in the judicial alethurgy has the weight of truth, he accepts them as truth. Without any commonality with the jailors, "with those who command" and form the manifestation of truth (shapes of the shadows), the caveman trusts his gaze and obeys. Foucault's genealogy then is what he offers as a method of investigating the alethurgies and regimes of truth.

Foucault explains that "The role of genealogy is to record its history: the history of morals, ideals, and metaphysical concepts, the history of the concept of liberty or the ascetic life; as they stand for the emergence of different interpretations, they must be made to appear as events on the stage of historical process" (Foucault 2021b: 152). In other words, as Dreyfus and Rabinow define it, the genealogist is the one who records the history of the developments of humanity in form of interpretation. What is the genealogist's approach? "The world is not a play which simply makes a truer reality that exists behind the scenes. It is as it appears. It is the profundity of the genealogist's insight" (Dreyfus and Rabinow 1983: 109).

Now that we have the common ground, having bracketed the concept of truth, and are still able to discuss two different theories of truth while standing inside Plato's cave, this is the right time for me to pose my third series of questions to Foucault: How far can we rely on the genealogist? Is genealogy capable of detecting *all* regimes of truths and alethurgies? In order to answer these questions, we first need to know where the genealogist stands inside the cave. Is he one of the prisoners? Jailors? Or one of the people outside the cave? I believe this is the time to discuss this serious question once again, in the singular position of Plato's cave.

Foucault explains "What is the source of history? It comes from the plebs. To whom is it addressed? To the plebs. And its discourses strongly resemble the demagogue's refrain: 'no one is greater than you and anyone who presumes to get the better of you—you who are good—is evil'" (Foucault 2021b: 158). If the historian, the one to whom the history is addressed is one of the *plebs*, and the history itself also comes from the plebs, and the historian does not have superiority over the others, he must be one of the prisoners. If he is one of the prisoners, can he encounter the beings? Having a certain historical standpoint, is he able to do genealogy? Derrida (1978) got close to asking this question in "Cogito and the History of Madness." Although he tried to investigate the possibility of Foucault's project of writing a history of madness, to write about the secret and enclosed being of madness through history, which is on the horizon of reason, and he did not focus on the historicity of history and the historical position of the historian in Foucault's work, but he did briefly point out the impossibility of being both encompassed in a horizon (to have a certain historical standpoint) and of investigating another horizon, one which we cannot encounter. Hence Amy Allen raised the question: "Where, after all, does the archaeologist who attempts to trace the outlines of our historical a priori stand?" (Allen 2016: 134), replying merely that "Perhaps Foucault would simply refuse this way of posing the question" (Allen 2016: 135). In short, he too is one of the prisoners.

Thus, as our discussion of Gadamer shows, Foucault too will not be able to encounter the beings. Neither is he capable of performing a genealogy of the shadows. He will have a certain historical standpoint and consequently he will not have access to the whole horizon of time (his future). That requires another scene, another experience. That is why Herodotus, although being a historian and a mortal man with a certain historical standpoint, added the oracular voice to his narrative. He had access to the past, the time of the events he was narrating (relative to the present), and the future (of the event, up until his own present time). But he did not have access to the future dimension of history. As a result, he needed a voice beyond the boundaries of time and with different experiences, capacities, and faculties of the truth. After Croesus, like Socrates, tried to examine the oracles, the oracle of Delphi responded to this offense singularly in his message to Croesus in hexameters. It began his response by:

"*I know the grains of sand on the beach and measure the sea;*
I understand the speech of the dumb and hear the voiceless."

(H 1:47)

In the first line, the oracle claims that it is capable of experiencing both microscopic and macroscopic matters *beyond any boundaries*. The second line explains that it has different faculties of experiencing the truths, which are different from our faculty of understanding truth, and he is also capable of experiencing the truths that are not subject matters of our experiences. Herodotus knowing his historical standpoint and his limits of experiencing the truth, added the prophecies to his historical narrative in order to be able to "sketch a sophisticated collage of the different dimensions of time" (Kindt 2006: 43). Similarly, as long as the genealogist does not have access to the whole horizon of time, he will not necessarily be able to detect all the manifestations and the regimes of truth or how the shadows are manipulated. History is all he has, all we have as prisoners, but it is not necessarily sufficient for Foucauldian truth. The genealogist's standpoint attracts our attention to the necessity of a genealogy of the genealogist as well.

What we have seen in this chapter is that each of our theories of truth is either partially effective or only capable of detecting certain aspects of the truth independently. But only in the allegorical method of understanding the truth, only when we applied all the theories to the cave, have we succeeded in seeing if we can posit a complete picture of different aspects of the truth operating simultaneously, of all the players in the game.

Conclusion

We began by identifying what ἀλήθεια comports to English. After tracing the differences between the two different subgroups of ἀλήθεια, namely truth ἄλλη θεία (other divine) and Truth (divine, oracular, and from dreams), we introduced the mode and instruments of each of these truths. Accordingly, truth is the subject-matter of the non-cognitive concept of understanding and consequently, the notions of origin and the so-called necessity of knowing its what-being are not a priori to it. Therefore, its mode is to be understood. This identification helped us to understand that what we were trying to accomplish through the allegory of the cave is to understand ἄλλη θεία (truth), which, unlike the inexponible experience of Truth, is an intentional and sharable experience. In addition, experience as the instrument of the truth is always the experience of the subject. Therefore, the truth, truth, and Truth, are not objects or objective beings, but they are what is experienced by the subject who experiences them, each in their different modes and dimensions.

The significance of the allegory of Plato's cave is that it shows us the only method in which the horizon and conditions of truth (ἄλλη θεία) can be discussed is via allegory. We can only discuss truth from the standpoint of the interpreter of this text, as an observer outside the horizon of the prisoner inside the cave. The impossibility of encountering the beings and fire inside the cave is due to the mode of conception (incomprehensibility) of what they signify and model; however, the fact that this allegory is written by a human being, that someone by means of allegory succeeded in making our encounter with the hypothetical incomprehensibles possible, postpones the possibility of their existence and undermines the hypothesis itself.

We discussed how Foucault was not unfamiliar with the reason behind our differenciation between the divine truth (Truth) and the other divine truth (truth), what he himself called the different procedure of truth; the divine half and the human half. But his interpretation of the truth–subject relationship was affected by shifting his attention from the experience of truth (including prophecy, dreams, perhaps even madness) to truth-telling. Furthermore, we discussed how these two almost became the same thing for him; however, it was his attention to truth-telling and the manifestation of truth that allowed him to question the formation of shadows and the existence of a judicial/testimonial regime of truth in our allegory of the cave. In return, we tried to investigate the position of the genealogist inside the cave and the reliability of genealogy. We understood that the genealogist will be one of the prisoners and consequently, he will have a certain historical standpoint that limits his access to the future dimension of time. Therefore, he will not necessarily always have access to the truth but he still will be able to detect many regimes of truth.

Our interpretation of the allegory of the cave was a way to picture a complete view of the concept of truth in a unique medium that can display all signifieds of the concept of truth through a fiction, through bracketing both the name and the inaccessibility of the horizons. The allegory is the very common ground that provides a possibility of dialogue on the concept of truth, while offering a possibility of understanding it.

3

Nothing to Do with the Truth? New Reflections on Foucault's Reading of Artemidorus

Sandra Boehringer
Université de Strasbourg

Translated by Meryl Altman[1]

"Between each of us and our sex, the West has placed a never-ending demand for truth: it is up to us to extract the truth of sex, since this truth is beyond its grasp; it is up to sex to tell us our truth, since sex is what holds it in darkness."

So wrote Michel Foucault in Volume 1 of his *History of Sexuality, La Volonté de savoir* (*The Will to Knowledge*) (Foucault 1980: 72; 1976: 102).

Foucault uses this formulation, which historicizes the relationship between the subject and truth, to describe the apparatus of sexuality as it develops in the age of *scientia sexualis*, in a "society of the norm" (Foucault 1996: 197; 1994b: 75) where power "produces reality; it produces domains of knowledge and rituals of truth" (Foucault 1995: 195; 1975: 227).[2] With this historicization, this description of a transformation which occurs in the West, he clearly invites us to look to the present day, to analyze contemporary forms of governmentality and the games of truth that belong to our own "society of the norm." But he invites us equally to look toward the past, toward those periods when that very demand for truth, which now binds sexuality and the subject so tightly together, did not yet exist, or at least did not produce itself through the same "games." Foucault directs our gaze to the time "before sexuality," as it was called in 1990 in the famous title of the collection edited by David Halperin, John Winkler, and Froma Zeitlin.

In 1984, the Volumes 2 and 3 of the *History of Sexuality* appeared, *L'Usage des plaisirs* (*The Use of Pleasure*) and *Le Souci de soi* (*Care of the Self*). For the reading public of that day, that is to say for those who knew Foucault through his writing rather than through attending his lectures at the Collège de France, it was Greek and Roman antiquity—really the six centuries from the fourth century BCE to the second century CE—which constituted the first stage of the argument, an argument advanced *through contrast*. The strongly marked difference of *dispositif*, "apparatus," between the different historical periods underpins his argument, putting into practice the principle of "refusing universals"[3] that Foucault held so dear. Readers became familiar with the Foucauldian chronology that can be expressed by the formula, "ancient *aphrodisia*; Christian flesh; modern apparatus of sexuality." And the gulf between the *aphrodisia* and the modern apparatus was further underscored by Foucault's unexpected leap back in time from the nineteenth century in Volume 1 (1976) to the ancient world in the Volumes 2 and 3 published in 1984.

This quick summary of the development of Foucault's work may seem obvious: it is the standard consensus that has framed Foucault scholarship for quite some time. And yet, over the last twenty years, certain things have changed, as new information has become available to us. First of all, the publication of Foucault's lectures at the Collège de France is finally complete, along with their translation into English; and secondly, in 2013 the Foucault archive was acquired by the Bibliothèque Nationale de France (BNF). Access to the notes Foucault used in preparing for his public talks, his reading notes, and draft manuscripts of his works (which I was able to consult at the BNF, and some of which have now been published), can help us to better understand how Foucault's thinking evolved. The posthumous publication of the talks he delivered in the United States and of *Les Aveux de la chair* (*Confessions of the Flesh*) as Volume 4 in the *History of Sexuality* now make it possible for us to take a new look at the work of the "Late Foucault" (Foucault 2011: 2; 2009: 3) and at the way he constructs the history of the "forms and modalities of the relation to self by which the individual constitutes and recognizes himself *qua* subject" (Foucault 1986: 6; 1984a: 12). I should also note here that, as Daniele Lorenzini has wisely pointed out (Boehringer and Lorenzini 2022: 5–6), the author's death in 1984 meant that critics were unable to gather responses from Foucault himself to the questions raised by the joint publication of *L'Usage des plaisirs* and *Le Souci de soi*; that practice of exchange and discussion, which had always followed the publication of his major works and had enabled Foucalt to clarify what he was doing (through interviews, debates, and so on), was no longer possible.

These recent and forthcoming publications, along with the work of editors and specialists (particularly Frédéric Gros, Daniele Lorenzini, and Phillipe Chevallier in France, and Paul Allen Miller and Niki Kasumi Clements in the United States) have begun a truly massive undertaking. This very broad and rich site for work in progress will lead to many more studies on a range of topics, including how Foucault developed his history of the games of truth in one's relation to oneself, and the role of Western antiquity in this development.

My argument here will unfold in the context of that flurry of new publications, but from a rather specific angle. I have chosen one particular document that Foucault used to unveil the historicity of the "never-ending demand for truth": an extract from Artemidorus of Ephesus' *Oneirokritikon*, the only complete ancient work of dream-interpretation that has come down to us.

In the first section of this chapter, I will briefly present the main elements of Foucault's analysis of sexual dreams, highlighting the points relevant to my analysis. In the second part, I will propose my own analysis of this approach to Artemidorus' work, starting from the margins and from his classification of sexual dreams. Finally, in a third section, I will begin to set out some hypotheses about what role this document plays in the history of truth as Foucault outlines it in his last works.

What do these sexual dreams, gathered from individual dreamers and collected together by a knowledgeable traveling expert from the second century CE, have to do with truth? Nothing? Let us look more closely.

How to Interpret Erotic Dreams: Artemidorus in *Le Souci de soi*

At the time when Michel Foucault first became interested in Artemidorus' book, in the late 1970s, very few studies about it had been published. We must not be fooled by our current sense of familiarity with this ancient manual, as we owe this familiarity mainly to Foucault.

Of course, psychoanalysts had been acquainted with Artemidorus' work for a long time by way of Sigmund Freud, who comments on it at length in *Interpretation of Dreams*, the *Traumdeutung* (1899). But the inventor of psychoanalysis was relying on the German translation made by Friedrich Salomo Krauss in 1881, and that text had been expurgated, leaving out the chapters on sexual dreams (I. 78–80)—something Freud did not fail to find ridiculous.[4] The French translation by the Dominican friar and philologist André-Jean Festugière, which is still the standard translation in France, appeared in 1975: this is the edition Foucault used. The Greek text was Pack's 1963 edition, which Festugière and later Foucault reference.[5]

As recently published letters show, Foucault maintained a cordial intellectual friendship with Festugière.[6] He was thus among the first to read this translation (perhaps even before it was published) and it is to this version that he refers. Nonetheless, I should point out that Festugière's translation is not easy to use when working on the question of sexuality: for instance, when Artemidorus gives the example of a man filled with desire for his young male lover (*paidika*), Festugière translates this with a more general and neutral term, as *l'objet aimé*, the object of love.

Artemidorus is better known today: he is translated, and numerous *Companions* and other books about dreams comment on his work. Still, studies and commentaries devoted to sexuality in Artemidorus are quite rare, even though translators tend to introduce their commentaries on the section about sexual dreams with a sentence such as "The section on the sex-dreams is probably the most famous of the entire *Oneirocritica*" (Harris-McCoy 2012: 461).[7]

Thus William Harris (2009), *Dreams and Experience in Classical Antiquity*, has no section devoted to the question of sexuality. And he's not alone: in the recent, and very interesting, edited collections about Artemidorus, we find all sorts of information about social hierarchies in the Greek cities of Asia Minor, about theater, about death, about money and credit, about animals, about colors, about the names given to plants, to weights and measures, to different foods etc.,[8] but there are very few discussions of sexuality.

Two in-depth studies do exist that bear on sexual dreams in Artemidorus' book: one by Simon Price ([1986] 1990) and the other by John J. Winkler (1990). Price underscores the enormous difference between the *Oneirokritikon* and Freud's *Traumdeutung*, which belong to different apparatuses and work by different logics. He barely refers to Foucault. Price's argument does not really have to do with sex; according to him, what has kept us from understanding Artemidorus' logic is our anachronistic way of thinking about dreams.

Winkler's approach, on the other hand, is very much centered on the question of sex. He is concerned to demonstrate that Artemidorus' work is "anthropological" in nature, by showing that his classification of sexual acts corresponds to shared social norms. He refers to Foucault only twice in this long chapter, which might seem surprising (we know that the two men met, in the United States, and that they felt warmly toward one another). That said, Winkler's argument does not have to do with the role of dreaming, or of sex, in the subject's relationship to himself or herself. Winkler's aim is to show what social codes regarding sexuality, and what relations of domination, are revealed by the dream narratives in Artemidorus' book. It is important to notice that both Price and Winkler were writing *after* Foucault's book had already appeared; between 1980 and 1984, Foucault was advancing across almost uncharted terrain.

This is probably one of the reasons for the strange way Foucault approaches Artemidorus at the beginning of *Le Souci de soi*: page after page seem to have been written by a classical philologist who is following standard academic practices in presenting his sources. But this becomes understandable when we remember that the audience for Foucault's book would have been unacquainted with this highly technical text. Very few of them would have heard him speak on the topic in his lectures of February 4 and 11, 1981 at the Collège de France, and even fewer people heard his 1980 presentation at the New York Institute for the Humanities, one section of which is devoted to Artemidorus,[9] or his talk in 1982 to the philosophy department at the University of Grenoble (Foucault 1994d).

In *Le Souci de soi*, there are about fifteen pages of commentary that do not touch on the question of sexuality at all (Foucault 1986b: 4–16; 1984b: 16–30). This is because the reader, to understand the commentary Foucault will go on to provide concerning sexual practices—the reason he chose to discuss this text—must first understand the context of the work's writing, and its didactic and technical nature. It is a work Artemidorus composed in order to demonstrate the scientific process of interpretation, and to transmit the rudiments of his practice to his son: it is a technical manual.

As Foucault explains, Artemidorus draws his own distinction between two different types of dreams, the *enupnion* and the *oneiros*, so as to focus only on the category useful to the professional interpreter, the *oneiroi*. The *oneiroi* are expressions of the sleeper's soul, unlike the *enupnia*, which are literal translations of the dreamer's physical state. Within the category that Artemidorus stays with, the *oneiroi*, one must then learn to distinguish between, on the one hand what he calls "theorematic" dreams (a direct warning from the soul concerning an imminent event, which is thus easy to decipher) and on the other hand "allegorical" dreams, which are the ones that need to be studied carefully, the ones from which the interpreter can draw important predictions about the dreamer's future. After this general introduction, Foucault takes up the small section Artemidorus devoted to the dreams of the *aphrodisia*. He notes that no sexual position can be morally evaluated in itself, that any sexual position can be an omen of either a lucky or an unlucky event. The whole art of the interpreter consists in knowing his client perfectly, because the dream's meaning is deduced using a number of criteria, in particular the socio-economic situation of the dreamer, his family situation (whether his father and mother are dead or living, how many children he has) and any plans he may have to travel. There are some general rules for the interpreter to apply, but only careful observation will reveal which element will be the decisive factor.

So for example, to be penetrated in a dream is not necessarily bad; it is not necessarily bad for a man to dream that he has milk in his breasts and is breastfeeding an infant; it need not be a bad omen to dream that one sexually penetrates one's son or that one makes love with one's mother. (In a sense this is something Artemidorus has in common with Freud: one can dream of anything and everything, and recount one's dream with no fear of moral judgment!)

But since the predictive value of the dreams (whether they are judged to forecast a favorable or unfavorable outcome) cannot help us see how the ancients thought about the sexual practices that appear in those dreams, how was it possible to make use of this document for the project of *The History of Sexuality*?

Foucault announces his objective at the start, with the short paragraph that abruptly opens Volume 3: the point is to show *the stability of ancient values in an Imperial society undergoing ethical change* (and by ethical change, he means in particular the growing value accorded to the conjugal relation, the growing devaluation of relationships with boys, the importance of care of the self, and the emergence of a new relationship of the subject to his sexual activity). According to him, the contrast between the ancient values, on the one hand, and on the other hand the texts produced at the same time Artemidorus was writing by the philosophers, doctors, and moralists of the first and second century (Soranus, Plutarch, Epictetus, Musonius Rufus), would thereby appear more clearly. This might seem like a strange line of argument: after all, such a contrast could have been demonstrated using much older documents, dating from the fourth century BCE. But to follow out Foucault's reasoning: since a particular sexual act in a dream is not, in itself, a favorable or unfavorable sign, what enables us to gain access to the values of individuals who come from a variety of social milieus is not the *content* of their sexual dreams, Foucault explains, but rather the *logic* that governs the reading of the omen conveyed by the dream, and the *classification* of dreams, by the interpreter who is an expert in this technique, as a function of the sexual acts that are dreamed about.

The logic involved is explained at length in the course *Subjectivité et vérité* (Subjectivity and Truth): Foucault is talking about about *socio-sexual isomorphism*. At the end of *L'Usage des plaisirs*, he uses the expression "the principle of isomorphism between sexual relations and social relations" (Foucault 1986: 215; 1984a: 237) to describe the mode of valorization of sexual relations in fourth-century Athens. This idea has been much-discussed by Foucault scholars. As Foucault explained in a 1981 lecture: "In this ethical perception to which Artemidorus bears witness, a sexual act will have a positive value inasmuch as its intertwinings, its intrications, its *sumplokai* extend or reproduce the same model of relation as that linking individuals involved in the whole social field" (Foucault 2017a: 79; 2014a: 81). The omen is thus bad if the sexual act of which he dreams transforms, reverses, or overturns the social hierarchy that exists in the dreamer's waking life.

To this examination of sexual hierarchy Foucault also adds the "principle of activity" (Foucault 2017a: 84–90; 2014a: 86–92): the sexual act is "always conceived of in terms of the model act of penetration, assuming a polarity that opposed activity and passivity" (Foucault 1986: 215; 1984b: 237). This very binary perception (which would generate a great deal of controversy in the 1990s) was strongly influenced by the work of his friend Paul Veyne. In 1978 Veyne had published a landmark article, "La famille et l'amour sous le Haut-Empire romain" (The Family and Love under the High Roman Empire). In this article, Veyne mentions Artemidorus' classifications in two short lines, including a small error which he would correct in a later article (Veyne 1982)—perhaps thanks to Foucault? In the Bibliothèque nationale, we find a copy of this article, inscribed by Paul Veyne to his friend (see Figure 3.1).

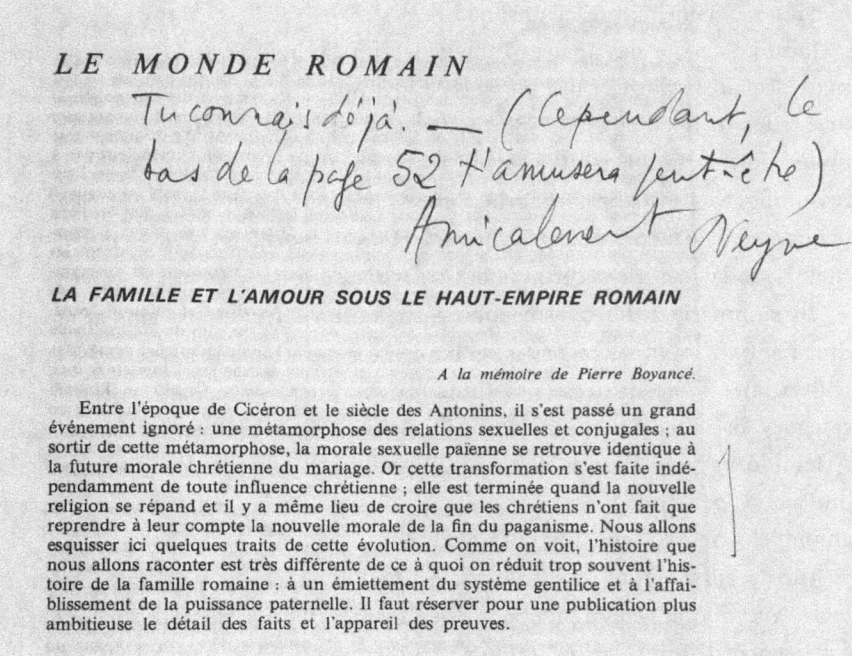

Figure 3.1 *Tu connais déjà (cependant, le bas de la page 52 t'amusera peut-être). Amicalement, Veyne.* "You already know about this! but maybe you'll enjoy the bottom of page 52. Warmly, Veyne." From an off-print of "La famille et l'amour sous le Haut-Empire romain" (1978), with a manuscript inscription from Paul Veyne to Michel Foucault.[10] BNF, Fonds Foucault, NAF 28730, Box 28, f. 843.

Veyne describes the relation of penetration using the fairly violent expression "bisexualité de sabrage" (bisexuality of the saber),[11] and, like Kenneth Dover, whose book *Greek Homosexuality* appeared in the same year, 1978, he foregrounds the fact that it is anachronistic to speak of a division between "homosexuality" and "heterosexuality" when discussing ancient Greeks or Romans, since for them this division did not exist—as Foucault says again at the end of his commentary on the *Oneirokritikon*.

The other aspect of Foucault's analysis has to do with the classification of sexual acts that appear in dreams. The six criteria to be used by the interpreter (the *stoicheia*) are described later by Artemidorus, in a specific section of their own in book four.[12] Here in book one (I, 78–80) he deploys two of those six criteria: one is νόμος, which can be translated as "social convention"; the other is φύσις, which is often translated as "nature," although the meaning of the Greek word is complex and somewhat contested. Sexual acts in dreams are classified into three categories: as κατὰ νόμον, conforming to social convention, as παρὰ νόμον, not conforming to social convention, or as παρὰ φύσιν, not conforming to nature, outside nature, against nature.[13]

John J. Winkler has analyzed the general meaning that the expression παρὰ φύσιν, "against nature," can have in certain kinds of texts. He shows that Seneca, in a letter to Lucilius (122.7-8), uses *contra naturam* to refer to hot baths, to potted flowers, to the habit of eating a large meal after sundown. At this level of reasoning, we must admit that the force of the expression is much weaker than in our own day: it does not speak of perverts or of monsters, as when transphobic rhetoric today describes certain bodies as *unnatural*.

To summarize: the classification κατὰ νόμον includes dreams where the dreamer (who in this category is, with one exception, a man) has sexual relations with women (wife, mistress, prostitute) or with men (slave, patron, friend). The category also includes dreaming of incest with one's brother. In this scenario, Artemidorus' prediction is different depending on whether the dreamer is the one who is penetrated or the one who penetrates. To be penetrated is generally an unlucky omen. Generally, but not always.

The dreamed-about acts that are classified as παρὰ νόμον include dreams of incest and of oral genital practices. The dreamer (who in this category is always a man) may dream of sexual union with his young child, or with his father. In the case of an incestuous dream with the dreamer's mother, the modalities of the sexual union are detailed in a way that a modern reader would not expect, a way we would be more used to seeing in descriptions of relations with a prostitute, mistress, or wife. For example, Artemidorus distinguishes between sexual acts according to whether the mother is dead or living, and also whether the act occurs face-to-face or with the mother's back turned. The face-to-face position is considered as conforming to what is done in the world of nature (a bit later in his treatise Artemidorus develops this point in discussing various animal species). Once again, the act itself may be either a positive or a negative sign—the art of the interpreter involves being sure that he knows his client well. For instance:

> As for dreams of performing oral sex oneself, if this is on someone one knows, whether male or female, it will set the dreamer at odds with that person, as it will no longer be possible to join mouths in a kiss. But if on someone one does not know, this is a harmful dream for anyone except those who use their mouths for their work, by which I mean pipers, trumpeters, orators, sophists, and any others of that sort.
>
> (I.79.125)[14]

Finally, the last category, acts classified as παρὰ φύσιν, includes a dreamer having sexual relations with himself (self-penetration or self-fellation), a woman dreaming of having sexual relations with another woman, a dream of sexual relations with a god or goddess, with a cadaver, or with an animal. We should note that Foucault includes, as part of the category *para phusin*, sexual relations which are not face-to-face, and also oral genital relations. However, in Artemidorus' text, those acts are discussed in a different section, *before* he creates the third category, *para phusin*. I will come back to this point below.

The rest of Foucault's analysis is fairly rapid. He notes the eminently social and economic character of the predictions, the absence of any erotic aspect in what a dream is determined to mean (we are very far away from Freud now). He develops the principle of social and sexual isomorphism that governs the analysis of dreams, comes back to the issue of penetration in analyzing the chapter Artemidorus devotes to the penis, and opines that this text makes it possible for us to gain access to "aspects of manners and customs" (Foucault 1986b: 34; 1984b: 48). But above all—this is where he concludes his discussion—the process of interpretation makes it possible to understand what the main issue is: "what might be called the subject's 'style of activity' and [...] the relation he establishes between sexual activity and the other aspects of his familial, social, and economic existence" (Foucault 1986b: 35; 1984b: 49). A little before this, he writes: "The sexual dream uses the little drama of penetration and passivity, pleasure and expenditure, to tell the subject's mode of being, as destiny has arranged it" (Foucault 1986b: 33; 1984b: 46).

Foucault's conclusion is not simple. We do not find here, says Foucault, any "clear and definitive line of division between what is natural and what is 'contrary to nature'"; but, he writes, we do see the expression of "a few major prohibitions that are manifested in the form of intense repulsions: fellatio, sexual relations between women, and above all, the usurping of the male role by a woman" (Foucault 1986b: 35; 1984b: 46). Artemidorus' text represents the ancient apparatus of a *before sexuality*, of a sex without truth, and *at the same time*, according to Foucault, this sexual dream says something about the subject, something less intimately invasive, but which all the same is particular to that individual subject,[15] especially when he dreams about acts that are strongly prohibited.

Sex *para phusin*, or What the Margin Reveals

Next I would like to concentrate on the part of Artemidorus' text which Foucault did not study at such great length, the part that has to do with dreams *para phusin*, which he nonetheless uses to support his interpretation that Artemidorus' system of classification gives us information about the moral *value* connected with sexual relations at the time when Artemidorus lived. As is well-known, the best way of bringing to light the tacit logics governing what is "normal" and "mainstream" is to analyze what is excluded or pushed to the margin.

The section about dreams "against nature" includes a passage describing two possible dreams by women.

> If a woman dreams of penetrating another woman, she will share her secrets with the woman penetrated; but if she does not know the woman she penetrates, she will find herself pursuing matters which come to nothing. If a woman dreams of being penetrated by another woman, she will be separated from her husband or widowed: but she will still learn the secrets of the woman with whom she has sex.
>
> (1.80.23)

Classicists have usually read this passage as proof of a lively repulsion with regard to sexual relations between women, since these dreams are grouped together with practices of necrophilia, autophilia, zoophilia, and what might be called "theophilia." For some commentators, this is because one of the two women would be taking the place of a man (that is Foucault's reading); for others, it is because she would be using artificial (thus not natural) means to succeed in penetrating the other woman; and sometimes people even say that the ancients would have considered one of the women to be afflicted by a deformation of the clitoris, which would thus be an aberration of nature. According to these commentators,[16] we would be dealing with something incredible, something extraordinary such as a sign from a God, a *thauma*, or a *monstrum*, and these women would be committing acts which society frowns on, to the point of making them taboo, casting social silence over such terrible practices.

However, a very different picture emerges from the research I have conducted on sexual motifs in the ancient texts dedicated to *mirabilia* (extraordinary phenomena), texts which describe the *monstra, portenta*, and *thaumata* (signs from the gods and other astonishing events). Unlike infants born with physical deformities, unlike the so-called hermaphrodites, who are (sometimes) considered as disruptions of the natural order, and also unlike changes of sex, which are miraculous in nature and (sometimes) defy the laws of nature, sexual relations between women do not appear in these works of paradoxography, or in scientific treatises concerning the natural world. In the Imperial period, relations between women did not constitute a *monstrum*, in the sense of a divine sign, nor an error of nature. In satirical authors, such as Martial and Juvenal, allusions of this type can certainly be found. But this is because the satirists adapted the motifs of the discourse on *mirabilia* in a comical, rhetorical way, to turn the motif into something socially extraordinary. In short, let us not confuse the original discourse with the satire.

In 1982, Paul Veyne took a rather different approach to relations between women in his summary of Artemidorus: he simply left them out. "Abnormal relations are incestuous. Relations that conflict with nature include bestiality, necrophily and intercourse with divine personages," he writes, in an article nonetheless entitled "L'Homosexualité à Rome" (Veyne 1997: 27; 1982: 26)—an article published in the journal *Communications*, alongside a text by Foucault. It is clear that Veyne, like Foucault, did not know how to make sense of the fact that relations between women were included in this category. So where Foucault had enlarged Artemidorus' category, Veyne instead reduces it.

Let us return to the original category in Artemidorus. In my view, what justifies inclusion in the category *para phusin* cannot be the frightening or monstrous aspect of the dream, because Artemidorus describes many *other* types of sexual relations that might be described as monstrous or frightening, in dreams which he does *not* place in the category *para phusin*: penetration of one's mother from behind ..."a woman dreamt that stalks of wheat had grown out of her breast and bent round to enter her vagina"[17] ... and so on. No, this category *para phusin* simply includes anything unintelligible, anything to which the interpreter cannot apply the criterion of insertive *versus* receptive sex that is used to interpret the other scenarios. Therefore, and contrary to what Foucault and others say, *the logic of the classification is not a moral logic.*

That reading is falsified by the presence of a god, and also by the presence of an animal. The dreams involving sexual relations are dreams of *sunousia*—literally, "being with"—and the prefix *sun*, "with," reminds us that the term is transitive, relational, even though the act will be evaluated from only one point of view. There must be two involved, two of the same "nature" in the sense of the same "species," that is to say, two mortal human beings. The non-human essence of the god, the cadaver, the animal, scrambles the interpretation; as for the dream of having sexual relations with oneself, the interpretive problem is probably the fact that there is no "two" to activate the "*sun*." And where the criterion of interpretation is whether the dreamer is in an insertive or a receptive position—a criterion which takes the penis as a central point of reference—well, in the case of two women, the predictive readability of the dream is compromised, so to speak.

The second point of my argument is as follows: the discourse deployed in this manual is a "scientific"[18] and didactic discourse, with its own rules and its own expectations. As Artemidorus explains in his introduction, he wants to differentiate himself from charlatans and hucksters. His book is rigorously constructed, based on experience and analysis; as a good interpreter, he wants to provide a comprehensive manual, where anyone with a question can find the answer. To do this, he has to take all possibilities into consideration and list as many permutations as he can, while also explaining what elements a good analysis should take into account, and providing an interpretive grid suitable for use by a near-beginner.

Third point: while Artemidorus' text is unique insofar as it is the only treatise on dreams that has come down to us in its entirety, it would be a mistake to think it was the only one of its kind, or to see it as detached from other didactico-scientific genres of its time. There are numerous formal similarities with the predictive discourses of astrologers, as has been noted by specialists in those disccourses who do not work on sexuality. Like the professional interpreter of dreams, the astrologer must follow a rigorous method: he needs to know all about people's families, to investigate them as individuals, and also to envisage all possible scenarios. This can be seen in Ptolemy, and also in Manetho, Vettius Valens, and Firmicus Maternus (astrologers of the second, thirrd, and fourth centuries CE). When we study the passages that have to do with sexual dispositions and practices, they point in the same direction: the man of science must anticipate, foresee, and predict *every* possible situation that could arise, in order to show himself infallible in the eyes of his clients: his professional reputation depends on this. Every imaginable scenario, however crazy it may seem, must be taken into consideration. Here we are seeing the same totalizing impulse that we see in the *progymnasmata*, preparatory exercises for orators in the Second Sophistic, which sometimes present quite grotesque situations.[19] In short, this discourse of applied "science" could not afford to overlook anything: the practitioner sought to use his skills to earn a good living, and to attract clients.

So what Artemidorus has, rather brilliantly, done here is to create a new box for what could not be put into any of his other boxes. Thus he can exhaustively patrol and map every possible corner of experience, even those where his basic criterion of analysis cannot be applied. What does not get labeled *para phusin*, that is to say, *everything else* (everything that is *kata phusin*), is simply what can be easily deciphered, from the practical viewpoint of the oneirocritic. We are very far away from any monstrous tribades, any belief in perverse practices, or any expression of a rejection or a taboo.

In short, it is difficult to see this as expressing the sexual norms of its era. Furthermore, I do not think that the text enables us to distinguish "a subject's 'style of activity.'" The soul sends its messages by way of allegory, and the analogy deciphered by the learned and skilled expert is what enables him to reach the correct diagnosis. That someone dreams about a particular sexual act is a message, not an attribute of the dreaming subject himself. The isomorphism is contingent, not essential.

Artemidorus in the Foucauldian History of Truth: Some Questions and Some Clues

At this stage of my analysis, the question I want to ask is not how can Artemidorus help us understand ancient sexuality? Rather, I want to *try* to see what Michel Foucault was wanting to do and what he was able to do, with this extremely complex text which most of his readers had never heard of, and which, as Paul Allen Miller has remarked in his recent book on the Collège de France seminars, had no particular influence on the culture of the ancients, either. I want to try to understand what role this text plays in a Foucauldian history of truth.

First and foremost, when I argued that the logic of Artemidorus' classification was not a moral or ethical logic, it seems that Foucault himself suspected this, because he seems somewhat uneasy with this document, both in the section where he analyzes it and again in his conclusion. For one thing, he groups together in the same category a set of elements that Artemidorus did not group together in that way. To the category *para phusin*, "against nature," he adds some elements (fellatio, cunnilingus) that Artemidorus did not put there: Artemidorus listed those acts under the previous heading, the group of elements that conform to *phusin*—they are *para nomon* (against custom) but not *para phusin*. So what we are seeing here is a kind of circular reasoning. Foucault brings together the elements that he thought the ancients considered repugnant and unnatural to create a group he himself labels "*para phusin*," and then he deduces from this that they were "*para phusin*" for the ancients.

Next, let us observe that for Artemidorus sexual dreams are not really a special category of dream that call for a special evaluation based on convention and nature, which we could then read as a moral evaluation of sexual practices. As Foucault also points out, sexual dreams are scattered throughout the book and can be found in many sections devoted to a wide range of themes (such as lakes, animals, or parts of the body). They are not singled out by any special emphasis or any special prudishness, they are interpreted according to the same criteria as other, non-sexual dreams. However, in Pack's edition of the text, there is one peculiar detail, which perhaps misled Michel Foucault into thinking that the theme of the *aphrodisia* would be an important factor in the analysis and the thematic grouping. Figure 3.2 shows the pages of Pack's edition, annotated by the hand of Paul Veyne and found in the Foucault archive. In the left-hand margin, Veyne supplies the page numbers from Festugière's French translation that correspond to this passage in the Greek as edited by Pack.[20]

Since the smudge on the first page (which may be a water stain made by Foucault himself) makes the image difficult to read, here's an enlargement of the most important section:

78 Ἐν τῷ περὶ συνουσίας [ἀφροδισίων] λόγῳ διαίρεσιν τὴν
ἀρίστην ποιούμενος εἴποι τις ἂν πρῶτον περὶ τῆς κατὰ
φύσιν καὶ νόμον καὶ ἔθος συνουσίας, εἶτα περὶ τῆς παρὰ

λουτροῦ παντοδαποῦ, περὶ τροφῆς πάσης ὑγρᾶς τε καὶ
ξηρᾶς, περὶ μύρων καὶ στεφάνων, περὶ [ἀφροδισίων] συνουσίας, περὶ ὕπνου. ταῦτα μὲν περιέξει ἡ πρώτη βίβλος· ἡ   p.16
δὲ δευτέρα * * περὶ ἐγρηγόρσεως ἀσπασμάτων κόσμου

As you can see, the word *aphrodisia* appears within brackets, which means that it is an *addition made by the editor*, a word that did not appear in the original Greek text but that the editor inserted to make the text easier to read and

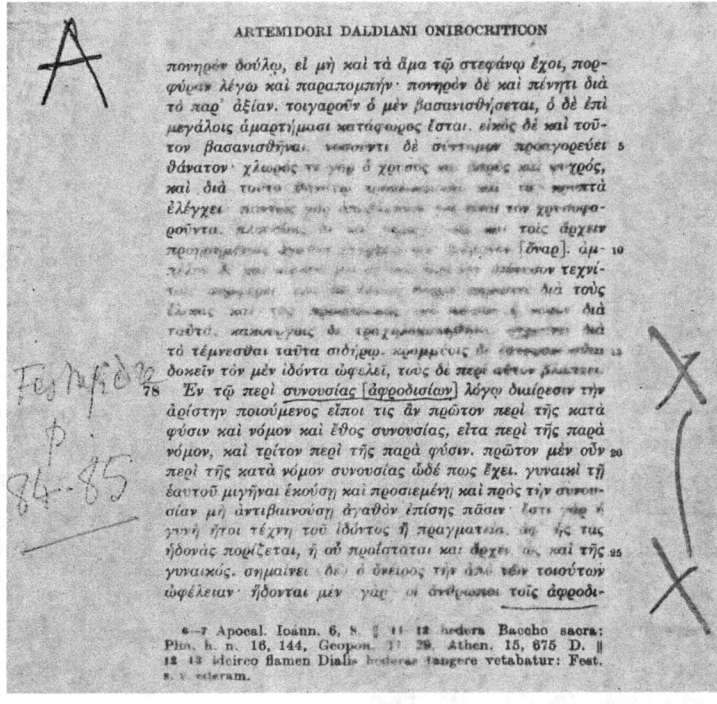

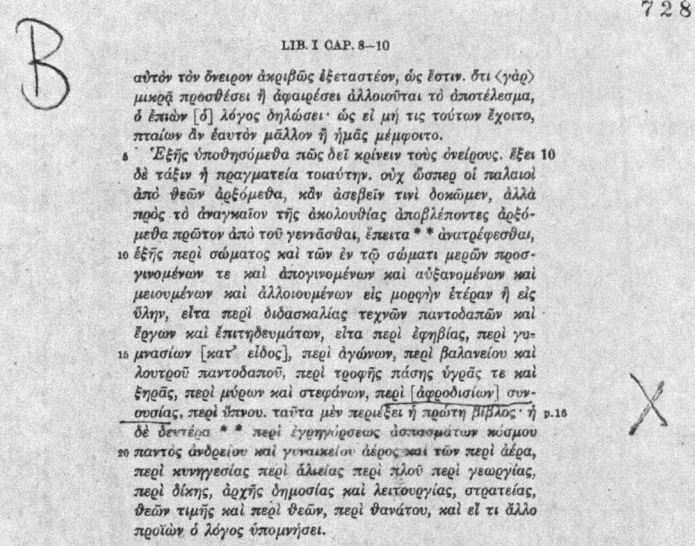

Figure 3.2 A and 2 B Annotated photocopies from the 1963 Roger Pack edition of the Greek text of Artemidorus' *Interpretation of Dreams*. BNF, Fonds Foucault, NAF 28730, Box 28 "Ultimes papiers 'sur le bureau,'" Folder 5, ff. 727–728.

understand. In reality, the word *aphrodisia* rarely appears in Artemidorus' text. The important word for Artemidorus is *sunousia*—literally, "being together." This connects to what I said earlier about the prefix "*sun*," "with," and the simple, non-moral descriptive criteria which govern the "classification" of dreams to make them useful for the novice interpreter. I do not mean to say that this text has nothing to do with the *aphrodisia*. But I want to point out that this reorganization of the *aphrodisia*, which makes them a coherent whole, is at odds with Foucault's own definition of the *aphrodisia* as he describes it in *L'Usage des plaisirs*.

It is also significant that the practice described in the treatise entitled *Oneirokriticon* derives from the Greek word *krinein*. The primary meaning of *krinein* is not "to interpret": that is a secondary meaning, derived from the primary meaning, "to separate, to distinguish." What we are dealing with is truly an art of classification, a *technê* which the dream-interpreter must learn and acquire, based on selected dream-elements which he must choose according to a set of rules that have nothing to do with morality. These last two points may seem to be minor details, but they can help us see how Foucault might have been tempted to make a connection, however modest, between the sex of dreams and a reading that would give it an intelligible meaning. How should we understand this temptation of Foucault's? And how should we understand the choice he made to devote such a long section of his work to this text?

Here again, the Foucault archive can provide some helpful clues. In his introductory note to the 2018 edition of *Les Aveux de la chair*, Frédéric Gros retraces the chronology of Foucault's work during the last years of his life, based on materials from the archive. In 1982, when Foucault delivered the text of his book *Les Aveux de la chair* to the publisher, he signaled that he wanted to delay its publication so as to give himself time, with Paul Veyne's encouragement, to prepare a volume devoted to Greco-Roman antiquity which would appear first.[21] We also know from his reading notes and from Daniel Defert's detailed chronology that Foucault had been working since 1977 on the early Christian writers and their development of elaborate techniques for speaking the truth about oneself in the interest of salvation.[22] His work between 1978 and 1980 focused on the theme of the Christian obligation of truth-telling, as it relates to marriage, virginity, fidelity, and control over one's erotic impulses. Greco-Roman antiquity had not yet featured in his agenda, with the exception of Artemidorus' *Oneirokriticon*, and a few other texts from the Imperial period, which appear in the French draft of his presentation for the New York Institute for Humanities seminar on the topic of the early Christian writers and the concept of *libido*.

At this point, as he was preparing the NYIH seminar that would deal with issues of virginity and concupiscence, Foucault was working through two related problematics: first, to identify the persistence in Christianity of a more ancient sexual ethics; and second, to understand the shift "from an economy of pleasures to an analytics of the self."[23]

The section of the fourth seminar devoted to Cassian, to whom he would return in *Les Aveux de la chair*, deals with the way Cassian defines spiritual combat against temptation, more specifically against the spirit of fornication.[24] The highest stage to be achieved through such combat is the ability to gain mastery over one's erotic dreams, which can lead to nocturnal pollutions. The goal is to become capable of mastering this involuntary part of oneself, by ensuring through constant self-examination (the examination of conscience) that there is nothing voluntary left for it to feed upon.

According to Foucault, Cassian

> comes back to this theme very often: the proof "that we have attained this purity will be that no image deceives us when we are resting or relaxed in sleep" [J. Cassian, Institutes, VI, 10] or again "This is integrity's end and definitive proof: that no voluptuous arousal comes to us during our sleep, and that we are not conscious of the pollutions to which nature constrains us". [Ibid., VI, 20][25]

In my view, the connection Foucault is making between Artemidorus and the early Christian writers has less to do with sexuality and more to do with the relationship between the dreamer and the dream. The strong contrast which emerges between Artemidorus' conception of dreams and the Christian conception has to do with how dreaming itself is perceived.

- In Christian thought, a dream is an element of oneself which can lead us to damnation, to the Fall; whereas in Artemidorus, a dream is a positive sign, meant to prepare us for the events of life.
- In Christian thought, dreaming is something to be understood and mastered, through the practice of examination of conscience, in order to speak the truth about oneself; for Artemidorus, dreaming is a natural phenomenon produced by the soul, which reveals nothing of a deeper nature that the dreamer needs to decode, no hidden nugget of truth.

This opposition holds true even when the dream-scenes are particularly erotic.

It seems to me that, in the development of Michel Foucault's thinking between 1980 and 1984, Artemidorus plays a clearer, better articulated role in the genealogy of relations between subjectivity and truth—as explored in his 1981 course at the Collège de France—than he does in the *History of Sexuality*, which is formulated as a genealogy of "desiring man." By this I mean that the importance of Artemidorus' work to Foucault can be clearly understood when we see it as a counterpoint to his discussion of Cassian. Readers lost this context in 1984 when they encountered *L'Usage des plaisirs* and *Le Souci de soi*, because as Foucault changed the order of publication, the volumes seem to take off from a different counterpoint: a strong contrast between the ancient and the modern.

When we trace the steps by which Foucault's thinking developed, it is clear that his reading of Artemidorus was shaped much less by the question of sexuality than by the question of truth itself. Foucault's reading occurs in the context of an approach that looks forward in history, reaching toward the centuries to come. But if we read Artemidorus in his own social and cultural context, and if, as would be logical, we look more closely at the influences which come to him from the other end of the chronological axis (from the Greece of the Archaic and Classical periods), we see clearly that sex as it is described in this treatise has very little to do with any kind of truth of the subject (and Foucault says this). Nor does it have much to do with moral models or norms, a style of living or a style of habits (and about this, Foucault hesitates).

Once we become aware of Foucault's process, of his continual back-and-forth dialogues with early Christian writers, we can see the logic of *Les Aveux de la chair* as a shadowy presence behind the Artemidorus of *Le Souci de soi*—even though it might have made more sense, given the point in his argument Foucault had reached at the end of *L'Usage des plaisirs*, to deploy Artemidorus as a clear counterpoint to the *modern* apparatus of sexuality, where sexuality is "constitutive of the bond that requires people to be tied to their identity under the form of subjectivity" (Foucault 1994c: 570; 1999: 130). Or, at least, it might have made sense to anchor Artemidorus' book more firmly in its own context of production and its own pragmatics.

Along those lines, there is more work to do, to understand this very special and unusual text and to recontextualize Artemidorus in his own moment *before sexuality*. That task is now left up to us, as we move forward: after Foucault, but also and always *with* Foucault.

4

To Dream the Impossible Dream

Parrhēsia and Rhetoric (*De Oratore* 3)

Paul Allen Miller
University of South Carolina and Ewha Womans University

Crassus: He who by the testimony of all the learned and by the judgement of the whole of Greece was the first not only in practical intelligence, acuity, attractiveness, and subtlety, but also truly in eloquence, variety, and abundance, on whatever side he had positioned himself, he was easily the first speaker. From those who treated, performed, and taught these things that we are now investigating, although they were all called by a common name, which named every thought of the best things and every exercise in them philosophy, Socrates, by means of his disputations, tore away this common name and created a division between the knowledge (<u>scientiam</u>) of thinking wisely (<u>sapienter</u>) and that of speaking beautifully (ornate), which cohered in the thing itself (<u>re cohaerentes</u>). Plato transmitted his genius and his varied conversations to eternity in his writings, since Socrates himself left not a single letter.

(Cicero, De Oratore 3.60)

Unlike the rhetorician or Sophist, the philosophical master thus had to believe what he taught. Unlike the prophet, he had to speak in his own name, and not about the future that will come, but about the concrete present in which he finds himself. Unlike the sage, whose esoteric pronouncements on what there is involves an endless interpretation, he had to concern himself with the concrete "ignorance" in which each person finds himself.

(Rajchman 1991: 129)

In the last three years of his lectures at the Collège de France, Foucault focused increasingly on the question of what it meant to be a speaker of truth, how one fashioned oneself to speak that truth to others, and the relation between philosophical veridiction and other forms of discourse in the ancient world. This exercise culminates at the beginning of *Le courage de la vérité* with a schematic rendition of four basic forms of truth-telling: prophecy, wisdom, instruction, and *parrhēsia* ("frank speech"). These correspond to: an enigmatic mode of revelation; a mode that seeks to demonstrate what is being or nature; a mode that seeks to transmit established bodies of knowledge; and a polemical mode that asserts the truth concerning individuals and situations. One may argue whether this schema covers all possibilities, but it is coherent, examples of all four of these modes can be found, and Foucault makes clear that each of these four possibilities may co-exist within the same speaker (Foucault 2009: 14–27). In many ways, these four cardinal points constitute a grid of intelligibility that, while it may have historically specific manifestations, Foucault argues is, if not universal, at minimum very long-lasting in the West. It is for this reason, he says, that antiquity is privileged in his study of "different modes of veridiction. Because, in Antiquity one finds them well distinguished and incarnated, given shape, almost institutionalized in different forms" (Foucault 2009: 25). In his "history of the ontologies of true discourses" antiquity assumes pride of place for the analytic clarity and categorical purity it diplays in their different kinds (Foucault 2008: 285).

Foucault argues that Greco-Roman culture also tends to want to join the parrhesiatic mode with that of wisdom, so that if we consider the *Alcibiades*, Plato's *Seventh Letter*, or Seneca's *Letters to Lucilius*, all three combine philosophical demonstrations with modes of discourse in which the addressees are confronted with truths that range from the mildly discomfiting to the frankly dangerous. The philosophical master, unlike the prophet, must speak in his own name, and unlike the sophist, who merely passes along a technique, must believe what he teaches and directly address his charge. There is nothing necessary, Foucault specifies, about this ancient pairing of philosophy and *parrhēsia*. Within Medieval Christianity the parrhesiastic mode is more commonly identified with the prophetic, as the great preachers indicted their listeners for their sins while evoking the last judgment. Wisdom, on the other hand, within the Medieval universities, was identified with teaching, the transmission of knowledge and authority. In the modern world, Foucault suggests that we often see the prophetic mode joined with the discourse of politics and revolution, while philosophy has become the mode that attempts to speak the truth of Being, and science largely replaces instruction. As for *parrhēsia*, it ceases to have a clearly identified separate existence, but it can still be recognized in revolutionary indictments of the existing state of things, in philosophical reflections on ethics and our conception of the human, and in science when it assumes the form of the criticism of existing prejudices or dominant institutions (Foucault 2009: 27–30).

What is opposed to all four of these modes, but most especially to the parrhesiastic and ancient philosophical mode, is rhetoric. As Foucault made clear at the beginning of his final course at the Collège de France in 1984:

> You see then how the practice of *parrhēsia* is opposed point by point to what is in sum the art of rhetoric. Very schematically, one can say that rhetoric, as it was defined and practiced in Antiquity, is at bottom a technique that concerns the manner of saying things but in no way determines the relation between the person who speaks and what he says. Rhetoric is an art, a technique, an ensemble of procedures that permit the person who speaks to say something that is not at all what they think, but it is going to have as its effect to produce in the addressee a certain number of convictions, induce a certain number of behaviors, establish a certain number of beliefs.
>
> (Foucault 2009: 14)[1]

Foucault here reproduces the essential Platonic opposition between philosophy and rhetoric most memorably etched in Socrates' comparison of the *rhētor* to the pastry chef, who gives the audience what they want, even if it is not good for them, as opposed to the philosophical doctor, who prescribes a bitter but curative pill (*Gorgias* 462c–466a3, 475d, 477e7–479e9, 503d5–505b12, 521e3–4). If we were to imagine the four points of veridiction as describing a rectangular plane, then rhetoric in Foucault's vision would be a non-coplanar line that traverses that defined space. It both passes through and is not defined by it. And this is what makes Crassus' statement in Cicero's *De Oratore* quoted at the beginning of this chapter so interesting, because it seems to argue just the opposite, that rhetoric, at least in its origins, was congruent with the space of philosophy and veridiction and that the loss of this unity is something to be mourned. Even so, Foucault rarely mentions Cicero in these lectures and never *De Oratore*.[2]

My point here is not to detect a lacuna in Foucault's research. There have been more than enough attempts to claim that Foucault did not really know Latin or Greek or that he did not understand the ancient world. Foucault's position is perfectly orthodox. Cicero's statement is the outlier here, and it is undoubtedly strange. For what would it mean to argue that, at their origins, philosophy and rhetoric, truth and enjoyment, were not only not opposed but one? From our post-Cartesian perspective, his statement is almost unintelligble. If Foucault offers a grid of intelligibility that makes sense of and operates within the dominant modes of truth-telling, from the dawn of Platonic philosophy to the present, Cicero offers the dream of an alternative form that both occupies a space between Foucault's cardinal points and exceeds them. It is a "dream" in the Freudian sense: it is both a wish-fulfillment and an engima, one that reads contradiction as overdetermination and unites the normally antinomian figures of the philosopher and the actor into the singular figure of the ideal orator: a world in which mind and body, *res* and *verba* are one (Michel 1960: 451; Connolly 2007: 109, 202–5). Yet, if the task of philosophy today remains, what Foucault said it was in the "Introduction" to Volume 2 of the *History of Sexuality*, "to undertake to know how and to what extent it would be possible to think differently" (Foucault 1984a: 14–15), then Cicero, if we take him both literally and seriously, grants us an unparalleled opportunity to rethink the most basic sets of oppositions that lie beneath the history of truth in the West.

In what follows, I first outline Foucault's understanding of the opposition between veridiction and rhetoric as it has been articulated since Plato's *Gorgias*. I focus on the parrhesiast as the ideal speaker of truth, a speaker whose subjective being is one with the act of veridiction. Next, I turn to the orator in the *De Oratore*, a text Foucault does not engage in his published work. Cicero's ideal orator is an impossible figure who transcends the oppositions Foucault defines and that are dominant within the philosophical tradition. We finish by asking what would it mean for such a figure to exist, how would it reconfigure what we understand as truth itself and the meaning of thinking as well as speaking.

I

An act of persuasion ... is not primarily a signifying operation and hence its mode of repetition is quite different. Rather than attempting to identically reproduce the proposition as a meaning in the mind of the audience, persuasive rhetoric attempts to make the proposition compelling, to give it a certain force.
(Muckelbauer 2008: 17)

Rhetoric ... from the point of view of philosophy is nothing other than the instrument through which the person who wishes to exert power can do nothing other than repeat very precisely what the crowd, or the leaders, or the prince wants. Rhetoric is a way to persuade people of what they are already persuaded.
(Foucault 2008: 211)

If the concern of the rhetorician is persuasion, the concern of the philosopher, the sage, the teacher, and the prophet is truth. Socrates as the archetypical philosopher differs from the other three figures by, unlike the prophet, undetaking an inquiry; unlike the sage, not claiming to reveal a secret truth; and, unlike the teacher, not speaking from the standpoint of one who knows. Rather, the Socratic parrhesiast knows that he does not know and wishes to convince you of the same, so that you too may become a seeker of truth, a lover of wisdom, a philosopher (*philo-sophos*; Foucault 2009: 82). Such a philosopher is not the academic who merely professes philosophy, who exposes the already known to a group of students or colleagues, but one who stakes his being on the truth he utters, and thus opens himself to a fundamental risk when he approaches his interlocutor (Foucault 2008: 318). According to the classical schema, in this way the actual philosopher, as opposed to the professional academician, contrasts with the *rhētor* on every point. For the latter is neither bound as a person in any fundamental way to the content of what they utter, nor do they expose themselves to the potential anger of their interlocutors, insofar as they seek to please and thus sway them. The goal of the *rhētor* is not to confront the audience with hard truths, but to convince them that what the speaker has on offer is what they wanted all along. The philosopher, however, Foucault contends, rather than affirming the identity and thus the desires of his interlocutors offers them instead the possibility of "freely" constituting themselves as "subjects of the courage of truth" (Brion and Harcourt 2012: 298).[3] The philosopher binds himself to the truth of his statements. The philosopher and the *rhētor*, then, exist at opposite ends of the spectrum. What is never contested at any point within this discourse however, both Foucault's in 1983 and 1984 and that of the larger tradition, is the existence of these categories as separate defined entities, the separation of true speech from that designed to please and persuade (Muckelbauer 2008: 81–2). Yet such was not always the case. The term rhetoric appears for the first time in extant Greek in the *Gorgias*, and it may well have been coined by Plato to establish the practice taught by Gorgias as a foil to the truth-seeking of Socrates (*Gorgias* 449d1; Schiappa 1990; Luzzatto 2020). Rhetoric and philosophy as defined entities are co-constitutive. Before the one came to be, the other did not exist.

It would be a mistake to assume Foucault understood this dichotomy between rhetoric and philosophy to be anything less than an artifact of history. In his initial 1971 lectures at the Collège de France, presciently entitled *La volonté de savoir, The Will to Know*,[4] he argues that the concept of truth we recognize today became established during the fifth and fourth centuries BCE, at the very moment when the division between philosophy and rhetoric was first instituted (Foucault

2011). In making this argument, Foucault follows Marcel Detienne's, *The Masters of Truth in Archaic Greece* (1996), which described the notion of "truth" operative in pre-classical Greece as one produced by divinely inspired poets, prophets, or kings. This archaic model understood truth as constituted not by the correspondence between a proposition and its referent but as a set of authoritative pronouncements and their preservation in communal memory. Lurking behind Detienne's inquiry (and Foucault's as well) is Heidegger's investigation of the changing meaning of *alētheia* ("truth," or for Heidegger "unhiddenness") from the Homeric to the Classical period. The implicit argument of all three thinkers (Foucault, Detienne, and Heidegger) is that our familiar correspondence theory of truth is only truly established with the advent of Platonic metaphysics, the fullest statement of which is found in the Myth of the Cave with its clear distinction between epistemic subjects and objects.[5]

Even here though, Foucault does not simply assume that truth in post-Platonic philosophy is always or only the correspondence between a statement and an external reality that exists prior to that statement, while rhetoric or persuasion is a mere focus on the form of discourse, and therefore it is opposed to referential truth. Indeed, his contention is just the opposite. For Socrates, Foucault reminds us, knowledge of the truth does not exist prior to our practice of the discourse that produces it. Truth is not simply "out there," under cover, waiting to be observed. Rather, truth in the Socratico-Platonic sense arises and has its authenticity precisely in the back and forth of dialectic, question and answer, refutation and agreement, in the encounter with the other. If the truth were in fact a set of pre-existing relations or a separate ontological reality from the practices through which we discover it, then the discourses of philosophy and science would consequently be reduced to the series of ornaments and figures we deploy to make it receivable, memorable, and persuasive. In short, they would be reduced to rhetoric (Foucault 2008: 303). Philosophical veridiction, then, is related to the truth of being not because that truth pre-exists the act of its articulation but rather because, in the act of its discursive fashioning, Socratic truth is shown to have the power to transform the life and the soul of both the speaker and the interlocutor. It has what we somewhat bombastically call "impact." Philosophical discourse inscribes its truth within our reality and changes it (Foucault 2008: 308–9, 315–16). Thus, within the *Gorgias*, Socrates welcomes his chance to test his views against those of Callicles. Callicles becomes the touchstone (*basanos*) of Socrates' soul, the abrasive material whose application reveals whether the currency of Socratic thought is gold or dross. The test of truth is not the transmission of accurate information or even the revelation of a pre-existing reality but the spark of englightenment produced in the moment of discursive abrasion in the living dialectic, what Plato in the *Seventh Letter* refers to as *tribē* or "friction" (Plato, *Seventh Letter* 334b; Foucault 2008: 229–34, 337; Miller 2021a: 144–7; 2022).[6]

For Plato, Foucault tells us, to be a philosopher and to practice *parrhēsia* is not a matter of performing a profession or elaborating a theoretical discourse but of adopting a defined manner of being in the world (Foucault 2008: 271–2; 2009: 15). Socrates in his frankness and his openheartedness, but also in his refusal to compromise, displays his *parrhēsia* throughout his dialogue with Callicles in the *Gorgias*. Callicles in fact warns Socrates that his form of speech—his style—will leave him ill-prepared to defend himself should he find himself in court accused of a crime. This warning, as every reader of the *Gorgias* knows, is only too apposite since a few short years later Socrates would find himself accused of impiety and corrupting the youth. Nonetheless, even on trial for his life, Socrates refuses to compromise and insists on speaking in his own manner (*Apology* 17a–18a), even refusing to use a speech Lysias had prepared for him (Cicero, *De Oratore* 1.231). The result is conviction and execution. Yet he never flinches and never ceases both to abrade and upbraid his listeners. *Parrhēsia* in the Socratic lexicon is not only the substance of what it means to practice the philosophical life, but also, by definition, to practice *parrhēsia* is to refuse to utter the pleasing "verities" of rhetoric (Foucault 2008: 343).

The essence of Socratic *parrhēsia* is a freely chosen personal relation between speaker and statement, the reduction of their distance to an absolute minimum (Foucault 2008: 64–5; Lawlor 2016: 170). *Parrhēsia*, as Foucault makes clear, is not performative in the sense of speech act theory (Foucault 2008: 59) but neither is it purely constative in the sense of reportage, the observation of a pre-existing fact. Rather *parrhēsia* names an act of veridiction undertaken in an atmosphere of potential risk to the speaker, in which the speaker utters a truth to which he or she is fully committed, like Socrates on trial, Plato before Dionysius the Younger, or later Christian martyrs and social revolutionaries (Foucault 2008: 55–6). Rather than confirming the interlocutor's or the audience's pre-existing prejudices, *parrhēsia* creates a break in the fabric of being, the existing verities, and thus opens a risk, and that risk is the possibility of thinking differently, the possibility of freedom (Foucault 2008: 61, 64).

The central question for ancient veridiction and for Foucault, then, becomes, how does one form oneself to be a speaker of truth, and perhaps more importantly, how does one form oneself to be an effective speaker that can create this break and take the risk necessary to lead the souls of one's fellow citizens or prince?

Who is capable of being an artisan of *parrhēsia*? What is the expertise, or what is the *tekhnē*, what is the theory or what is the practice, what is the factual knowledge but what is also the exercise, what is the *mathēsis* and what is the *askēsis* which are going to permit the possession of this *parrhēsia*? Is it rhetoric or is it philosophy? And this rhetoric/philosophy question is also going to traverse, I think, the whole field of political thought.

(Foucault 2008: 180)

Parrhēsia, thus, cannot be separated from persuasion even as it is fundamentally concerned with truth. It is an act that seeks to speak to and change the souls of those it addresses, while simultaneously leaving them their freedom (Foucault 2008: 98).

Here we face the fundamental epistemic and philosophical crux of the matter, and one which reproduces itself on the level of the political. What would it mean for there to be a *tekhnē* or an *ars* of *parrhēsia*, as Foucault avers? If a *tekhnē* is a repeatable skill that can be taught and that produces reliable, consistent results—such as cobbling or stone cutting, to take classic Socratic examples—then what exactly is the technique that can be taught that will reliably allow one to speak the truth, to fully embrace that truth, and to do so in a way that both takes a risk and opens the possibility of the other's freedom? What is the craft through which the subject freely and absolutely links itself to the enunciation of a truth (Foucault 2008: 64), a truth that qua truth is self-identical and without any foreign or obscuring element, that is pure (Foucault 2009: 201–2)?

At minimum, this *tekhnē* is a paradox. For if parrhesiastic speakers must identify their being with the truth they enunciate, and this relation must be without the admixture of foreign elements, then how can there be an art or skill of *parrhēsia*, how can there be a *tekhnē* of that which defines itself by the absence of intervening artifice? If rhetoric is defined as an art or skill of manipulating language for the purpose of producing an effect, then how can the *tekhnē* of *parrhēsia* not itself also be a form of rhetoric, a style of speaking, a formalized practice of the *logos* (cf. Foucault 2008: 285-6)? Thus, we see that, while philosophical *parrhēsia* constitutes itself from Plato on in its opposition to rhetoric, it must also presume the rhetorical as a skill separate from the enunciation of the truth per se so that the division on which its existence depends is consistently undermined by its own condition of possibility as an identifiable, formalizable, and hence transmittable, form of speech incarnated in the figure of the "artisan of *parrhēsia*."

Parrhēsia is, then, beyond simple free speech (*isēgoria*). It is an art open to all, but it cannot be practiced by all. In democratic Athens, *parrhēsia* entails the attempt to persuade your fellow citizens to follow you over your rivals, with all the attendant risks. If the assembly is displeased, if they feel you have attempted to assert your power too vigorously, they can vote for your exile (Foucault 2008: 99, 147, 172; Rajchman 1991: 120–1). Free speech is a necessary presumption of the existence of true discourse within a democratic regime and so of democracy itself. At the same time, true discourse cannot be equally shared by all speakers, and all speakers cannot have equal access to the podium whether literally or figuratively. We see this regularly in scientific and institutional settings in modern democratic societies: the need to establish rules and norms to determine who speaks, whose speech is authoritative, and how the truth of speech is validated. Democracy both renders true speech possible, insofar as that discourse is authentic, and incessantly threatens it. As Socrates argues in the *Gorgias*, the temptation of the speaker is to flatter the democratic audience. The parrhesiast, however, is the opposite of the flatterer. Political *parrhēsia* can only exist in a democratic system, where speech is ostensibly free, yet must always be in tension with that system (Foucault 2008: 167–8, 183). It is for this reason that Plato concludes that for democratic man *parrhēsia* is both necessary to live justly and impossible (Foucault 2009: 43–5, 205). *Parrhēsia* is the art of authentic speech addressed to an audience constitutionally inclined to reject and even punish it.

II

All this means that "philosophical" texts of this kind—however analytic, demonstrative, logical, or "treatise-like" they seem—are also doing "rhetorical" work. Using the figurative language of personification, they incorporate the social and aesthetic affinities and aversions of the readers' and writers' lived experience.

(Dressler 2016a: 117)

From the juvenile *De Inventione* down to his final theoretical essay, *De Officiis*, Cicero dwells on the importance of combining rhetoric and philosophy ... He consistently recognizes the differences between the two types of discourse and the difficulty of succeeding in both of them.... He also knows the history of Greek philosophy well enough, and that of Greek and Roman rhetoric, to be aware that his ideal combination is not only difficult to approximate but something that many experts on either side would actually oppose.

(Long 1995: 50–1)

What for Foucault is not so much a contradiction but an aporia, the relation between authentic true speech and the craft necessary to produce it and to make it receivable by its audience, is for Cicero the center of his concerns in *De Oratore* and his later philosophical and rhetorical practice. Far from seeing truth and persuasion as opposed to one another, Cicero's argument in *De Oratore* is that the persuasive speaker is only successful when he is sincere. As Foucault argues in the case of Socratic question and answer, Ciceronian truth does not pre-exist the moment of its discursive articulation and discovery (*inventio*) but arises in the act of its articulation, in the moment when the categories of thought are applied to a defined matter or instance (*res*), which both produces and is delimited by the speaker's words (*verba*) and thoughts (*sententiae*). Rhetoric "is not a question of playing with human passions, but of finding in them the truth beneath their appearance" (Michel 1960: 243).

In Book 2 of *De Oratore*, Antonius tells us that there is nothing greater in speaking than when the auditor is "more ruled by a certain violent attack (*impetus*) or disturbance of the soul than by judgment and council" (2.178; Remer 2017: 14–15). In isolation, this passage could seem to argue for an appeal to emotion rather than reason, for the power of rhetoric over the truth of philosophy. Is this not a formulation for wielding a certain violent passion that overpowers the audience? As Antonius' exposition continues, however, it becomes clear that this "attack" is achieved not through the application of *tekhnē* or a form of manipulation, but through a kind of passionate embrace brought about by the language and the body of the orator in the throes of his conviction, by a seamless identification of the speaker with the spoken (Morstein-Marx 2004: 272). This is as true of Crassus as of Antonius:

> Crassus, I am accustomed to shudder when these [acts] are performed by you, so great the violence of spirit, so forceful the attack (*impetus*), so great the pain is accustomed to be signified by your eyes, your face, gesture, and finally by that finger of yours; so great is the river of best and most weighty words, so full, then true (*verae*), so new the thoughts (*sententiae*), so that you yourself seem to me without pigments or childish rouge not only to inflame the judge, but also to be ablaze (*ardere*)!
>
> (2.188)

The *impetus*, the "blow," the "attack," that the auditor of the ideal orator should suffer in their experience of persuasion is a moment of ecstatic communion with the impassioned speaker, who unleashes a gushing torrent of words. His sentences and gestures are not meretricious adornments. The speaker is ablaze with new thought, true thoughts!, whose convulsive force carries off the will of speaker and auditor alike.

The corollary of this position—that the goal of oratory is to move the auditor, that the auditor is moved through a kind of violence or attack that affects the speaker as well, and that this is an index of the speaker's truth—is that the effective orator, no matter which side he argues in a case, must always be speaking the truth. Antonius says as much a few lines later:

> But if any contrived pain were suspected and if in this type of oration there were nothing but the false and that simulated by imitation, perhaps some even greater art would be required: now I do not know what happens to you and the rest, Crassus, but for my part there is no cause why I would lie (*permentiar*) in the presence of the most thoughtful and well-disposed men: by god, I myself have never wished to excite in the judges pain, pity, envy, or hatred by speaking without myself being moved by those same feelings by which the judges themselves are to be moved.... For just as there is no material easily lit aflame, which would be able to catch fire unless a flame is put to it, so there is no mind so prepared for the force it is to grasp, which would be able to be lit afire unless one who was already aflame and burning (*ardens*) should draw near.
>
> (2.189-90)

Antonius here couches the whole of this description as a response to Crassus' earlier depiction of the theatrics of Antonius' defense of Norbanus, whom Crassus refers to as a seditious madman, hardly an endorsement of the justice of Antonius' cause (2.124-5). But neither accuses the other of lying, rather the truth of their discourse lies in the power with which they burn (*ardere*), not in its reference to a prior reality untouched by discourse and experience, and that truth we are told lies in the arguments and commonplaces the orator marshals, from which the emotions arise. Eloquence is a fire: to communicate, you must be a torch (Michel 1960: 243-7). The commonplaces of argument may pre-exist the facts of the case and the orator's use of them, but the emotions are no less authentic, and it is the emotions themselves, which arise in the orator and are thus shared by the audience, that guarantees their truth in the actuality of their enjoyment, an actuality beyond mere pleasure that is inseparable from the reality of the pain experienced by both orator and audience. "It should come as no surprise," Antonius contends, "that the proper advocate is possessed so often by such powerful and contrary emotions about the affairs of others, since there is such force (*vis*) in the thoughts (*sententiarum*) and commonplaces (*locorum*)." There is no need to counterfeit the emotions. "The nature of that oration, which is undertaken for the purpose of moving the spirits of others, moves the orator more even than anyone of those who hear" (2.191; cf. Connolly 2017: 164; Remer 2017: 50–2).

What is the ontology of this force? Where does it exist? How is its truth related to its status as a form of violence (*vis*, *impetus*) and its ability to remake our consciousness, to change what we think and feel, to alter our experience. There is indeed something fearful and sublime in this moment, which is not per se irrational, but depends on the force of thought and arguments as we experience them in their performance. For these pleadings arouse emotions in the audience and in ourselves just as poetry, theater, and stories do. These uses of language produce an effect in the real beyond discourse, produce a truth that is experienced, a force that is at once rational—produced by the *loci*—and beyond the rational, a *jouissance* of the body (2.192). Such a truth can never be limited to one side of a question (cf. Barton 2001: 2).

There follows an extended comparison between the genuiness of the emotion produced by the orator's performance of pre-existing *sententiae* and *loci* and the actor playing a tragic part with genuine emotion, which in turn becomes the agitation and agony of the tragic poet who creates it. The orator, however, as both performer and author occupies both positions:

> Nonetheless in this genre I have often seen, how the eyes of the human actor (*hominis histrionis*) seem to burn through the mask as he says:
>
> You dared for him to be apart from you, to come to Salamis without him?
>
> You did not fear your father's aspect?
>
> He never said "aspect," but that a furious Telamon did not seem to me to rage with grief for his son. And with his voice bent to a wretched sound, he said
>
> Now bereft of sons in my old age
>
> You have tortured me, bereaved me, destroyed me, with no thought
>
> Of a dead brother, nor his small son entrusted to your guardianship.
>
> With weeping and lamentation he seemed to speak. If that actor (*histrio*), although he would perform these things daily, was nonetheless not able to perform them properly without pain, why would you think Pacuvius to have written them with a quiet and gentle mind?
>
> (2.193)

The mask of the actor pre-exists the performance, like the *loci* of the orator. The performance is made possible by the conjunction of the pre-existing form with emotional content, with the actor's burning eyes, like those of Crassus in Antonius' description (2.188). Pacuvius, as the author, experiences the truth of these emotions, and yet they do not exist for him before the poetic act, before he becomes Teucer in the moment of creation. Pacuvius in producing his poetic discourse must be truly moved. But it is the production of the discourse that produces the affect/effect rather than its referent in the real. Antonius continues the analogy between the poet and the orator in the next chapter, where he also makes mention of the inspired nature of the poets in Plato and Democritus. But he draws a distinction. The orator does not seek to imitate the emotions of ancient heroes, as Pacuvius did, nor to be the actor (*actor*) behind the role or mask of another,[7] but to become the *auctor* ("author") of his own (2.194). Nonetheless, the play on words between *auctor* and *actor* indicates the close relationship between the two, as each adopts a role, which both pre-exists the moment it is put on and only comes to life in the truth of the performance.

After Antonius has finished his exposition of invention in Book 2, Crassus in Book 3 is supposed to explain the function of ornamentation, but he begins by objecting to the separation of form and content on which the division depends. Indeed, he argues that a strict separation between words and the subject matter cannot be maintained. Such a position is a truism of modern literary and translation studies. Nonetheless, we seldom draw its full consequences. For if the world of meaning (*res*) cannot be rigorously separated from the forms that signify it (*verba*), and if all our meanings are, therefore, of and in the world and so can never simply or cleanly refer to that world as a separate but somehow intelligible entity, then the division between the material and intelligible, between ornamentation and argument, and between rhetoric and philosophy is, at least in part, illusory:

> Indeed for those ancient ones seem to me to have seen something greater to be embraced by the mind than what the sharpness of our ingenuity can perceive, those who said that all these things, both above and below, were one thing and were bound by one force (*vis*) and by one agreement; for there is no type of thing, which would be able to stand in itself apart from the rest, nor is there anything that if the other things were without it, would they be able to preserve their own force and eternal nature. Yet if this line of thought seems beyond what is able to be understood by human thought and perception, that true voice of Plato is certainly not unheard by you, Catulus, that said all the learning of the noble and human arts can be held by a single chain of interdependence; for, where the force of its reason is seen, whereby the causes and ends of things are

known, it's as if a certain wondrous harmony and agreement of all the forms of learning is found.

(3.20-21)

Indeed, while Platonism is not normally considered a monism, it is the case that Plato sees the reality of the world as a harmonious whole, not a Manichean dystopia divided between warring principles. This vision of an underlying unity, beyond the limits of the individual objects of our perception, is in fact a vision of truth as enjoyment, as a shattering experience of recovered union that, if experienced in its full intensity, would mean both the annihilation of the individual object and the experiencing subject (Braunstein 2020: 56–7). It would mean that on some level not only do we not stand apart from the world and choose *verba* to speak about discrete *res*, but the *res* speak themselves into being through us. Such an understanding of eloquence "calls into question both the notion of the autonomous subjet and dominant philosophical beliefs about truth" (Connolly 2007: 150).

Nonetheless, we experience the world as individual subjects not as a totalizing oneness, and the task of the orator is to recognize that the varieties of human enjoyment are as varied as our individual modes of insertion in or emanation from the enfolding oneness. This can be seen, Crassus says, in the different arts, giving examples from painting, sculpture, and poetry, before discussing the stylistic variety of individual orators (3.25-28). The speaker who can produce these forms of enjoyment, who crafts the rhythms of his prose as the poet makes his verse, he tells us, is like a god among men (3.53). And it is for this reason that the true orator must have a complete command and understanding of all aspects of life, including philosophy and psychology. He must be both knowledgeable and moral: for through his aesthetic shaping the true orator is able to move those who listen wherever he is inclined. To give this power to the ignorant and rash would be like giving arms to a madman. Eloquence is thus among the highest virtues, we are told, because, even if the Stoics contend all virtues are equal in the world of appearance, some may be deemed more beautiful (*formosa*) and radiant (*inlustris*), such as this force (*vis*), "which having embraced the knowledge of things in this fashion explains the perceptions of the mind and its counsels in words" (3.54-55).

True wisdom (*sapientia*), then, consists of "thinking and speaking" as a single exercise joined together in terms of "reason and force." This can be seen, Crassus claims, in such early Greek statesmen as Lycurgus, Pittacus, and Solon, as well as Romans such as Coruncanius, Fabricius, Cato, and the Scipios. All these men were examples of what Crassus would consider orators who were exempt from the censures of flattery and amorality that Socrates laid down in the *Gorgias*. More importantly, Crassus notes, at this point in history, the teachers of doing well and speaking well were one and the same (3.56-57).

Crassus then names Themistocles, Pericles and Theramnes as those who excelled in both speaking and doing in the Greek polity. It is notable that Themistocles and Pericles are also named by Callicles in the *Gorgias*, as *rhētores* who were devoted to their communities. Socrates contested this claim on the grounds that none of them actually made their citizens better men or cared for their souls (503–504e). Crassus continues by mentioning Gorgias, Isocrates, and Thrasymachus as examples of those who, while less involved in politics, were nonetheless eloquent and "teachers of this same wisdom" (3.59). Yet there began to grow up a third group who, although they abounded "in talent and learning, by a certain judgment of mind, shrank from civic life and business and had contempt for the activity of speaking" (3.59). These latter men devoted themselves to poetry, geometry, music, or dialectic, all means of sharpening the mind, recreating the soul, and so of making men better (3.58), but not ends in themselves. As some thinkers withdrew into these more private devotions, the pursuits of thought became increasingly alienated from action in the world, whether accomplished by speech or other means.

The chief figure and the first to codify this growing split, Crassus tells us in the passage quoted at the beginning of this chapter, was Socrates. It has not generally been appreciated how radical a statement Crassus is making here. Elaine Fantham does not discuss it in her book (2004). David Mankin, who appreciates this account as the intellectual center of Book 3, does not connect it with Crassus' acceptance of the Eleatic philosopher's contention that the universe is one. He is content with the notion that future orators, those who follow Cicero's argument, will "combine their real-life experience with both wide knowledge ... and methods of argumentation to be obtained from the study of philosophy" (Mankin 2011: ad loc), a position that continues to see rhetoric and philosophy as separate. Similarly, Michel argues that it is unclear whether Cicero gives the advantage to rhetoric or philosophy, when the putative artificiality of the division is the point (Michel 1960: 84). Connolly comes much closer to doing Crassus's position justice when she argues:

> Unifying these two flows [of rhetoric and philosophy] in his voice and physical motions, Cicero's orator literally embodies learning, giving vitality to philosophical disourse and its "thin and bloodless style" (... 1.56). His eloquence exhibits a charm not owed to cosmetics but to blood (... 3.199).
>
> (Connolly 2007: 109).

In the unity of rhetoric and philosophy, of truth and enjoyment, there is no firm distinction between argument and style, *inventio* and *ornatus*, but rather each courses with the same blood, the same warmth, the same passion and potential violence.

Particular attention should be paid to the Latin in this quoted passage. Cicero uses the singular *scientiam* for the knowledge of thinking wisely and speaking beautifully. It is one thing, one knowledge. But Socrates created or at least formalized, since Cicero acknowledges antecedents, a division within knowledge itself. This division is both recognized and denied in the phrase *re cohaerentes* in which the accusative plural participle modifies a now implied *scientias*, which remains unstated. But those "knowledges" "cling together" in a single "thing" (*re*), the matter spoken of, that only exists as a defined *res*, because it is spoken of, because it has been differentiated from other matters in the choric space of the real. The seeming flaw in grammatical agreement between singular noun and plural adjective enacts the very separation of that which must not be put asunder, even as on the semantic level it maintains its "coherence" in the thing itself. The next sentence qualifies the split between rhetoric and philosophy not as one between tongue and mind or spirit, but between tongue and heart (*cordis* 3.61). Thought and wisdom are not separated from feelings or experience even once the schism has occurred.

The orator, thus, as Crassus describes him some chapters later, is the "actor of truth itself" (3.214-15). He does not merely imitate the truth through his style and delivery, he enacts it. The term *actor* can mean either theatrical performer or merely one who "does" (Wisse, Winterbottom, and Fantham 2008: ad loc; Mankin 2011: ad loc). To be the "doer" of truth through one's performance, is to bring a truth into being, one so powerful, we are told, that even your enemies may shed tears. This action is then opposed to the stage actor (*histrio*) who simply imitates a pre-existing truth. The orator brings into reality a truth that did not exist in the same form before: he does this not merely through ideas or concepts, nor even through his words, but also with his body. The full epistemic implications of this formulation, even though it is perfectly consonant with Crassus' earlier statements on the originary unity of rhetoric and philosophy and his evocation of the Eleatic philosophers' vision of oneness, have been shied away from by most commentators as an offense to common sense. Instead, we are instructed here to understand the "actor of truth" as "the doer in reality," which softens the antithesis and defeats the point of using *actor* here in contrast to *histrio*.

We may think this notion of the doer of truth is a fanciful construct. But aside from what Cicero's text manifestly says, there are many examples of truth as an action performed by a subject. The notion that truths cannot be enacted through our performance is indeed belied by our experience every day. Darwin, Marx, and Freud not only observed their worlds but fundamentally changed them. The minister pronouncing two people married makes it so, and we body into truth the realities of our gender and sexuality every day (Butler 1990). Artistic truth is performed truth. Such truths are not always salutary, and few are actually permanent. But those that are the hardest to refute are often the ones most deeply felt. The world in which actual humans live is a world of embodied, sometimes ecstatic, but deeply invested truths. From the perspective of humans' lived experience in the world, the conjoining of truth and enjoyment, and hence of philosophy and rhetoric, goes without saying. Truth is something humans do in the world and the *logos*, reason, is their instrument.

III

> We can say in a general fashion that *parrhēsia* simply cannot be defined within the field of rhetoric, as an element coming under rhetoric. . . . As you have seen, *parrhēsia* is defined fundamentally, essentially, and primarily, as truth-telling, while rhetoric is a manner, an art, or a technique of disposing of the elements of the discourse in a persuasive manner.
>
> (Foucault 2008: 53)

Foucault in his 1979/80 course at the Collège de France introduces the concept of the *alèthurgie* or "act of truth" to name the "ensemble of possible procedures . . . through which one brings to light what is posited as true in opposition to the false, the hidden, the unsayable, the unforeseeable, the forgotten" (Foucault 2012: 8). Reflecting on this form of analysis at the beginning of his 1984 course, Foucault argues that the "alethurgical" analyzes the type of act "through which the subject speaking the truth *manifests* itself, by which I mean to say, represents itself to itself and is recognized by others as speaking the truth" (Foucault 2009: 4). *Parrhēsia*, on this analysis, is a formalized act of truth, which is classically performed by the philosopher, who with his interlocutor produces through his discourse a truth that did not exist before the act's performance. In the figure of the rhetorician, though, these two moments of truth and performance become alienated from one another, the act becomes separated from its truth, and the subject is no longer tied directly to the performance.

In Cicero's dream of the perfect orator, however, these valences are reversed. The orator persuades precisely because the performance of his conviction is so powerful and so genuine that he becomes like a torch who lights the fire of his auditor's conviction as well. There is no space visible between the truth and its performance. The ideal orator is a figure who transcends the contradictions of the discursive moment, of language's alienation from meaning, of the democratic speaker from the audience's desire, of truth from its material realization.

Still, the attentive reader may object that, while the parrhesiast must risk his life in the act of truth, the rhetorician is judged by his ability to produce desired effects and avoid consequences. As Callicles reminds Socrates, rhetoric is a means of avoiding risk when on trial. But is that always true? Cicero at the beginning of Book 3 tells us how shortly after the conversation depicted in *De Oratore*, Crassus was called back to Rome, where he gave such an impassioned speech in defense of the senate that he collapsed and died a few short days later. More directly, we know that as a result of the attacks Cicero launched on Marc Antony in his *Philippics* after Caesar's assassination, Antony will order the orator's death, his head and right hand cut off and nailed to the rostrum in the Forum.

While the ideal orator was just that, in real life Cicero sought to unite the philosophical parrhesiast with the master of eloquence. For that he ultimately paid the price. Foucault was no doubt correct for the purposes of his genealogy of the modern subject to accept the opposition between philosophy and rhetoric, which was instituted with the *Gorgias* and has remained dominant ever since. Yet figures like Cicero offer a glimpse of a literary and rhetorical counterhistory in which truth is not merely a ratification of what is but is fully rooted in our embodied experience of language, action, and performance, and so affirms the possibility of difference in thought and speech.

5

From True-Confessions to True-Discourse in Late Foucault

Niki Kasumi Clements
Rice University

In a worn green folder in the archives at the Bibliothèque nationale de France, Michel Foucault announces the questions haunting him since 1963: "Why are we obliged to tell the truth about ourselves? Which truth?"[1] Foucault handwrites these questions to himself in English in October 1980 in preparation for his first Howison lecture at UC Berkeley, "Truth and Subjectivity" (Foucault 2016a). This lecture starts with nineteenth-century psychiatrist Dr. Leuret extracting confessions from Patient A through water-torture; by confessing his madness, Patient A constitutes himself as a mad subject whom the good doctor cures.[2] Foucault reads modern disciplinary subjects—like Patient A—as obliged to participate in constant *truth-confessing*, particularly of one's sexuality. Confession and subject formation are inextricable in this disciplinary logic structuring modern carceral society.

In this same archival draft, Foucault develops these questions as "both a philosophical and an ethical problem, both an institutional and an epistemological problem."[3] Readers can see themes that thread through Foucault's monographs in the 1960s and 1970s yet with a twist towards his 1980s attention to ethics. There is the epistemological question of how knowledge is produced, institutionalized, and normalized (Foucault 1972; 1994e). There is the question of how institutions and power relations are not isomorphic yet bound together through asymmetries of authority and patient (Foucault 1977; 1990). We can even glean the bourgeoning ethical question of how telling the truth might also critique and challenge dominant norms. Still, the question of ethics in this 1980 draft remains far from Foucault's 1983 exhortation at the Collège de France toward a modality of true-discourse known as παρρησία (*parrhēsia*) where philosophical critique remains in "a permanent and restive exteriority with regard to politics"(Foucault 2010: 354).

It is widely known that Foucault develops his understanding of *parrhēsia* between 1982 and 1984, where although the term's valence changes, a commitment to *true-discourse* runs through his lectures (Foucault 2016b: 11).[4] What scholars have not yet addressed is archival evidence of how Foucault first engages *parrhēsia* years earlier. Working through Foucault's archives at the Bibliothèque nationale de France, I was surprised to come across Foucault's reference to *parrhēsia* in a typed draft for his 1980 Howison lectures at the University of California, Berkeley.[5]

This reference is in the same 1980 draft beginning my chapter here. How might Foucault's questions—"Why are we obliged to tell the truth about ourselves? Which truth?"—as philosophical, ethical, institutional, and epistemological problems, correlate with his interest in *parrhēsia*? Why might Foucault address truth-confessing as a problem (for Patient A and modern subjects) in tandem with a bourgeoning interest in true-discourse as a critical practice (of ancient parrhesiasts)? What happens in this shift from the truth of oneself to the truth "in general" as later Foucault notes?

In this chapter, I address these questions through Foucault's engagement with *parrhēsia* between 1980 and 1984. I identify Foucault as moving from the problem of *truth-telling* as a technology of power and domination to the possibility of *true-discourse* as critiquing power and domination (Foucault 2005: 510). Speaking of the relation between subjectivity and truth, Foucault confirms in 1984 "in fact, that has always been my problem, even if I have expressed in different terms the framework of this thought"(Foucault 1988: 1). Moving from concerns regarding subjection through normative orders of truth (identified with power/knowledge) to the subjectivation enabling their critique (identified with ethics) helps Foucault gradually articulate the ethical dimensions of the form of self-relation that leads to *parrhēsiastic* articulation of the truth.[6]

Why is this analysis important now, more than forty years after Foucault's death? Beyond the need to understand *parrhēsia* as a critical concept in Foucault's late ethics, his navigation of *parrhēsia* illuminates something crucial in his inquiry into how subjects constitute themselves in relation to truth. Such a critical analysis of *parrhēsia* has only recently become possible through the scholarship of (and on) Foucault that extends beyond his published monographs, to the publications of his lectures at the Collège de France and abroad (Lorenzini, Revel, and Sforzini 2013: 9–11; Clements 2021a: 5). The archives at the Bibliothèque nationale de France (BNF) offer a vital and still underexplored site for understanding Foucault's historical and theoretical wrestling with the questions that haunted him; my chapter here relies on archival work I have undertaken between 2019 and 2023.[7] This ongoing research confirms for me the importance of the archives for understanding how Foucault forges his concepts through his shifts in methods, texts, and contexts.

This subtends my larger argument—inaugurated here yet that I am developing in a monograph—that Foucault did not go in search of "ethical" materials or questions to theorize. Instead of "an ethical turn," Foucault's historical research on confession and the experience of the self as a privileged locus of truth led him to the question of how the subject forms themself as a teller of truth. As Foucault engages texts and practices in Western antiquity, he comes to see different ways that selves relate to truth through this question of *parrhēsia*. Neither *parrhēsia* nor ethics suddenly appear as concepts in 1982, as the published records suggest. That Foucault drafted these concepts together in 1980 challenges us to see his own surprise in how different possibilities for technologies of the self route two paths of truth-confessing and true-discourse.[8]

Parrhēsia in the Fonds Foucault

Foucault does not often date his drafted materials. Yet, the worn green folder for his 1980 Howison lecture, "Truth and Subjectivity," bears Foucault's handwriting:

> Berkeley 1ère conférence
> —
> version longue
> et version brève
> oct 80 [9]

After this handwritten page, we find an unfinished fifteen-page typescript in English dated "Paris 1980." Within his schematic treatment of Greco-Roman spiritual direction, Foucault treats "the importance of the common life in the philosophy schools."[10]

In this context, Foucault uses the term *parrhēsia*—I believe for the first time—in reference to Epicurean community:

> And at the point of juncture between this friendship and this hierarchy, there was the obligation of the parresia, to which Philodemus consecrated a complete treatise. Parresia was the opening of the heart, the candour which should pass not only between the discipline and his master, but in the relationships of the members of the group amongst themselves. However it must not be thought that this implies the necessity of saying everything to the other. It is rather a question

of an ethical and technical rule concerning verbal relationships between members of the group."[11]

Foucault refers to the second-to-first century BCE Epicurean philosopher Philodemus of Gadara and his treatise *Peri parrhēsias* to orient his exploration of *parrhēsia* as "the opening of the heart." He notes the two-fold operation of *parrhēsia*, both in the direction of conscience (between master and disciple) and as the "candour" (*la franchise*) characterizing all relationships in the community.[12] Whether in vertical or horizontal relations, *parrhēsia* defines "an ethical and technical rule concerning verbal relationships."[13] In this earliest reference to *parrhēsia*, then, Foucault also invokes the "ethical" in relation to speaking the truth.

In his French manuscript draft for the English lecture he gives at Berkeley, Foucault directly relates *parrhēsia* to confession and *truth-telling*. Although preserved in a different archival Box 62, the overlap is clear:

> Ce thème de l'aveu nécessaire pour le progrès de l'âme, on le trouve chez les épiucuriens. Le Περί παρρησίας de Philodème est très révélateur sur ce point.[14]

Foucault frames Philodemus' treatise as important for understanding confession (*l'aveu*) in Epicurean spiritual direction. Yet as he hand-edits this French typescript for the Howison lecture, he notes in the margins "*non sauter*" thereby deleting his reference to Philodemus and his *Peri parrhēsias*. He rejects the connection intended between confession (*l'aveu*) and the direction of souls in the Epicureans. When he delivers his Howison lectures, Foucault instead ties *confession* (*l'aveu*) to the monastic practices of *exagoreusis* in John Cassian. This is the contrast Foucault makes in his treatment of *parrhēsia* above: "the necessity of saying everything to the other" is tied to Christian monastics, while the ethical and technical rule of *parrhēsia* is tied to Epicurean philosophers. Federico Testa stresses how Foucault situates Epicurean *parrhēsia* as both "the foundation of a confessional practice" that "will be appropriated and transformed by Christianity" *and* "its ambiguous role and singularity" (Testa, 2024). As Foucault works out the status of truth-telling, he stresses differences between the injunction to say everything (*tout dire*) for late ancient Christian monastics, and the ethical obligation to speak truly (with *la franchise*) for Greco-Roman philosophers. It makes sense, then, that Foucault would delete his correlation between *l'aveu* and spiritual direction in Philodemus.

Between 1980 and 1982, Foucault wrote and preserved a few more treatments of *parrhēsia* with a stress on *la franchise* or *franc parler* in Philodemus. Foucault crosses out a short but suggestive treatment of *parrhēsia* on the backside of a page on Musonius:

> appelaient <u>Parrhesia</u> : aptitude à dire hardiment ce qu'on pense, capacité à sourire en toute liberté à son interlocuteur, vertu du « franc parler », à pouvoir dire à quelqu'un sans restriction ce qu'on pense de lui.[15]

This is in another archival Box 52, titled "Le souci de soi," within a section called "III. Les épreuves du corps et de la conduite." Foucault identifies *parrhēsia* with speaking with complete freedom, as a virtue of "frank speech" and the ability to state what one thinks about someone else "without constraint" (*sans restriction*). It is curious that this material on *parrhēsia* does not appear in the *History of Sexuality*, Volume 3 that carries the same name as this box: *Le Souci de soi*. Indeed, Foucault does not refer to *parrhēsia* in any of his volumes for the *History of Sexuality*. The one reference to Philodemus is in a section on "The Culture of the Self" ("La Culture de soi") in Volume 3 (Foucault 2015: 1014–15).

Archival Box 79 has a related set of typescripts in a more developed form which Foucault gave page numbers (typically signaling material he was preparing for publication). In a folder called "Culture de soi et rapport aux autres," the typescript titled "II <u>Rapport aux autres</u>" includes material on Philodemus and spiritual direction, developing the relation between self and other in practices of self.[16] It is in relation to Galen of Pergamon that Foucault ties the imperative to speak freely that he elsewhere relates to *parrhēsia*:

> Ce dont on a besoin, disait-il, c'est d'un conseiller qui parle « franchement » ; il faut pour cela s'adresser à quelqu'un qui est connu pour n'être pas un flatteur, un de ces hommes sages qui ont su vivre comme il faut et dont on testera, par différents moyens, la sincérité: et ce qu'on lui demandera, c'est de dire, sans rien déguiser, les défauts qu'il a pu observer chez son interlocuteur.[17]

The doctor, like the spiritual director, must "speak 'frankly'" (*parle "franchement"*) when giving advice; one must find a doctor who is sincere and who does not avoid mentioning faults. The guide must avoid flattery and directly state the problems and how to address them.

In the archives, then, we can see Foucault's broader discursive frame for understanding spiritual direction, the care of the self, and care for others in relation to *parrhēsia*, "franc parler," "la franchise," and speaking "franchement." These drafted materials share themes with Foucault's published monographs *L'Usage des plaisirs* and *Le Souci de soi*, raising the question of why he chose to exclude *parrhēsia* from direct treatment in his final monographs. If *parrhēsia* is as important to his attention to ethics as I am suggesting, why is it not present in his final works?

In fact, in the early 1980s, Foucault researched and drafted material for a separate book on ancient ethics called *Le Gouvernement de soi et des autres*. According to Daniel Defert, Foucault considered the work "ready to be edited."[18] Foucault conceived of this book as separate from the "sex series" yet still dedicated to the Greco-Roman (and, to a lesser extent, ancient Greek) materials in Volumes 2 and 3 of the *History of Sexuality* series.[19] As Frédéric Gros argues in his course context for Foucault's 1982 Collège de France lectures, *The Hermeneutics of the Subject*:

> The subject matter of this book is precisely what forms the content of "The Hermeneutics of the Subject"...it is like the substitute of a projected and thought-out book which never appeared, a book devoted entirely to these techniques of the self in which Foucault found, at the end of his life, the conceptual crowning achievement of his work, something like the principle of its completion.
>
> (Gros 2005: 515)

In preparation for the course publication, Daniel Defert had loaned five folders to Gros, François Ewald, and Alessandro Fontana that are now housed at the BNF (Gros 2005: 516); Gros's treatment of this material remains the definitive (and I believe the only) sustained treatment of this book and deserves careful attention (see Gros 2005: 507–46). For our current purposes, we can note Gros's framing of "the relevance of the problematization, from 1983 at the Collège de France, of *parrhēsia* as 'courage of truth': so a problematic that is wholly in line with a set of unpublished studies of the politics of the self can only be recaptured on the basis of this set of studies" (Gros 2005: 517).

Indeed, in a folder titled "Écouter, lire et écrire" Foucault takes four pages of notes on *parrhēsia*, beginning:

> B. C'est la parrhesia
>   - Étymologiquement, c'est le « tout dire »
>   c'est la franchise, la liberté de parole, cette ouverture qui fait qu'on dit
>   ...
>   - En apparence c'est un terme qui désigne une qualité souhaitable chez toute personne qui parle
>   Mais c'est aussi un terme technique et qui se rapporte essentiellement à ce que doit dire le maître, et à la manière dont il doit le dire
>   → Philodème[20]

Foucault identifies three aspects to *parrhēsia*: first, the etymological sense of the "say everything" (*tout dire*) with frankness and freedom of speech; second, the desirable quality of speech (contrasted with flattery or empty-speech); third, the technical term for what and how a spiritual director must speak. And this attention to the *parrhēsia* of the director connects to the *parrhēsia* of members of the community in the following archival Box 73:

> Philodème en la *Parrhesia*, le franc parler du directeur, appelle et rend possible le franc parler des disciples et leur bienveillance réciproque ( ). D'ailleurs il ne faut pas oublier le lien essentiel que les épiucuriens établissaient entre amitié et utilité.[21]

Parrhēsia as the "franc parler" of the director enables the "franc parler" of the disciples and their openness to each other; *parrhēsia* is not just a verbal relationship, but encompasses broader ethical relations. Friendship enables disciples to advance in philosophical ways of life, through the obligation of *parrhēsia* as the opening of the heart, not only between the disciple and master but also between members of the community.

This reading of *parrhēsia* and Philodemus deserves special care because of how Foucault keeps returning to its significance, even though it does not appear in his published monographs. *Parrhēsia* as the "opening of the heart" enabled by and enabling the "franc parler" of a spiritual director and community members does not only appear in one draft of his 1980 Howison lectures, but is reiterated across four different archival Boxes—Boxes 76.1 (in French), 40.1 (in English), 62.4 (in French), 79.2 (in English)—and in other parts of Foucault's archives on ancient Greek and Roman ethics. So Foucault comes to *parrhēsia* as a concept by 1980 yet develops its importance and shifts its valence through 1984. So how and why does he pursue its modification and centralization as a concept over his last four years, notably in relation to questions of ethics?

Public *Parrhēsia*

We can at this point follow the scholarly work done on Foucault's public references to *parrhēsia*. On the basis of extant publications, scholars who have written on *parrhēsia*—including Edward McGushin (2007), Frédéric Gros (2012), Maria Andrea Rojas (2012), Fabienne Brion and Bernard Harcourt (2014), Carlos Levy (2014), Laura Cremonesi (2015), Stuart Elden (2016), Daniele Lorenzini (2017; 2023), Corey McCall (2017), Bernard Meunier (2021), and Michel Senellart (2022)—rely on the dating of 1982 for when Foucault starts his work.[22] Elaborated by Frédéric Gros and translated by Graham Burchell into

English first as "boldness" or "speaking freely" in Foucault's 1982 Collège lectures, *parrhēsia*'s centrality to Foucault's last three years of lectures is well known. Henri-Paul Fruchaud and Daniele Lorenzini's edited volumes stage *parrhēsia* in Foucault's international lectures in 1982 at the University of Victoria, 1982 at the University of Grenoble, and 1983 at UC Berkeley (Foucault 2017b; 2021c; 2016b; 2019). The 2008 through 2021 publications of these lectures by Foucault—in French and English editions—have been vital for understanding Foucault's treatment of *parrhēsia* in 1982, 1983, and 1984 (Foucault 2010; 2011; 2019; 2021c).[23]

Foucault's first public treatment of *parrhēsia* occurs in January 1982 emphasizing true speech as a social practice, stressing the necessity of a guide (*hēgemōn*), "an intense affective relationship of friendship," and *parrhēsia* as "a certain 'ethics of speech'" (Foucault 2005: 137). On March 10, 1982 Foucault offers his longest exposition on *parrhēsia* at the Collège that year as "speaking freely" (*franc-parler*) in opposition to flattery (Foucault 2005: 372). Foucault walks back his claim that *parrhēsia* is "telling all" and specifies instead:

> It seems to me that the term *parrhēsia* refers both to the moral quality, the moral attitude or the *ēthos*, if you like, and to the technical procedure or *tekhnē*, which are necessary, which are indispensable, for conveying true discourse to the person who needs it to constitute himself as a subject of sovereignty over himself and as a subject of veridiction on his own account.
> (Foucault 2005: 372)

Parrhēsia, then, refers to the "moral attitude" and "technical procedure"—the *ēthos* and the *tekhnē*—needed for the subject's self-constitution. Paul Allen Miller notes how for Foucault *parrhēsia* "was a technique used by the master to engender a transformation of the disciple, making his self visible through the frank speech of the other" (Miller 2021a: 178). This quality of speech reflects less about the content (i.e. the truth) and more about the *kairos* (i.e. the occasion and timeliness); as "a specific, particular practice of true discourse," it is not the truth of oneself but the practice of self-constitution and care for the self that matters (Foucault 2005: 384).

This self-constitution is not, however, a solipsistic or individual endeavor. As editor of these lectures, Frédéric Gros stresses the social dimensions of this care of the self: "The Hellenistic and Roman care of the self is not an exercise of solitude. Foucault thinks of it as an inherently social practice" (Gros 2005: 536). Foucault considers *parrhēsia* in other social sites, notably in Galen of Pergamon's use of *parrhēsia* in the medical *technē* as paralleling how Philodemus conceives of *parrhēsia* as a philosophical *technē* (Gros 2005: 396–9).²⁴ For his May 1982 conference at the University of Grenoble, Foucault similarly describes *parrhēsia* etymologically as a "telling all (*tout dire*)" of the disciple to his director, opening his heart to reveal the movement of his thoughts; yet he also clarifies in conversation with his host, Henri Joly, *parrhēsia* does not reduce to "juridical confession" (Foucault 2019: 4–5, 37).

During Foucault's last two years, *parrhēsia* comes to encompass a broader semantic range than "frankness" or "free speech," acquiring a pronounced political valence.²⁵ Opening his Collège de France lecture on January 2, 1983, Foucault refers to Philodemus' treatise on *parrhēsia*, and its political and religious use which he claims is yet "extremely incomplete for individual spiritual direction" which suggests his dissatisfaction with his earlier designation (Foucault 2010: 46). Foucault returns to *parrhēsia* on February 9 to respond to a dissatisfied auditor, who challenges Foucault's reading by differentiating *parrhēsia* from *isēgoria*, which is the Athenian citizen's legal right to voice their opinions. Foucault then modifies the importance of *parrhēsia* as not the freedom of speech granted to every citizen (as in *isēgoria*) but as a more specific political practice that puts the speaker at risk (see also, Miller 2021a: 135).

In his following 1983 lectures, Foucault stresses the distinctly political function of *parrhēsia* where one courageously speaks truth to power, especially when an interlocutor is threatened by such critique: "Parrhesiasts are those who, if necessary, accept death for having told the truth. Or more precisely, parrhesiasts are those who undertake to tell the truth at an unspecified price, which may be as high as their own death" (Foucault 2010: 56). In one of the earliest treatments of Foucault's *parrhēsia*, Edward McGushin describes: "In *parrhēsia*, furthermore, one speaks one's mind in a situation where the stakes are high. This is because one speaks a truth to someone who does not want to hear that truth—one's opinion is critical or offensive. The listener is in a position to retaliate if he is inclined to do so" (McGushin 2007: 7). In Fall 1983, Foucault's lectures at Berkeley expand this political and philosophical form of *parrhēsia*, now extending from the fifth century BCE to the fifth century CE, from Euripides to John Chrysostom (Foucault 2019).

In Spring 1984, Foucault delivers his last lectures at the Collège de France, redescribing radical *parrhēsia* as a relation between subjectivity and truth, in word and deed, as an art of living. He stresses *parrhēsia* as necessary for philosophers in a directly ethical register. Like Socrates whose *daimōn* compels him to question the mores of Athens even while respecting its laws unto his own death, the parrhesiast follows "his duty, obligation, responsibility, and task to speak" (Foucault 2012a: 18). Foucault admires Socrates' ethical emphasis on the "alethurgic" form, or the alchemy by which subjects produce truth by manifesting it in deed and word (Foucault 2012a: 3; see also, Lorenzini 2023).

Foucault describes the development in his own thought via Philodemus, Plutarch, and Galen: "So this is how I was led to focus on this notion of *parrhēsia* as a constitutive component of truth-telling about self or, more precisely, as the element which qualifies the other person who is necessary in the game and obligation of speaking the truth about self" (Foucault 2012a: 7).[26] It is not just a quality of speech, but a form of relationality both to oneself and to others. So we can see Foucault himself connecting *parrhēsia* with the opening questions for my chapter; he was led to focus on *parrhēsia* through questions of speaking the truth and relations to self and others, using Socrates before the Athenian assembly, Plato before Dionysius the tyrant, and Diogenes before Alexander the Great as examples. Yet here speaking the truth requires a bold risk-taking instead of a passive obligation and subjection.

In 1984, Foucault describes Socrates as practicing all four modalities of truth-telling: prophecy, wisdom, teaching, and *parrhēsia* (Foucault 2012a: 24–30). As Gros stresses, *parrhēsia* "is no longer practiced within an individual relationship of direction but is instead an address in a public arena" (Gros 2010: 380). The boldness, then, is not about the master-to-student dyad or parrhesiast-to-ruler but the courageous person who speaks out in public aiming to turn everyone's attention toward the truth they speak. Different modalities produce different discourses of truth, and Diogenes the Cynic comes to exemplify the parrhesiast for his complete eschewal of societal norms (recall Diogenes barking to Alexander the Great to get out of his sunlight or, more vividly, masturbating in the public square).[27] Foucault surprisingly extends Cynic modes of life even to early Christian witnesses and martyrs of truth who take on the "idea of a mode of life as the eruptive, violent scandalous manifestation of the truth" (Foucault 2012a: 181).[28] Foucault correlates such challenges to authority with *parrhēsia*, while also identifying "a positive and a negative conception of *parrhēsia*" within Christianity (Foucault 2012a: 337). While the mystic poses positive parrhesiast challenges to social orders, the ascetic is the anti-parrhesiast bound in relations of obedience and the denial of self in Christian monasticism (Foucault 2012a: 337).

In this last lecture, Foucault also returns to the "opening of the heart" as positive-*parrhēsia* in fourth-century Cappadocian Gregory of Nyssa. Foucault cites Nyssa's description of the pre-lapsarian human as looking "on God's face with free assurance (*en parrhēsia*)" (Foucault 2012a: 332). This *parrhēsia* is part of the human condition before the fall from paradise, "in *parrhēsia* with God: openness of heart, immediate presence, and direct communication of the soul and God" (Foucault 2012a: 333). And as Michel Senellart argues of Foucault's Christian *parrhēsia*: "It is the relation of confidence in God which, for the Christian, anchors the courage of truth" (Senellart 2022: 21). Like the Epicurean relation to one's director and community, and in overlap with Cynic attention to an "other world" possible, Nyssa's *parrhēsia* signals the possibility for relations other than subjection and blind obedience.[29] Nyssa also plays a central role in Foucault's 1982 Collège de France lectures affirming the "care of the self" (ἐπιμελεία ἑαυτοῦ) in continuity with Socrates eight centuries before.[30] This correlation between the care of the self and *parrhēsia* no doubt contributed to Foucault's appreciation of Nyssa alongside Socrates for ethics; Philodemus occupies a midpoint between Socrates in the fifth century BCE and Nyssa in the fourth century CE.

*

Between 1980 and 1982, Foucault develops his understanding of *parrhēsia* as linking truth, subjectivity, and discourse. From an "opening of the heart" (1980) to a quality of speech (1982) to a political stance (1983) to an ethical way of life (1984), *parrhēsia* accrues an epistemic weight: it becomes the means by which one has access to the truth even when at odds with dominant forms of knowledge and power. *Parrhēsia* accrues a political weight in the founding of democracy as a form of government and an aptitude of the citizen beyond *isēgoria*. *Parrhēsia* also accrues an ethical weight as basic to self-formation in community, a disposition cultivated in vertical and horizonal relations with others, as well as a risky speaking truth to power.

In Foucault's reading of radical ancient figures—like Socrates, Diogenes, and even Nyssa—knowledge of truth enables *parrhēsia* as contesting forms of domination, enacted through the cultivation of ways of life that challenge the social *nomos*. *Parrhēsia* requires a philosophical way of life and reflection on truth. Therefore *parrhēsia* as "true-speech" has a number of characteristics: (1) one speaks truth to power, (2) one shows through their way of life the quality of this truth, (3) one puts oneself at risk, and—it is not often enough remarked—(4) one speaks the truth of injustice impacting others: one speaks on behalf of others as well as oneself. In short, there is the possibility (however slim) of effecting more just social formations without any guarantee of how those in power will respond. Foucault in 1984 reframes positive true-speech as a practice of freedom, while the anti-parrhesiast pole closes a long arc of his thinking about truth-telling as obligation.

By 1984, *parrhēsia* also becomes Foucault's privileged site for considering the interrelation of three constitutive elements in the relation between subjectivity and truth: "It seems to me that by examining the notion of *parrhēsia* we can see how the analysis of modes of veridiction, the study of techniques of governmentality, and the identification of forms of practice of self interweave" (Foucault 2012a: 8).[31] Foucault poses the question of the subject and truth through modes of veridiction (knowledge), techniques of governmentality (power), and forms of practices of the self (ethics)—and he refuses to reduce subject formation to a single theoretical movement (Foucault 2012a: 9). I relate this "triple theoretical shift" of Foucault to how Gros notes the three dimensions of *parrhēsia* (political, ethical, philosophical) provide "an interpretive grid rather than the definition of essences" (Gros 2019: xix). Ethical praxis is bound up in relations of knowledge and power; these three axes do not delimit essences but map an analytical grid of relations in constant interplay. *Parrhēsia* exposes how ethics might challenge relations of power and knowledge.

Coming to *Parrhēsia* through the *History of Sexuality*

I return us to Foucault's handwritten questions with which I opened this chapter: "Why are we obliged to tell the truth about ourselves? Which truth?" The obligation to confess the truth of one's sexual identity poses a modern problem—this is the practice of *truth-confessing* vividly staged by Dr. Leuret that Foucault traces back to Christian monasticism. By contrast, speaking truly requires ethical relations to others—this is the practice of *true-discourse* Foucault identifies in the *parrhēsia* of Socrates, Diogenes, Philodemus, and Nyssa. So how does Foucault begin with the problem of obligatory truth-telling (about oneself) and end up delineating how *parrhēsia* enables risky true-speech (about injustice)?

We can better understand these moves by analyzing the archival investigations that preoccupied Foucault in the 1970s and 1980s. Truth-confessing is a central problematic of Foucault's *History of Sexuality* series; as he frames it in his 1976 Volume 1, "we demand that sex speak the truth"(Foucault 1990: 69). We can see this problematic maintained in the title for his drafted Volume 4, posthumously published in 2018 as *Les Aveux de la chair* (*Confessions of the Flesh*; Foucault 2018). We have all become confessing animals, and like Patient A, we participate in our own subjection.

Foucault started his *History of Sexuality* series research by identifying sixteenth- to eighteenth-century Catholic confessors and Reformers as antecedents to nineteenth-century psychiatrists—all of whom extract confessions from subjects obedient to them (Clements 2022a). To trace how these mechanisms were shaped (and therefore expose them as contingent), Foucault conceives his original six-volume series as connecting sixteenth- to eighteenth-century confessional practices to nineteenth-century strategies of subjecting women, children, queer men, and racialized populations. Foucault's research for Volume 2, *La Chair et le corps*, retitled by 1977 *Les Aveux de la chair*, brought him to the direction of conscience in the confessors' manuals of the sixteenth to eighteenth centuries. The penitent and confessor both follow strict norms in order to produce a "good confession." Between 1974 and 1977, Foucault researched the relation between confession and sexuality in his drafts for Volumes 2 (*Les Aveux de la chair*) and 3 (*La Croisade des enfants*), where the battle against masturbation and nocturnal emissions overlaps with the injunction to tell-all to one's confessor.[32] The confessor mediates the penitent's self-relation through a direction of conscience that extracts confessions of the subject's sexual identity.

Foucault begins studying early Christian authors in 1977, finding antecedents to early modern confession in the monastic practices of *exagoreusis* and truth-telling (Chevallier 2011). Identifying obedience and sexual desire at the heart of the monastic subject, Foucault centers fourth- to fifth-century monastic John Cassian and his practical texts—the *Conferences* and the *Institutes*—as shaping the mechanisms for modern confession and the interrogative practices that produce subjectivity (Clements 2021a). Foucault stresses the hierarchy of director over monastic in Cassian's direction of conscience, where the supplicant is obligated to confess everything and obediently follow the director's commands. In his elaboration of pastoral power between 1978 and 1979, Foucault analyzes these mechanisms of individualization and totalization as institutionalized in Catholic confession first as sacrament in 1215 and then as frequent post-1550s Council of Trent (Foucault 1999; 2007; see also Sforzini 2018).

In lectures between 1980 and 1982, Foucault focuses his analyses of obligatory truth-telling in *exagoreusis*, the "dire vrai" binding novice and elder in late ancient desert monasticism. Why are we obliged? Foucault responds to his question by tracing truth-telling in Western discourses. Which truth? Foucault responds by identifying where sex and subjectivity are elided—where, following the influence of Peter Brown, Foucault comes to understand "why sexuality became in the Western Christian culture the seismograph of our subjectivity" (Clements 2022b: 11). These two currents—the obligation of truth in veridiction and sexuality as the heart of subjectivity—recur through *Confessions of the Flesh*, as Foucault continues to draft and redraft this Volume 2 between 1979 and 1982 (Chevallier 2022; Clements 2022a).

Yet in the period between 1980 and 1982, Foucault also recognizes that there are other relations between truth and discourse possible than those routed through disciplinary subjection. In his lectures at the Collège de France, Berkeley, and Louvain, Foucault charts the possibilities for subjectivation that recognizes how subjects can also participate in their own formation. As Laura Cremonesi notes, "Foucault therefore seems to read *parrêsia* as a center we can 'follow on the surface' for the evolution of a specific configuration of relations between subjectivation, truth, and relations of power" (Cremonesi 2015: 83; citing Foucault 2012: 321). Foucault comes to see the direction of conscience in Stoic, Epicurean, and Neo-Pythagorean communities as opening up a different way of thinking about subject formation and truth-telling beyond obedience, submission, and self-renunciation.[33] And we have seen in this chapter how *parrhēsia* is central to such communities.

Different forms of the direction of conscience (*la direction de conscience*) contribute to forms of examination of conscience (*l'examen de conscience*) as a practice—and Foucault stresses the differences between Roman (notably Stoic) and early Christian examination.[34] Foucault frames Stoic direction as a relation between intimates; for example, Marcus Aurelius gives advice to his beloved teacher Fronto and the two support each other in a shared journey. In Stoic contexts, one examines one's conscience to recognize the truth about their progress; in Christian contexts, it is to recognize the truth about their desires and who one *is*. Truth-telling and subject formation become bound together in the relation of (philosophical and monastic) direction; yet while truth-telling requires obedience in Christian contexts, true-discourse enables confident relations to self and others in Greek and Roman *parrhēsia*. By 1982 at the University of Grenoble, Foucault frames his project through "the question of *parrhēsia* in spiritual direction" (Foucault 2019: 14).[35]

The materials for *parrhēsia* and the examination of conscience also connect to the drafted book on ancient ethics and practices of the self that Foucault never completed, *Le Gouvernement de soi et des autres*.[36] As he reads Greco-Roman texts, Foucault comes to see different ways of relating truth and subjectivity through direction and examination—ways that challenge hierarchies of truth-confessing, and the practices of obedience and self-renunciation that he identifies with Christian monasticism. This way of considering direction and examination as sites of ethical subjectivation—and not just obedient subjection—fosters an ethical line of inquiry and the rearticulation of relations between subjectivity and truth for Foucault in his last four years.

My archival work suggests that Foucault deepened his interested in the Greco-Romans through this question of the examination of conscience, notably as framed through the research of Ilsetraut Hadot and Paul Rabbow.[37] Recall the typed draft for his 1980 Howison lectures, where Foucault refers to *parrhēsia* as "the opening of the heart" in the treatise of the Philodemus. In a reading note in Box 23, Folder 10 titled "Philodème," Foucault takes notes on Ilsetraut Hadot's reading of Philodemus on *parrhēsia* in ancient schools of philosophy in her book on Seneca and spiritual direction.[38] Hadot notes how *Peri parrhēsias* concerns the direction of conscience where the master trains the disciple in true-discourse; such truth telling requires the disciple to truthfully open their heart to their director (Hadot 1969: 64–5). Foucault shares Hadot's stress on navigating the tension between friendship and hierarchy that we saw earlier in this chapter.

Foucault does not directly attribute his reading of *parrhēsia* or spiritual direction to Hadot or Rabbow. Instead, he notes the need for analysis of *parrhēsia* due to the dearth of scholarly treatments extant at this time. In his 1983 *The Government of Self and Others* lectures at the Collège de France, Foucault refers to an article in the *Realencyclopädie der classischen Altertumswissenschaft*, an article by Giuseppe Scarpat in 1964 (from which Foucault seems to draw many of his sources), and the importance of Marcelo Gigante for his understanding of Epicureans (notably from Gigante's entry on Philodemus) (Foucault 2010: 46).[39] Foucault's archives also have his photocopy of Philodemus' *Peri parrhēsias* in the 1914 Greek text edited by Alexander Olivieri.[40] In these treatments, *parrhēsia* signals a reciprocal confidence, trust, and benevolence needed for true discourse to be offered and evaluated in good faith. *Parrhēsia*, then, opens Foucault's attention to the ethical relations binding communities of philosophers practicing true-discourse.

Parrhēsia as Ethical Challenge

With this brief history in mind, I want to expand on two questions that Foucault's edited drafts of the 1980 Howison lectures raised. First, how does Foucault come to the notion of *parrhēsia*? Tracing Foucault's reading notes and bibliographical references, he seems to come to *parrhēsia* by 1980 through scholarship on direction of conscience and examination of conscience that started with the early modern confessors yet bring him to the works of Ilsetraut Hadot and Paul Rabbow on Greco-Roman practices of truth-telling.[41] Foucault had explored the questions of obligation and subjection in Christian spiritual direction, yet engaging ancient texts contributes to Foucault's focus on ethics and the consideration of different forms of subjectivation, different forms of self-formation in relation to truth.

Foucault conceptually differentiates the "dire vrai" *true-discourse* in the examination of conscience of Philodemus from the examination of conscience and *truth-confessing* in Cassian's Christianity; the latter leads to confession of one's truth to "le bon confesseur" whose relation to the penitent mirrors that of Dr. Leuret and Patient A. By contrast, the examination of conscience in ancient philosophical communities enables relations to self and others that differ from the confessional relation to the truth of one's sexual identity. Analyzing different forms of *parrhēsia* contributed to Foucault's recognition that ethical relations of self-to-self and self-to-others were also possible, seeing the relation between subjectivity and truth as not only one of submission (*truth-confessing*) but also of normative critique (*true-discourse*).

Foucault's treatments of *parrhēsia* are very developed by March 1982 at the Collège de France and the focus of his public lectures in May 1982 at Grenoble and June 1982 at the University of Toronto, Victoria. He extends these *parrhēsia* lectures at UC Berkeley in October/November 1983, as well as through his 1983 and 1984 Collège lectures. *Parrhēsia* increasingly takes on a critical function in Foucault's work, as a political practice by 1983 and a riposte to social orders in 1984—from *parrhēsia* as foundational to democracy to *parrhēsia* as the critical activity of the Enlightenment. As Corey McCall notes of the relationship between *parrhēsia* and Kantian critique:

> Although Foucault was able to do little more than outline the project that would link the ancient conception of *parrhēsia* to the modern conception of critique, it is clear that this was his intent…this genealogy of true political discourse links up with the critical attitude, the conditions under which one begins to question the various political games of truth under the particular experiences of power relations that constitute individuals as the subjects that they are in relation to others.
>
> (McCall 2017: 336)

Despite differences in context between ancient Greece and eighteenth-century Europe, Foucault—in McCall's reading—engages *parrhēsia* as the critical attitude through which political and ethical challenges might be leveled.

Second, how does *parrhēsia* as speaking the truth relate to Foucault's interest in ethics? I add to other scholars' work the additional dimension of reflection on

Foucault's 1980 attention and deferral of concerns for *parrhēsia*. We can see Foucault move from *truth-confessing* (central to his discourses on power-knowledge) to *true-discourse* (involving the ethical relation). Year by year in the 1980s, Foucault comes to see *parrhēsia* as not only an opening of the heart nor only a reflective attitude toward politicians but also a lived disposition that allows for relations of self-to-self and forms of subjectivity able to challenge the forms of power and knowledge through which they are subject.

In Foucault's "triple theoretical shift"—between knowledge, power, and ethics—*parrhēsia* becomes a way of understanding how "practices of the self" constitute human experience alongside (and in tension with) forms of governmentality and games of truth. In his 1983 and 1984 articulations, *parrhēsia* becomes the central vector for analyzing ethics (via practices of the self), processes of knowledge (games of truth), and power (forms of governmentality) as constitutive of human experience. Yet now, it is not just obligation, obedience, and subjection to forms of power and knowledge—it is also the ability to critique and challenge such regimes in order to forge different possibilities for self and others to live and "think differently." And this brings together the forms of archeology, genealogy, and ethics that Arnold Davidson has long described (Davidson 1986).

All subjects are shaped through social power and games of truth (noted as governmentality and truth in his 1980 Collège de France lectures)—yet *parrhēsia* opens up a way of understanding how subjects can also forge ways of life in an ethical challenge to social norms. Subjects are not only subjected—they can also cultivate new practices, challenge operations of power, and counter normalizing discourses for themselves and others. The logic of reversible power relations is set up in *History of Sexuality*, Volume 1, yet remains insufficiently theorized until Foucault sees the relation between subjectivity and truth unfold differently in ancient texts in the 1980s. Foucault defers his discussion of *parrhēsia* from 1980 to his 1982 Collège lectures as he conceptually works out relations between subjectivity and truth that do not reduce to obligation and subjection.

Parrhēsia illuminates how Foucault sees human experience as not only constituted by forms of power and knowledge, but also as able to critique, challenge, and produce forms of life. It stages the possibility of challenging the two questions so central to modern subjection—why are we obliged? which truth?—where subjects need not obediently confess their sexual identity in order to be named and cured. Instead, subjects can also participate in the shaping of communities and practices that challenge their unjust or tyrannical aspects. Ethics emerges as an explicit axis in Foucault's thought in the years he develops his understanding of *parrhēsia*, notably as he rethinks social relations that can challenge hierarchical authority and obedience. Foucault exposes the institutional and ethical problems that he works to address over his last four years.

It is significant that Foucault comes to *parrhēsia* and ethics together at a time when he was working through confessional practices in (first early modern and then late ancient) Christianity, identifying both continuities and differences with ancient philosophical practices. Reconsidering the relations between subjectivity and truth in Foucault's ongoing analyses of ancient Greek to Roman to Christian forms of life also opens his conceptual apparatus from power/knowledge (*pouvoir/savoir*) to include ethics (*éthique*) in the final years of his life. We can therefore situate Foucault's inquiries into *truth-confessing* and *true-discourse* as part of his conceptual shifts in his genealogy of the modern subject.

6

Confessing in Communities

The Genealogical Exclusion of Joy from Late Antique Christianity

Alex Dressler
University of Wisconisn

And when one will hear it said in the seventeenth century . . . that confessing is a way of directing consciences, one can say that exagoreusis *has prevailed over* exomologesis . . .

(Foucault 2021a: 294)

Therefore, after saying, I will confess to the Lord, *the psalmist added this final passage,* And I will sing to the name of the Lord most high, <u>to make sure that we do not take it to mean confession of sins</u>. <u>Singing belongs to joy,</u> *but repentance of sins to sadness.*

(Augustine, *Exposition of the Psalm* 7(2), 19;
(trans. Boulding et al., 2000.1, 128, underlining added)

A Genealogy of the Joyful Subject

Foucault identified the concept of confession in Volume 1 of the *History of Sexuality*, making it the key to his conception of the relationship of subjectivity, power, and freedom for the rest of his life; a thinker of unparalleled suppleness, he never strictly opposed confession and freedom, as though confession, subjecting the confessor to various systems of knowledge and power, was the opposite of emancipation, but he tended in that direction.[1] Seeking the historical origin of confession as a means of subjection in Greco-Roman antiquity, the philosopher-historian discovered two forms of subjectivity. On the one hand, monastic Christians of Late Antiquity developed a special form of confession that Foucault termed "the hermeneutics of the self": in this hermeneutics, the goal of discourse was to discover the truth of oneself within a regime of power that unified identity and obedience.[2] On the other, before that fateful "coupling of the verbalization of the sin ... and the exploration of oneself" (Foucault 2016a; 225), Greco-Roman philosophers developed an "aesthetics of existence": choosing from a more general assortment of "techniques of the self," which confession would later monopolize, individuals would not *resist* domination in the name of a self whose inmost truth they sought to disclose and avow, passively accommodating themselves to its discovery; the ethical subject of the pre-Christian experience sought, rather, to wrest control of domination for themselves, asserting an active form of mastery over their own conduct (Armstrong 2008: 27). In doing so, they were cultivating a relationship to truth that was surprisingly "aesthetic": instead of seeking some personal, private truth, they accepted themselves as a human being—more often than not, in the ancient sources, a man, a politician, a philosopher, and a slaver—and sought in their own way to express that truth, which thus "took on the brilliance of a beauty that was revealed to those able to behold it or keep its memory present in mind."[3]

The aim of this chapter is to revisit Foucault's reconstruction of early Christianity with an even broader, though perhaps more traditional, understanding of aesthetics. While the model of confession that I will find there comprises the familiar Foucauldian concepts of discourse, power, truth, and death, it nevertheless entails a few concepts that are less common in Foucault: community, beauty, joy, and life. Foucault was attentive to some of these aspects of the *earlier* models of confession in Late Antique Christianity, and I will use his analysis of those accounts as a basis for my own alternative account of the later forms. But except for the suggestive outline that he provides in the last minutes of the lectures on *The Courage of Truth*, he never really develops the positive function of Christian speech as a source affects that produce communities.[4]

Following the barest notice of this alternative sense of confession in Foucauldian scholarship, I will discuss the one lexical sense of "confession" that Foucault never mentioned.[5] Derived from Christians' liturgical reliance on the psalms of the Hebrew Bible, confession in these contexts exhibits traditional aspects of aesthetics, including poetry, performance, beauty, and the senses—as Augustine says in the first epigraph of this chapter: confession constitutes the praise of God, the avowal of thanks, and the orally expressed experience of joy.[6] The use of confession that interests Foucault in his "genealogy of the modern subject" is a less happy form, the ancestor of the modern "incitement to discourse" of the "confessing animal" familiar from Volume 1 of the *History of Sexuality*; this, in the now published Volume 4 and the late lectures, the philosopher traces from the enclosure of confession in Late Antique monasteries through the Fourth Lateran Council to psychoanalysis and beyond.[7] At that point, by a shift in the Greek that lies behind the Latin word *confessio* from *exomologesis*, including the public proclamation of faith and praise, to *exagoreusis*, the exclusively monastic confession of sins, Foucault leaves popular Christianity behind, only to return to it, time and again, in the form of pastoral care, but at that point it will be too late.[8] Confession then appears as the chief technology of pastoral power, the individualizing instrument of mortification and obedience, and thus only the background of those later medieval struggles of resistance that Foucault called counter-conducts: asceticism, mysticism, the formation of religious communities, and eschatological or millenarian beliefs.[9]

In this chapter, I suggest that public confession can be a popular, collective, affectively rich, aesthetically complex, and ultimately joyous practice of counter-conduct, as well as a technology of the self. My aim is not to critique Foucault on historical grounds, but rather to demonstrate the value of two sets of characteristics of popular, public confession that the philosopher really elucidates so well: first, the material, physical, and even sensuous aspects of the collective experience of public confession; second, maybe more importantly, the flexibility of the idea of the aesthetics of existence, which appears in the tenth lecture on *The Courage of Truth* as a stylistics of the truth.[10] Linking truth and aesthetics, Foucault (2012: 163–6, 181–9) traces this "stylistics" from the Greek Cynics, through Christian ascetics, right up to modern revolutionaries and the "anti-Aristotelian" and "anti-Platonic" aesthetics of modern literature and art. From these examples, with unapologetic modernism, Foucault describes the aesthetics of the truth as "bareness of life" (Foucault 2012: 183), a quality at least opposed to traditional aesthetic forms and practices: "This is the idea that art itself, whether it is literature, painting, or music, must establish a relation to reality which is no longer one of ornamentation, or imitation, but one of laying bare, exposure, stripping, excavation, and violent reduction of existence to its basics."[11]

The traditional aesthetic technologies of representation ("imitation") and stimulation of the senses ("ornamentation") may have a bigger role in the aesthetics of existence than Foucault's particularly *ascetic* aesthetics allows. First, the "arts" of discourse and representation render the other technologies on which they operate more than usually malleable: inflection, repetition, variation—in short, stylization—modify and extend the meanings or functions of specific practices, opening otherwise overdetermined acts to local agency

(Staten 2019: 21–4, e.g.). Second, to quote David Graeber (2015: 99): "There is a certain communism of the senses at the root of most things we consider fun"; Graeber lists: "music, food, liquor, drugs, gossip, drama, beds." Many of these were combined in the festivals of the saints that provided the scene of the confession of praise in Late Antiquity.[12] More philosophical thinkers, such as Rancière, have found this "communism of the senses" in more attenuated modern forms of poetry and performance; these also occurred at those festivals.[13] In poetry and performance, the communism of the senses inheres in their ambiguous plurality: my saying the word *language* as I write it, for instance, and you "saying" it inside yourself when you read me writing it again: *language* (Derrida 1973: 7f., 12, 165f., e.g.). Whatever was shared between the page and us just now offers a good (albeit weak) example of this "communism of the senses."[14]

By expanding Foucault's archive of confessional sites with this aesthetic theoretical concept of "communism," I will link Foucault's claims about Late Antique Christianity in the lectures *On the Government of the Living* and in Volume 4 of the *History of Sexuality* to his final remarks about the "unconcealed life," the aesthetics of existence, and Christian mysticism as counter-conducts in the lectures on *The Courage of Truth* (Foucault 2012; 336–7). In doing so, I will argue that more traditional aesthetic practices, such as poetry and performance, are more integral to the aesthetics of existence than they otherwise appear.[15] On the one hand, this is a perfectly acceptable Foucauldian claim. As Foucault (2012: 164–5) points out, the whole point of calling the stylistics of the truth a *stylistics* is that it admits of multiple forms of elaboration: "[t]he dandy, the sexual nonconformist, the revolutionary, and the philosopher," for example (Miller 2021a: 188). On the other hand, increasing diversification of stylizations of the truth may problematize some Late Foucauldian assumptions: how far can the stylization of truth go before it ceases to be a stylization of *truth*, and becomes instead a mere show? And is it, when it becomes that, really a "mere show" or might it not have a Foucauldian value *apart from the truth*?

To answer this question, I will discuss two kinds of ancient Christian evidence: first, the publicly performed poetry of the renegade aristocrat Paulinus of Nola (354–431 CE); second, the theorization of Judeo-Christian poetry offered by Paulinus' exact contemporary, the better-known Augustine, in his *Expositions of the Psalms*. While my concern with regimes of appearance problematizes Foucault's late emphasis on truth, it also counteracts the predominance of death, risk, antagonism, individuality, and masculinity promoted by the philosopher's ancient archive—something that Foucault only begins to overcome in the very last lectures of *The Courage of Truth*.¹⁶ At the same time, the reinsertion of appearances, and thus maybe also ideology, into Foucauldian thought points the way to *class* as a category of that thought, and to class as a category of experience, even if Foucault misprizes it.¹⁷ There is a real practical necessity to this, at least for understanding Foucault: the assumption of poverty (Foucault 2012: 259–60) plays a key role in defining truth and the Marxian notion of changing the world in the last lectures. But is poverty intelligible without some relational concept of collectivity, such as class or status, and what role do traditional aesthetic forms such as poetry and performance play in producing such collectives in experience? These are the questions that I will ask, and in the end, I will seek some answers in ancient aesthetic forms and, following Chevallier (2011: 179–85), in Foucault's earlier work on aesthetics from the 1960s.

Collective and Aesthetic Aspects of Confession: Confession of Sin

In the 1979/80 course *On the Government of the Living*, Foucault derives the first form of confession, *exomologesis*, from the Latin Christian Tertullian's account of confession before baptism and after lapsing, or recanting Christianity—that is, recanting the confession of faith—in the persecutions. In this preeminently ritualistic practice, Foucault discerns two related features, the theatrical aspect of the practice and its transformative effects. In both cases, Foucault privileges death and the truth where life and a spectacular construction of community are equally salient. A glance at Tertullian's Latin will show, not that Foucault was wrong, but that he was selective (Chevallier 2011: 155–7), even as his analysis reveals affective and aesthetic dimensions that later Christians will harness for happier ends.

Identifying the aesthetic dimension of public confession, Foucault describes "the permanent drama of repentance, that kind of theatrical dramatization" (Foucault 2016: 210), which amounts to "the externalization of the conversion of thought" and "its transcription in comportment" (Foucault 2016: 209).¹⁸ The central passage is Tertullian, *On Penance* 9.1-3 (trans. Le Saint 1959: 31, modified):

> Exomologesis is, then, an ordinance [*disciplina*] which leads a person to prostrate and humble themselves. It prescribes a way of life which, even in the matter of food and clothing, attracts pity [*misericordiae inlicem*] .... It requires that you

habitually nourish prayer by fasting, that you sigh and weep and groan all day and night to the Lord your God, that you prostrate yourself <u>at the feet of the priests and kneel before the beloved of God</u>, making <u>all the brethren</u> commissioned ambassadors of your prayer for pardon [*omnibus fratribus legationem deprecationis suae iniungere*]. Exomologesis does all this <u>in order to render penitence acceptable [*ut paenitentiam commendat*]</u>.

Now Tertullian is not *obviously* describing acts of joy or praise or anything other than what Foucault says. And one can see, especially with the word that I have translated as ordinance, which in Latin is *disciplina*, or discipline, why Foucault would be attracted to the passage (cf. Chevallier 2011: 200–1). What in many ways *fails* to interest Foucault about this passage, even as he rightly elucidates it, is the *social dimension* of speech and language that Foucault locates on "the verbal-non-verbal axis" of confession (Foucault 2016: 212; Büttgen 2021a: 94–6). In contrast with the later monastic form, which, Foucault (2016a: 212) writes, "is obviously on the side of verbal formulation," the form of confession in Tertullian "is entirely on the side of non-verbal expressive elements, or, if one uses words . . . it is not at all to speak . . . it is to affirm . . . [S]peech here has the value of the cry, an expressive value, and not at all the value of the precise designation of a sin." Lacking the "precise designation of a sin," *exomologesis* could not, over any period, give rise to the incitement to *discourse* of the modern subject.

As a result, despite his brilliant elucidation of the social and symbolic aspects of the ritual, Foucault moves too quickly when he concludes (Foucault 2018: 367, trans. Foucault 2021a: 292): "The penitent's exomologesis is a double manifestation (of the renunciation of what one is and of the being of defilement and death that one renounces) as a purifying test of oneself conducted by oneself [*épreuve . . . de soi sur soi*]."

Perhaps it depends on the ambiguity of "conduct" in this formulation, but the description of *exomologesis* in Tertullian is by no means exclusively reflexive. One example of this, of course, is the priests who watch the penitent at their feet, the "brethren" who plead their case. More subtle, and subtly aesthetic, is the role of affects. The drama of *exomologesis* "attracts pity" (*misericordiae inlicem*)— whose pity? Surely, the pity of the congregation, if not also of God. It makes penitence acceptable, and the word that the Latin uses to describe that process (*commendat*) unquestionably implies a *subject* of acceptance—that is to say, a people who accept the confessing subject as an object, even of care.[19]

Foucault devotes little time to the intersubjective and affective dimension, especially after the 1979/80 lectures, but the next chapter in Tertullian makes the communitarianism of early Christianity and its power to transform individuals into communal beings the main attraction for prospective penitents. To those afraid to commit themselves to their community in this way, Tertullian says (*On Penitence* 10.4, trans. Le Saint 1959: 33, modified):

> But among brethren and people enslaved to the same household [*conservos*], where hope, fear, joy, sorrow and suffering are shared [*communis*], because the Spirit is shared between the Lord and Father [*communi domino et patre*], why do you think these men something other than yourself [*tu hos aliud quam te opinaris*]? Why do you flee, as from scoffers, those who share your misfortunes [*consortes*]? The body cannot rejoice at the suffering of a single one of its members; the whole body must needs suffer with it [*condoleat*] and help in its cure [*ad remedium conlaboret*]. Where there are two together, there is the Church – and the Church is Christ. When, therefore, you stretch forth your hands to the knees of your brethren, you are in touch with Christ [*Christum contrectas*] and you win the favor of Christ by your supplications. In like manner, when they shed tears for you, it is Christ who suffers, Christ who supplicates the Father. And what the Son requests is always easily obtained.

One does not need to be a Latinist to see that every step of this process identifies community. Starting with the overt statement of com-munion which binds human con-gregations to one another in the same way that the spirit effects the unity of God and Christ, every significant verb begins with the Latin prefix denoting togetherness: *com-*, *con-* ("with," *cum*). In the context of the definition of *exomologesis* in the previous chapter of the treatise, Tertullian suggests that the etymology of confession (*con-fessio* or "speaking with" in Latin), while it eventually denotes the first step on the path to individualization in monasticism, also denotes, in pre- (and possibly para-) monastic Christianity, the speech act of community par excellence.

For this reason, it is surprising that Foucault continues in the same course to compare this institution to earlier Greek rituals of supplication only to say that the public confession of early Christians "functions quite differently" (Foucault 2016: 213). If pre-Christian "supplication operates as the transfer of obligation through the manifestation of misfortune," and if Christian supplication derives from this, as Foucault (2014b: 106–8) claims, what happened to the transformative and communitarian power of the early form in the Christian transformation of confession? Was it entirely supplanted by truth and death? At any rate, "by using the vocabulary of supplication to manifest both that one is dead and that one is dying to death," Foucault (2016: 214) continues, "one brings out the truth of oneself." Of course, Foucault is not *wrong*; there *is* a close relationship to death at the heart of the initiation into Christianity.[20] And Foucault is also right to attribute some form of truth to the act of public confession: since everyone is a sinner in Christian thought of the time, anyone who avows this is telling the truth. It is just that, alongside a connection of truth and death *within* the subject, public confession also establishes a connection between truth *and life* within the subject and its community.[21]

If Foucault did not always recognize this, his interlocutors did. After the introduction of *exomologesis* in the Louvain lectures of 1981, one questioner objects (Foucault 2014b: 114): "being dead in the sackcloth and ashes, you seem to be saying ... one is thereby accepting death, when this mortification would seem to represent instead the will to return to life"; to this, Foucault responds: "To bear the sackcloth and ashes ... is to demonstrate that one is in truth someone who has chosen the path of death. What can one do once one has chosen the path of death ...? Well, one must die to the path of death ... in order to enter the true spiritual life that implies death to this life" (Foucault 2014b: 114–15). A little earlier, writing on the Iranian revolution and conscious of the spectacular "T'aziyeh performance, which is similar to Christian passion plays and was influenced by them" (Afary and Anderson 2005: 44; cf. Foucault 2005b: 216), Foucault recounts a conversation with the writer who commemorated recently assassinated political activists (Foucault 2005a: 201):

> I did not have to even ask him whether this religion ... is not profoundly fascinated with death .... I knew what he would have responded: "What preoccupies you, you Westerners, is *death*. You ask her to detach you from life, and she teaches you how to give up. As for us, we care about *the dead*, because they attach us to life. We hold out our hands to them in order for them to link us to the permanent obligation of justice.

While Foucault answers the objection of the interlocutor of Louvain in 1981, the interlocutor from Iran in 1978, in Foucault's appropriation, has, as it were, the final word.

At such moments, Foucault recognizes the selectivity of his account of Christian confession: it misprizes the ambiguity of the performative and expressive aspects of the "dramatic exomologetic character" of public confession. This is nevertheless precisely the point where individuals intersect with groups and death reveals itself to be a figure of renewed, revolutionary, and even *happy* life.[22] Identifying these points of play with the ambiguity of aesthetic forms, I'll explain now how poetic confession forms communities, using the fictive dimensions of discourse to unify life and death, self and group, suffering and joy.

Ars vitae, ars poetica: Confession—of Joy

Turning to later Christian aesthetic theory and practice, I will argue three things. First, Late Antique Christianity itself attempted to metabolize death or rid itself of the self-sacrifice that Foucault found at the heart of its model of subjectivity and subsequently "our own" (see below). Second, traditional aesthetic practices facilitate this process through the ambiguity of embodiment or "the communism of the senses" in modern aesthetic theory. Finally, I will assimilate regimes of truth, to which Foucault subordinates the aesthetics of existence, to regimes of appearance where the role of truth, as Foucault shows in his work on literature from the 1960s, cannot be taken for granted.

In his mishmash of exegesis, reader response, and sermon, the *Expositions of the Psalms*, Augustine develops a theory of Judeo-Christian poetry as an experience of community that uses language to synthesize ostensible opposites, including self and other. In addition to the second epigraph of this chapter, we find statements like the following (Augustine, *Expositions* 29(2).12, trans. Boulding et al. 2000.1, 313, modified):

> Confession is twofold [*gemina est*]; it can be of sin or of praise. When things are going badly for us, in the midst of tribulations let us confess our sins [*confiteamur peccata*]; when things are going well for us, in our joy in justness [*in exsultatione iusititiae*], let us confess praise of God [*confiteamur laudem*]. Only, let us never give up confession [*sine confessione tamen non simus*].

Augustine's extension of confession over the course of our entire lives appears to support Foucault's claim that, after enclosure in the monasteries, confession as "the verbalization of . . . sin" (Foucault 2016a: 225) will take its place among the intrusive technologies of pastoral care and thus inaugurate the whole future of disciplinary apparatus.[23] But, in contrast with that Foucauldian trajectory, confession here also encompasses praise, with its joyous aspect, to say nothing of justice, which also appeared in the imagined response of Foucault's Iranian interlocutor.[24]

Where Augustine in his *Expositions of the Psalms* outlined a positive model of confession as a community-building performance of praise from the Jewish background of Christian culture, Paulinus of Nola put this model into practice: he renounced his fabulous riches, relocated to the hinterland of southern Italy, and used poetry, art, architecture, and performance to put a properly aesthetic model of confession as a collective experience into practice among the rural proletariat.[25] He devoted himself to an earlier saint, in fact a Confessor, named

Felix, who acquired his status as such when he almost died in the persecutions but—and this is crucial—lived to tell the tale (Brown 1981, Chapter 3; Trout 1999, Chapter 7).

Instead of sermons, Paulinus performed poems for his mixed-class congregation every year. Here, he first explains the distinction between a martyr and a confessor exemplified in the life of Felix (Paulinus, *Poems* 14.4-10, in Dressler 2023: 139–40):

> A martyr without blood, he acquired that heavenly prize,
> when, not opting out of paying the price, as a confessor
> God took his devoted mind, in lieu of blood, on credit.
> Assessor of our secret hearts, He pays those who are prepared
> and those who *actually* suffer the same rate. Because He surveys
> their inner being enough, He waives the price of flesh with devotion
> justified: a bloodless martyrdom is best, at least if the mind is ready
> to suffer and devotion burns for God. The will that *will* endure it
> is payment enough. The ultimate test is the *wish* to earn it.

Two aspects of confession stand out from this passage. First, Paulinus refers to confessors, as *better* than martyrs ("a bloodless martyrdom is best"). Suggesting that it is better *not* to die, Paulinus attempts, from within Christianity, exactly what Foucault (2016a: 78) would say it was time for "us" to do—namely, "get rid of the necessary sacrifice of the self which was linked to [the] hermeneutics [of the self] since the beginning of Christianity." This contrasts with Foucault's otherwise accurate assessment of the confession of faith whose affective intensity and existential risk inform his later notion of *parrhēsia*: "[P]ractically up to the seventh and eighth century ... the word 'confessor' refers to someone who is prepared to make the profession of faith ... to the point of risking death."[26] Again the issue is one of ambiguity: while confession in this sense is predicated on death, it also offers the possibility of survival (Trout 1999: 185–6).

Demonstrating the temporality of such confession, not as a form of mortification but celebration, Paulinus performed such poems at the religious festival on Felix's feast day every January for fourteen years (*Poems* 21.138-43, in Dressler 2023: 142):

> From this it follows that, for witnesses
> made sacred by their suffering, for confessors too,
> our faithful populations cultivate
> with serious merrymaking the sacred days
> of exit from this fallen world to God ...

> Today's the day the old man died in body,
> avowing his confession prior to battle.
> After the battle, on the day of peace,
> a bloodless sacrifice and victor, He
> went home to heaven. He was happy to leave
> the earth because Christ called. Still He received
> the martyr's wreath because He had avowed
> the will to suffer the Passion in his mind.

Performed for a popular audience of rural laborers, the passage is ostensibly simple, but full of paradox. There is of course the joyous paradox of the peculiar martyrdom of confessors—in its life-affirming bloodlessness. But at a higher level, the affective dynamics of this experience of confession, the profession of faith without death, can be extended through the technology of verse and spectacle to the entire community.[27] Holidays help the congregation achieve collective holiness, not by pastoral scrutiny, but by recreation and freedom from labor.[28] Elsewhere, Paulinus explains his thus only quasi-pastoral purpose in cultivating popular festivals (*Poems* 26.107-15 in Dressler 2023: 145):

> Therefore, then, as the Lord did deck the sky with stars,
> the fields with flowers, and the year with time, so too He decked
> time itself with holidays. Thus, when the people's energy flags
> in daily acts of devotion, at least they get a break ...
> after a certain amount of time, the will comes back,
> and they do the holy rites gaily. After they settle into the festal
> year, their minds attend to the Lord. It is exhausting
> to be incorruptible always and serve justice. To people accustomed
> to be remiss, it's work to give up sin.

Hence the "serious merrymaking" that Paulinus reports in the first passage, and hence the joy—not without the touch of death, but hardly dominated by it—of the patron saint's peaceful demise in old age after a life of confessing faith. If the aesthetics of truth that Foucault traces from Socrates and the Cynics through Christian asceticism to modern revolutionary discourse, countercultural lifestyles, and the anti-aesthetic tendencies of modernism everywhere involved the "laying bare, exposure, stripping, excavation, and violent reduction of existence to its basics"—this is all Foucault, describing the aesthetics of *parrhēsia* (see "A genealogy of the joyful subject" above)—then confession as Paulinus practices it seems *also* to hold out the promise of a more collective aesthetics of abundance: gathering together, sharing senses, "deck[ing] time itself with holidays," as Paulinus says, with or without the tight discipline of the monastic order (Goldhill 2022: 330–6, 344–5, 360–1).

Most of the poems of nativity that Paulinus performs for his congregation thematize time. Foucault alludes to temporality in his account of *exomologesis*, emphasizing equally the prolongation and truncation that characterize the mournful performance of public confession, which makes it a ritual prelude to the longer lasting, even lifelong form of subjectivity of monastic obedience (Foucault 2013: 208; 2021a: 69). Paulinus deploys the same combination of prolongation and truncation, but to completely different effect (*Poems* 23.12-40, in Dressler 2023: 142–3):

> Just as with tuneful sound,
> the linnets fill the woods, just silent in their unkempt lodgings, happy now
> that spring has sprung, when the song of each bird tongue
> sounds different from the other as their wings are different color,
> so I remember this day too ...
> O God, O source of the word, assent with a nod *as* the word.
> Make me sing with the sweet voice of spring like a bird ...
> Dappled in her utterance, though in the single color of her feathers,
> she pours the liquid of transforming songs in not one tone ...
> In contrast, Christ, let grace and beauty spring from me
> *continuously*, even as I beg and pray that I may be
> like the bird in her variety, bestowing verses promised annually,
> with utterances of changing styles even in a single mouth.

If we think about the lives of rural laborers among whom Paulinus stages his performance and the "serious merrymaking" that he ascribes to holidays, the performance of poetry about the performance of poetry, constituted by this passage, opens sacral alternatives to the time of labor and domination that characterized the lives of Roman peasants (Goldhill 2020: 12–14). Here, I think, Paulinus is trying to do for a community, with poetry, what Foucault describes virginity doing for the individual in the *Confessions of the Flesh*: constituting a recreation of creation in the here and now by punctuating the dreary span of fallen time with its outermost limit—eternity.[29] But again in sharp contrast with virginity, and yet with all the possible empowerment that Foucault attributes to that condition, this invitation to eternity involves no sacrifice.

What is the relationship of this affirmative form of confession to sin? Is it utterly divested of sin? Not exactly, and recognizing the intersection of the confession of praise and confession of sin is the key to situating the public, poetic form of confession that I am describing in Foucault's schematic of counter-conducts and technologies of the self in later Christianity. When he first identified the counter-conducts of the later Middle Ages in the 1978 lectures, Foucault contrasted both forms of confession, the "doctrinal" confession of faith (*exomologesis*) and monastic self-examination (*exagoreusis*), with that form of counter-conduct that he identifies as mysticism.[30] In one of his most suggestively Hebraic passages, however, Paulinus uses poetry to assimilate mysticism and confession, ostensible opposites in the Foucauldian history of Christianity (Paulinus, *Poems* 15.26-9, 32-6, 45-6, in Dressler 2023: 109):

> And so, O lyre, rise. Extend your sinews one and all.
> Arouse the power of my soul. Let love my still unsinging
> insides pound until the shaken sound box (my heart) makes
> my teeth throb. May plectrum tongue pick mouth harp loud ...
> The chorister of my song is Christ. By Christ endowed
> <u>I dare to avow the holy and heavenly, sinner though I be</u>.
> It is not hard for you, all powerful God, to open my mouth
> in cultured song when you bid dumb things speak and dry things flow
> and hard things open. You made the donkey bray with speech ...
> Give me the word from your fountain. <u>Without you, I cannot avow
> your story. For indeed your martyr's glory is your glory</u>.[31]

Notice the celebration of the flesh and its joyful technologization of the body as the animated and animating instrument of such activity; even if this process does not entail the "endless [...] exploring" of "individual secrets" that Foucault attributes to monastic confession, it is viscerally reflexive. At the same time, Paulinus identifies himself in passing as a sinner in l. 37 (*audeo peccator ... fari*). With this, he illustrates Augustine's key claim about the inherent duality of confession. "What does it mean," Augustine asks about the line of the psalms which reads, "I will confess to you forever?" He explains (*Expositions* 29(2).22, trans. Boulding et al. 2000.1, 315): "It means, 'I shall <u>praise</u> you forever.' I have explained that there is confession of praise too, not only of sins. Confess now what you have done to God, and in the future you will confess what God has done for you."

Returning to the same theme in another psalm, Augustine quotes the psalm and then explains it (*Exposition* 31(1).5, trans. Boulding et al. 2000.1, 360): "*And you have forgiven the impiety of my heart*, because you hear the heart's confession <u>before ever it is spoken aloud</u>." Referring to perfect tense of the psalm, "you have forgiven," Augustine describes a condition that is equally past, present, and future—in short, eternity.[32]

This increasing synchronization of the different tenses and affects of confession, past confession of sins and present confession of praise, suggests that the duality of confession is not only serial, as Augustine explains in the earlier gloss, but also simultaneous. There are two ways of approaching this simultaneity of confession. The first pertains to the ambiguity of embodiment and sensation, which I described as the "communism of the senses" in the first section of this chapter. One possible description of this phenomenon in ancient literary criticism, denoted by the Greek *hupokrisis*, is "hearing-in-reading": originally denoting the oral "delivery" of discourse by the actor (*hupokritês*: Porter 2016: 334–5), through the constant reorganization of orality and textuality in Greco-Roman performance culture, the term comes to denote a subtler distinction between the uttering of a speaker and the hearing of their own utterance *by* the speaker (Porter 2016: 353–4, 357–64). As such, "hearing in reading" constitutes, in one aesthetic theoretical formulation (see n. 13 above), a "third thing that is owned by no one," and thus potentially owned by everyone. In the context of confessing sins, Augustine activates the ecclesiological potential of this aural dimension: "We have to distinguish as we listen, but the voice is one."[33]

Discerning this dimension of discourse when he reads in the Psalms, "You are he who will restore to me my inheritance," Augustine writes (*Expositions* 15.5, trans. Boulding et al. 2000.1, 183): "You will not restore to me what I never lost, but you will restore to those who have lost it the knowledge of that bright glory. Yet because I am among them, *you will restore it to me*."

By not differentiating the voice of the psalmist from his own voice even though they are two, Augustine enacts at the level of a reading what Paulinus' performance of poetry enacted at the level of a congregation. Given the conditions of psalmody in Late Antiquity, and Augustine's specific methods of interpreting psalms, the two sides of the voice discerned in "hearing-in-reading" evince an intersubjective dimension of discourse which is concurrently single and plural.[34]

As he continues his analysis of this psalm, Augustine corroborates the simultaneous plurality achieved in recitation with the serial plurality of repetition. "[M]y inheritance is glorious to me," says the psalm, and Augustine explains (*Expositions* 15.6, modified): "Glorious it is indeed, but not to everyone – only to those who can see. Because I am among them, *to me*." Is that "to me," repeated from the exegesis of the previous verse, "you will restore it to me," an instance of quotation or participation?[35] Whether or not "I" am included in "my inheritance" becomes, in the context of confession, a matter of whether or not I voice my inclusion; among the congregants, it is a matter of whether or not I hear and thus vicariously voice the part of another's voice that is not their own.[36] With such concurrences, con-fession induces community, through the communism of the senses.[37] The cultural historical background of this process is complex: where leftist anthropologists like David Graeber would find it in the context of Late Antique feasts, European philosophy of language finds it in the peculiar characteristics of language in time; the poems of Paulinus of Nola combine these contexts and add a more traditional (Classical Roman) consciousness of the need to communicate with a socio-economically diverse audience—which, in Late Antiquity at least, Foucault does not mention.[38]

The second way to approach the simultaneity of confession is indeed Foucauldian. Here I finally address the question of truth, even though, on Foucault's own treatment in the lectures *On the Government of the Living*, the role of truth is hardly straightforward. Invoking the ancient philosophical idea of the "liar's paradox" to explain the Christian's confession, "I am a sinner," Foucault says (2012: 214–5):

> [W]hen one says "I lie," it is impossible to say whether this proposition is true or false.... But the Christian, who is not a liar ... and who in his humility says, "I am a sinner ..." speaks both truth and falsehood, since he says something true, namely that he is in fact a sinner.... But what is the effect of the enunciation itself, in the form at least of its dramatic exomologetic character? Precisely that of showing, and not only of showing, but of carrying out that kind of detachment with regard to the state of sinner .... I am all the less a sinner as I affirm that I am a sinner.

What Paulinus is doing, in contrast with the earlier Christian forms of *exomologesis*, is bringing the act of confession and the various temporalities that constitute it under the control of the speaker and into the experience of the congregation, dilating the verbal axis of what Foucault defines as a non-verbal, but rather expressive event. Part of what this event expresses is a new, joyous relationship between the individual and the community.

Conclusion: Confession—of the Outside

From a Foucauldian perspective, there are pros and cons to this approach. On the con-side: my attention to traditional aesthetic forms has perhaps distracted from the aesthetics of existence, which, Foucault (2012: 162) explains, "has [...] been hidden by the privileged study of those aesthetic forms devised to give forms to things, substances, colors, light, sounds, and words." On the pro-side, the same attention to the "forms [of] things ... sounds, and words" has demonstrated—and this *is* Foucauldian—how traditional aesthetics relates to the aesthetics of existence (think of Foucault's invocation of Vasari and the *Lives of the Artists*, Baudelaire, and the rest, in the tenth lecture of *The Courage of Truth*). Maybe more importantly, such a discussion may make some contribution to fulfilling that poignant paragraph from the first hour of the last lecture, when Foucault "confess[es]" (Foucault 2012: 316): "I still don't know and have not yet decided. Maybe I will try to pursue this history of the arts of living ... precisely, after ancient philosophy, in Christianity." By relating these arts of living to a more traditional notion of the arts as they were practiced in popular Christianity, I have tried to show what that could have looked like.

True also to the communitarian background of Christianity in Jewish culture, I have tried to show how the arts of living incorporated communities, in addition to individuals, in arts of *shared* existence. This is obviously important to Foucault. In the first hour of the last lecture of *The Courage of Truth*, where he invokes Marx's injunction for philosophers to change the world, Foucault (2012: 313) describes the ostensible solipsism of the Cynic as a form of self-care, care of the self. In Volume 3 of the *History of Sexuality*, Foucault (1986: 51) called the care of the self "a true social practice," but for my money, he only really makes good on that claim here: "The care of others," he says in the last lecture, "coincides exactly with the care of self" (Foucault 2012: 312). Still, does it coincide *exactly*? Could it possibly? Should we want that? Do we, did Foucault, want the care of the self to be *just the same as* and *no more than* the care of children, lovers, friends, and political allies and fellow travelers?

The aesthetic form of collectivity that I have tried to use the poetry of Paulinus to carve out of Foucault's late work seems to me to provide a powerful answer to this question. The truth that the subject manifests is not just different from truth in the usual sense of the correspondence theory of truth. Scholars, such as Allen Miller (2022: 6–7, 41–2, 55–7, 89–90), tell us that the concept of truth in Foucault is different from that, because it is an emergent and transformative property. But it seems to me that another counter-intuitive property of Foucault's truth, which its production by aesthetic processes reveals, is that it is also not even always exclusively true. It is true and false, like the liar's paradox to which Foucault compares public confession. Foucault talked about the liar's paradox in his essay on Blanchot and modern literature, entitled "Thought of the outside," in 1969. He starts the essay with the statement, "I speak, I lie," and ends it with the following reflection on the origin of the paradox (Foucault 1998: 168): "At a time when language was defined as the place of truth and the bond of time, it was placed in absolute peril by the Cretan Epimenides' assertion that all Cretans are liars: the way in which that discourse was bound to itself undid any possibility of truth."

In the same essay, he denies the similarity of modern literature, which in the late sixties he obviously adored, to negative theology and Christian mysticism (Foucault 1998: 168):

> Despite several similarities, we are quite far from the experience through which some people are wont to lose themselves in order to find themselves. The characteristic movement of mysticism is to attempt to join . . . the positivity of an existence by opening a line of communication with it . . . . The experience of the outside has nothing to do with that.

I do not think Foucault would have agreed with that statement after nearly a decade of studying Christianity.[39] He might have; and that might be why in the end he preferred the complicated solitude of the Cynic (cf. Senellart 2007: 36–7). But he did want to find something else on "the outside"—the other side of the care of the self that *just is*, according to the last lecture, the care of others. Without contradicting that claim, the production of public poetry in Late Antique Christianity indicates the amount of work required to turn the care of self into the care of others: the work of mediation. Although it is unlikely that Foucault would have pursued the Christian arts of existence in Late Antique *aesthetics*, if he had, he would have found a collectivizing counterpart to the technology of pastoral care, and with it, possibly, a contribution to the history of "revolutionary subjectivity" that he considered writing with this material but never did (Foucault 2021c: 73–4).

7

Artemidorus as Symptom

Freud and Foucault

Richard H. Armstrong
University of Houston

ὁ Ἡράκλειτός φησι τοῖς ἐγρηγορόσιν ἕνα καὶ κοινὸν κόσμον εἶναι
τῶν δὲ κοιμωμένων ἕκαστον εἰς ἴδιον ἀποστρέφεσθαι.
*Herakleitos says there is one common cosmos for those who are awake,
while each of those who are asleep turns away to his own.*[1]

(Diels-Kranz fr. B89)

Introduction: Foucault's Freud and Situating Artemidorus

As it once became difficult to read Sophocles without reading Freud, it has now become difficult to read Freud without Foucault. Not that Foucault created the kind of extended, formal rereading of Freud's work that one might find in Hans Loewald, Jacques Lacan, Jacques Derrida, or Paul Ricoeur. It is more that the late Foucault's work on truth and the subject forms such a powerful contrast to Freud's project of psychoanalysis, which in its day was nothing short of an attempt to create a science of subjectivity centered on a desiring subject. If Freud felt psychoanalysis could give the lie to rationalism's *cogito ergo sum,* Foucault found with equal justification that *cupio ergo sum* is itself assailable—not an eternal psychobiological truth, but the product of particular discursive formations, something he was set on seriously questioning since at least Volume 1 of the *History of Sexuality*.[2] But Foucault's relationship with Freud is complex: at times oblique, even cagey, at other times almost celebratory, one can find grounds for accusing Foucault of deep ambivalence. As the psychoanalyst and philosopher Joel Whitebook puts it, this is not the *ordinary* ambivalence one expects to feel with Freud; "Rather, with Foucault, what we are talking about exceeds the limits of expectable ambivalence and, because of its compulsive and repetitive character, has something symptom-like, which is to say, something unmastered about it" (Whitebook 1999: 30). Hence, there was something quite on point in Derrida's comment that Foucault was playing a *fort/da* game with Freud (Derrida 1994: 234).

My chief objective in this chapter is neither a defense of Freud nor an interrogation into Foucault's ambivalence toward him. Rather, I am focused on something that organically links Freud's project of *Traumdeutung*[3] (dream interpretation) with Foucault's *History of Sexuality* in an intriguing way: the figure of Artemidorus of Daldis. Artemidorus is very much a figure of "unmastered" ambivalence in Freud's work, as I relate in detail below. The Greek is a pivotal figure in a sense, coming close to psychoanalytic *Traumdeutung* yet always failing to arrive at it, a precursor just shy of the last revelation, playing Virgil to Freud's Dante in the inferno of dreams. But Artemidorus also cuts a figure of feared identity for Freud; namely, the clever oneirocritic who, like a virtuosic tarot reader, unscientifically yet skillfully tells people what they want to hear. Artemidorus thus represents the risk inherent in making *Traumdeutung* a public matter anyone might dabble in outside of clinical supervision. It is not surprising, then, to see Freud playing his own *fort/da* game with Artemidorus, embracing him yet also clarifying quickly where ancient intimations of the unconscious must give way to the rigor of psychoanalytic *Wissenschaft*.

However, there is a third aspect of Freud's deployment of Artemidorus that speaks to how psychoanalysis in turn seeks to vindicate the *Oneirokritika*'s author; namely, by boldly demanding in the interests of *Sexualwissenschaft* an end to the censorship that prevents the Greek's most sexually explicit discussions from seeing the light of day (particularly 1.78-80). But what happened next signals Freud's ambivalence perhaps most revealingly: having cleared the way for these notorious passages to emerge in German translation, Freudian psychoanalysis passed over Artemidorus' vivid sex dreams in utter silence. These suppressed dreams were of no service to the *psychological* censorship of repression so central to the Freudian model of the psyche. This silence is not merely ironic, but symptomatic of the Freudian subject's need to hide sexual truth from itself in coded images; thus the naked penis dissolves into a menagerie of phallic symbols.

For this reason, I argue, Artemidorus' appearance at the beginning of *The Care of the Self* reads like the return of the Freudian repressed within Foucault's work, with the Greek now cutting a pivotal figure of a different kind. By presenting Artemidorus' sex dreams in the simplest of terms, Foucault can pivot the evidence of this text in the other direction, since "it offers a window into this world that is all but designed to contrast with that of psychoanalysis," as Allen Miller suggests (2022: 64). It is a world before *Sexualwissenschaft* and the assumptions underwriting the modern discourse of sexuality and repression, with a very different relationship to the emergence of truth in the dreamworld. Derrida described Freud as the "hinge" (*charnière*) in Foucault's thinking on madness and sexuality, but also the "ambiguous figure of a doorman or doorkeeper [*huissier*]" (Derrida 1994: 234). My argument here is that Artemidorus in turn became the doorkeeper that reveals a dynamic link between Foucault and Freud: instead of early evidence of the unconscious at work, Artemidorus is the dutiful cataloguer of *aphrodisia*, pleasures and bodies unyoked to the alienation of the modern subject. Thus, Foucault's unambivalence toward Artemidorus should be seen in the light of his ambivalence to Freud.

Foucault's Freud: Three Steps along the Way

We can hardly dismiss Foucault's relationship with Freud as tangential, given the evidence of Foucault's preoccupation with psychoanalysis in his earliest publication, his introduction to Ludwig Binswanger's *Dream and Existence*. In this work, Foucault deftly offers a dual reading of Freud's *Interpretation of Dreams* and Husserl's *Logical Investigations* that argues the deficiencies of both could potentially be repaired by a further development in *Daseinsanalyse*, Binswanger's existential psychology. Foucault gives Freud both credit and criticism for understanding dreaming: credit in that Freud "sensed clearly that the meaning of a dream was not to be sought at the level of image content"; and criticism in that the compromise represented by the dream was not one between repressed content and a censor, but rather "between the authentic movement of the imaginative and its adulteration in the image" (Foucault 1984c: 73). That is, the gulf to be breached is between the dreaming experience in real time (the Heraclitean *idios kosmos* of the dreamer) and its recollection upon waking in fragmented, dislocated images. Strange as it might seem to see Foucault arguing for an authenticity of the subject in the dreaming state,[4] this early work shows a sense of the dreamworld as a kind of thought from the outside, though an "outside" decidedly not to be located in the "other scene," the Freudian mythology of the unconscious. Hence, Foucault's earliest revision of Freud lay originally in the dreamworld.

A similar combination of appreciation and criticism can be found in Foucault's notes from the 1950s, as Elisabetta Basso's eye-opening *Young Foucault* shows in detail. In one manuscript, Foucault notes Freud's achievement as the culmination of contradictory impulses.

> Freud, while attempting to conform with the Darwinian model, liberated – in opposition certainly to his intention, and without always noticing it – a psychology with a naturalist epistemology. Instead of explanations that dispel contradictions, he offered explanations by means of contradiction; instead of the important notion of the conservation of life (or of adaptation – or of utility – or of interest) reigning over all of the life sciences, up to and including the science of man, he opposed a conflictual dialectic between Eros and Thanatos; instead of the evolutionary schemas that insist on the present succeeding the past, he offered a mode of analysis in which present and past culminate in an indissociable unity.
>
> (Cited in Basso 2022: 84)

In other notes from the 1950s, we see again Foucault's sense that Freud shifts from an older biological analysis of illness toward a newer "understanding of its psychological signification," but in a manner that tries again to situate psychoanalysis in a history of discourses.

> This transformation did not, however, take the form of a rupture; and the psychoanalytic "revolution" has the character more of a progressive, slow turn, from a psychology of evolution to a historical psychology of genesis. Moreover, the progressive point of view was never abandoned, and up until the most recent forms of the psychoanalytic approach to neurosis, the evolutionary horizon – the first homeland of Freudian thought – remains present, more real than a backdrop, truer than a myth, a veritable landscape in which the characters of the Freudian drama can move about.
>
> (Cited in Basso 2022: 55)

It seems from the outset that Foucault had a qualified sense of the historical shift Freud caused, without casting it in the heroic terms of an empirical romance, i.e., the story of a bold pioneer discovering the hidden bedrock of biological or psychological truth.

It is especially fruitful to our investigation to see how the "middle" Foucault of the late 1960s came to characterize Freud's achievement in broader, social terms. In his seminal essay "What is an author?", Foucault accorded Freud a special privilege of being the founder of a discursivity, like Marx, something that only begins in the nineteenth century in Foucault's reckoning. Here Freud and Marx become formal paradigms in discursive filiation: "They have created a possibility for something other than their discourse, yet something belonging to what they founded," he explains.

> To say that Freud founded psychoanalysis does not (simply) mean that we find the concept of the libido or the technique of dream analysis in the works of Karl Abraham or Melanie Klein; it means that Freud made possible a certain number of *divergences* – with respect to his own texts, concepts, and hypotheses – that all arise from psychoanalytic discourse itself.
>
> (Foucault 1979: 154–5; my emphasis)

Foucault holds there is a difference between founding a discursivity and founding a science. The discursive practice remains under the spell of its originator in a way that a science does not, since the creation of the former "is heterogeneous to its subsequent transformations" (Foucault 1979: 156). Those engaging in psychoanalysis relate back to the founder's work as a primary point of reference in a manner different from those working in scientific fields like astronomy or physics that have their own structural and intrinsic norms established beyond the work of Galileo or Newton. Thus, "re-examining Freud's texts modifies psychoanalysis itself," even if only in shifting emphasis (Foucault 1979: 156–7). Here Foucault hits upon a historical truth we see in psychoanalytic studies of various sorts, but perhaps most saliently in the early development of dream theory as reflected in the successive editions of the *Traumdeutung* (see below).

In the late Foucault, the focus shifts to practices of the self in the first and second centuries CE and to the *parrhēsia* of spiritual direction, first Stoic and then Christian. In this context, *parrhēsia* entailed virtue, duty, and a technical means of realization, "this virtue, duty, and technique must characterize, among other things and above all, the man who is responsible for directing others, and particularly for directing them in their effort, their attempt to constitute an appropriate relationship to themselves" (Foucault 2010: 43). It seems clear Foucault's fascination with plotting Freud on a discursive map led him to seeking a point of origin for the analytic situation and the confessional subject of modernity, even when Freud is not the stated target. We twice find in his lecture manuscripts for 1980/81 concluding references to "this question of the subject of desire that will traverse the West from Tertullian to Freud," though both times the phrase is left off in the lecture as delivered.[5]

Foucault was not above the oedipal gesture of pointing out Freud's error in interpreting *Oedipus Tyrannus*, as when he said in his lecture of 17 March, 1971, "Freud, advancing in the direction of the relations between desire and truth, thought that the Oedipus was speaking to him about the universal forms of desire; whereas it was telling him about the historical constraints of our system of truth (of the system that Freud was coming up against)" (Foucault 2013: 192). And Foucault would continue revisiting Oedipus in multiple lectures until 1981.

But I see Foucault's recourse to Artemidorus as rather different from Oedipus in its effect. Knowingly or not, Foucault homed in on the same oneirocritic that fascinated the early psychoanalytic movement as it sought a historical genealogy for its revolutionary focus on dreams. But for reasons internal to Freud's discursive practice, Artemidorus quickly became a problematic figure, while Oedipus, whose drama of truth seeking conformed to the very model of psychoanalysis, became the literal icon of the movement.[6] By returning to Artemidorus, then, Foucault hit upon a vulnerability in psychoanalysis that, unlike the overinterpreted Oedipus, remained unguarded. After relating the case of Artemidorus in early psychoanalysis in the following sections, I return to how this changes our view of Foucault's relationship with Freud.

Artemidorus as Symptom in Freud's *Traumdeutung*

Sophocles' Oedipus has a reception well beyond psychoanalysis, but Freud is often credited specifically for why we talk about Artemidorus at all. For example, Robert White prefaced his English translation of the *Oneirokritika* by saying, "The current interest in dreams and their meaning for man is one of the hallmarks of the intellectual life of this century. Freud's revolutionary theories of dream interpretation were doubtless initially responsible for this interest" (White 1975: vii). White went on further to stress the continuity with antiquity: "In a sense, Freud, Jung, and others were not so much innovators as restorers, since they were reassigning to dreams and dream-readings the importance they had held in antiquity, and which they had lost in more recent centuries" (White 1975: v). However, it is important to see how Freud's interest in Artemidorus emerged dynamically and gradually over the various editions of the *Traumdeutung*. The revisions are evidence not simply of Freud's further refinements of the book, but also of the immediate consequences of a discursive practice that was rapidly evolving beyond his control while emanating centrally from his work. In Foucault's terms again, Freud "made possible a certain number of *divergences*—with respect to his own texts, concepts, and hypotheses—that all arise from psychoanalytic discourse itself" (Foucault 1979: 154–5, my emphasis), such that the early defections of Alfred Adler, Wilhelm Stekel, and Carl Jung, who continued to participate in modified forms of this discourse for decades, can be seen as organic to this particular style of practice, not negations of it.

In the *Traumdeutung*'s first edition (dated 1900), there are only two mentions of Artemidorus, one of which is indirect and will be dealt with later (on

"Artimedorus' sex dreams" see section below). The more important mention uses Artemidorus to characterize the "decoding method" (*Chiffrirmethode*) of dream interpretation in chapter 2, in which the Greek is noted for his "interesting modification" of the method by considering the character and circumstance of the dreamer. This makes Artemidorus' method more nuanced than the "purely mechanical translation" based on a dream key found in a typical dream book. What entices Freud about this particular "interpretive labor" (*Deutungsarbeit*) is the focus on each piece of the dream in itself, and he introduces a geological analogy that is an anticipation of his dynamic model of the dream as a compromise formation created by competing forces of desire and repression.

> The essence of the decoding procedure, however, lies in the fact that the work of interpretation is not brought to bear on the dream a whole, but on each portion of the dream's content independently, as though the dream were a geological conglomerate in which each fragment of rock required a separate assessment. There can be no question that the invention of the decoding method of interpretation was suggested by disconnected and confused dreams.
>
> (SE 4:99)

Thus, at this early stage in the book, Freud rushes to identify Artemidorus with a method of interpretation that will mirror his own, claiming it arose from the need to interpret confused dreams, which for Freud represent those most subjected to the dreamwork of censorship. The vivid geological analogy foreshadows the dynamic dream theory that has yet to emerge at this point in the book. But he is then quick to discount the validity of Artemidorus' method based on the problem of the trustworthiness of the symbolic "key" it requires— the ancient dream book, for whose validity there is no guarantee (SE 4:100). Freud at this moment throws his whole project rhetorically into doubt: we might feel tempted to think of dream interpretation as a "fanciful exercise" (*imaginäre Aufgabe*) if no book can be produced with valid answers.

> But I have been taught better. I have been driven to realize that here once more we have one of those not infrequent cases in which an ancient and jealously held popular belief seems to be nearer the truth than the judgement of the prevalent science of today. I must affirm that dreams really have a meaning and that a scientific procedure for interpreting them is possible.
>
> (SE 4:100)

This passage reveals the ambivalent status of Artemidorus as a figure of the past who *confirms* the long-held belief that dreams have meaning, a man who diligently elaborated a systematic method suited to individual dreamers, not just disembodied images. But Freud will use his paradoxical notion of *Wissenschaft* to differentiate himself from *both* Artemidorus and "the prevalent science" of his day. The Greek's method is unscientific, but so is the science of Freud's own time in not recognizing the uncanny truth of folk psychology. Artemidorus thus cuts a figure like Sophocles, whose misguided theological drama of Oedipus hit on the oedipal truth buried in the mythic material of Greek folk psychology.[7] These Greeks anticipate prophetically and intuitively the truth that Freud will deliver scientifically.

In later editions of the *Traumdeutung*, we see however that Freud had been rethinking Artemidorus over the following decade and a half. An addition to a footnote made in 1911 shows Freud appreciating the "nicest instance of a dream-interpretation which has reached us from ancient times" as related by Artemidorus in Book 4.24 (Krauss 1881: 255). This is an anecdote about Alexander the Great, who when bogged down by the prolonged siege of Tyre dreamed of a satyr dancing upon a shield. Aristander of Telmessos interpreted the dream through wordplay, dividing the Greek word *saturos* (satyr) into *sa Turos* ("Tyre is yours"), and thus encouraged Alexander to fight on and take the city. It is important to see, however, how this example linking the verbal and visual became interjected into the text. Freud had added a footnote in 1909 that related how the "oriental dream books" base a great deal of their interpretations on the wordplay, which defy translation and lead to "unintelligibility of the renderings of our own popular dream-books" (SE 4:99, fn 1).[8] The anecdote of Artemidorus, then, speaks to this problem of translatability, and after citing the Greek anecdote, Freud cites a paper by Sándor Ferenczi to proclaim, "Indeed, dreams are so closely related to linguistic expression that Ferenczi [1910] has truly remarked that every tongue has its own dream-language." This addition shows Freud interacting with his followers on the question of the cultural specificity of dreams, and that Artemidorus' text was still under discussion. The dream of Alexander also illustrates wish fulfillment, with a manifest content that seems disturbing (a mocking satyr dancing upon a shield) revealing instead the latent wish for victory. The anecdote neatly shows how things are not what they seem in dreams, so it is no wonder Freud deemed it "the nicest instance" to come down from antiquity.[9] It also is a vivid demonstration of linguistic meaning devolving into the visual representation characteristic of dream regression.

Another footnote added to the *Traumdeutung* in 1911 mentions a classification of dreams held in common by Macrobius and Artemidorus, which was then moved into the main text in the 1914 edition, followed by a further paragraph explaining how the classification of dreams was related to the problem of interpreting them. Since some dreams were not immediately comprehensible,

> This provided an incentive for elaborating a method by which the unintelligible content of a dream might be replaced by one that was comprehensible and significant. In the later years of antiquity Artemidorus of Daldis was regarded as the greatest authority on the interpretation of dreams, and the survival of his exhaustive work [*Oneirocritica*] must compensate us for the loss of other writings on the same subject.
>
> (SE 4:4)

Artemidorus, the author of an "interesting modification" of the decoding method of dream interpretation in the first edition, has thus been promoted to "the greatest authority on the interpretation of dreams." This claim now promotes the authority of a man whose approach is clearly an important precursor to Freudian *Traumdeutung*, specifically for dreams that contain difficult, unintelligible content (i.e., where the work of the censor has been most effective).

Also in the 1914 edition, a new footnote appears at the place in chapter 2 where Freud first introduces the decoding method. I will cite this in full because it helps us to see not only the scholarly mediation of Freud's ideas about Artemidorus, but it shows him explicitly stating his grounds of difference early in the book.

> Artemidorus of Daldis, who was probably born at the beginning of the second century A.D., has left us the most complete and painstaking study of dream-interpretation as practiced in the Greco-Roman world. As Theodor Gomperz (1866, 7f.) points out, he insisted on the importance of basing the interpretation of dreams on observation and experience, and made a rigid distinction between his own art and others that were illusory. The principle of his interpretative art, according to Gomperz, is identical with magic, the principle of association. A thing in a dream means what it recalls to the mind – to the dream interpreter's mind, it need hardly be said. An insuperable source of arbitrariness and uncertainty arises from the fact that the dream-element may recall *various* things to the interpreter's mind and may recall something different to different interpreters. The technique which I describe in the pages that follow differs in one essential respect from the ancient method: it imposes the task of interpretation upon the dreamer himself. It is not concerned with what occurs to the *interpreter* in connection with a particular element of the dream, but with what occurs to the *dreamer*.
>
> (SE 4:98, fn1; original emphasis)

Here again we find the ambivalent game of identification Freud is playing with Artemidorus. In that the Greek relied on observation and experience, he did the equivalent of clinical work, like Freud, and did not just read books about dream interpretation. In that his interpretive principle was based on *association*, he approaches Freudian *free association* as a method of dream interpretation. The fatal error lies in assuming the interpreter's associations are controlling for the interpretation, whereas Freudian *Traumdeutung* uses the dreamer's, thus appropriately relocating the dream as a psychic act distinct from external agencies (i.e., messages from the gods, suggestions of the interpreter).

The invocation of Theodor Gomperz in this footnote, however, is both indicative and problematic in relation to what Freud is trying to do. Gomperz was a pillar of the Jewish *Bildungsbürgertum* in Vienna, in addition to being a renowned classical scholar, and Freud knew the Gomperz family reasonably well. As a university student, Gomperz engaged Freud to translate a volume of essays by John Stuart Mill that appeared in 1880, part of a much larger project of making Mill's thought accessible to the German-speaking world. Gomperz's wife Elise became a patient of Freud's in the 1890s and was later instrumental in helping Freud to obtain his position of *professor extraordinarius* at the University of Vienna in 1902 (Vogel 1986). In a letter to her written in 1913, Freud even recalls his first meeting with her imposing husband, "one of the great men in the realm of thought" from whom he heard "the first remarks about the role played by dreams in the psychic life of primitive men, something that has preoccupied me so intensively ever since" (Freud was writing the letter just after finishing *Totem and Taboo* [1913] 1955).[10] We might be tempted, then, to see Freud combining Gomperz and Artemidorus to synthesize a sense of tradition, one in which Freud can definitively insert himself. But as Andreas Mayer (2018: 96–7) points out Freud has seriously misrepresented Gomperz's view of Artemidorus, which was rather that the *Oneirokritika* is just cunningly dressed up pseudoscience. At a critical turn in his essay, Gomperz asks:

> What have we found in him, if we disregard all the ponderous sophistication and clever effort to concoct the appearance of science for a barren delusion? What was the (clearly folkloric) core of his teaching? Nothing other than this: if two things recall one another somehow, then the one is the portent of the other.
>
> (Gomperz 1866, 25)

Gomperz's whiggish view of intellectual history had little patience with this kind of text, but as he was dead by the time Freud added the footnote, the great scholar was not there to object. While still alive, he showed skepticism about Freud's own dream interpretation method, as did his son the philosopher Heinrich Gomperz, who had offered himself up to Freud as an experimental subject to test his theory of "wish fulfillment" soon after the *Traumdeutung* first came out (Marinelli and Mayer 2003: 16–19). Thus, Freud's interest in Artemidorus found no real support from the Gomperz quarter, much as he tried to make it appear this was the case in this footnote. The real enthusiasm for Artemidorus came from inside Freud's movement.

Freud, Stekel, and the Crisis of Interpretation

Freud's many additions to the *Traumdeutung* remain enigmatic if not put within the larger context of the dynamic changes occurring between 1908 and 1914 within the psychoanalytic movement. Freud's small circle of colleagues that began as a Wednesday discussion group in 1902 gradually turned into the Vienna Psychoanalytic Society, an association that in its earlier phases was well known for its frank and open discussion of eclectic topics and "intellectual communism" (Bronner 2019). As Lydia Marinelli and Andreas Mayer's (2003) important study shows, the *Traumdeutung* underwent significant editing during this period following Freud's interaction with his colleagues in Vienna and Switzerland. Not all this interaction was positive, but it certainly provoked Freud into further extending his dream theory. A central figure in this interchange was Wilhelm Stekel (1868–1940), who was among the very first to become an active promotor of psychoanalysis. Stekel's enthusiasm for symbolic analysis in particular propelled Freud into considering it to a larger extent than he had in the 1900 edition of the *Traumdeutung*, and one feature of Stekel's approach was his constant recourse to Artemidorus. In December 1908, Stekel read out "some characteristic passages from Artemidorus' dream book" before seven members of the Vienna Psychoanalytic Society (Nunberg and Federn 1967, 2:77), pushing the discussion further than Freud's initial mention of the Greek oneirocritic from the first edition. Stekel's gesture was not a simple matter of looking for a genealogy of practice, but rather a consultation in point of detail. This approach is quite evident in Stekel's subsequent book *Die Sprache des Traumes* (1911), in which he cites Artemidorus by name over thirty times in support of specific interpretations. Stekel insisted that symbolism is crucial to *any* dream interpretation (a point Freud strongly contested), and for this reason Artemidorus remains essential reading today.

> Without the knowledge of symbolism, *Traumdeutung* is impossible. The great error of modern dream researchers consisted precisely in the fact that they were unable to get accustomed to symbolism. That's where the ancients were superior

to us. How wonderfully is dream symbolism presented in the Bible! And how accomplished [*vollendet*] appears the symbolism in Artemidorus of Daldis, whose book *The Symbolism of Dreams* is still to this day worth reading for the psychoanalyst!

(Stekel 1911: 3–4)

It is worth noting here that Stekel, like Freud, refers specifically to Artemidorus' work as *Die Symbolik der Träume* ("the Symbolism of Dreams"), the title given to the *Oneirokritika* by Friedrich Salomo Krauss for his 1881 German translation. As we shall discuss below, Krauss became a visitor to the Viennese Psychoanalytic Society beginning in 1910 and added a perspective on folklore that fed Freud's interests in the years in which he was probing intensively into ethnography. Krauss's translation was specifically the key text in these discussions, and the psychoanalysts could thus consult with the one man in Vienna who had dedicated considerable time to the study and translation of the *Oneirokritika*.

However, Stekel's enthusiasm for Artemidorus was part of an overall approach to dream interpretation that made Freud deeply uncomfortable. For example, in a discussion of teeth in dreams, Stekel cites at length Artemidorus' discussion at *Oneirokritika* 1.31, which details how the mouth must be considered one house: the top teeth signify the important people and the bottom the inferior people in the household, and those on the right represent men and those on the left women (Harris-McCoy 2012: 83). After this citation, Stekel writes, "I cannot deny that many times I have often been able to confirm Artemidorus' rules" and then relates how a patient dreamed his false teeth fell out and three of them broke (Stekel 1911: 223). The man was in an unhappy marriage with two children; the "false teeth" represented his false (unfaithful) wife; free association led the patient to thinking of his wife dying, and then how his children had been ill, "So his children could die too. Then he's totally free. All three upper teeth gone" (Stekel 1911: 224). This interpretation is typical of Stekel's succinct, offhand manner of presenting the dreams in his book, and Freud sensed his follower was becoming *too much* like an Artemidorus in hawking a technique of symbolic exegesis.

The minutes of the Vienna Psychoanalytic Society show that various criticisms were lodged against Stekel's book when he presented it before the members (April 26, 1911). Hanns Sachs objected that the book moves too much into generalizations, and that "interpretation is sometimes made to look much too easy, and as a result a wrong impression of the psychoanalytic technique is created" (Nunberg and Federn 1974: 235). Sachs made a further technical point about the dangers of symbolic interpretation: "the physician takes upon himself too much of the work involved, thereby contributing to the strengthening of the patient's resistances"; he also found the failure to distinguish individual from typical symbolism to be a serious flaw (Nunberg and Federn 1974: 235). For his part, Freud read the draft of his own review (which he never published) to the group, in which he faulted Stekel for not keeping within limits on the topic of dream symbolism, which not all dreams utilize. "Through exclusiveness in the application of symbolism, dream interpretation has become uncertain and superficial. This, however, is connected with Stekel's overvaluation of the manifest dream content" (Nunberg and Federn 1974: 236).

Thus, we can see that Freud's need to "lock down" Artemidorus as an important predecessor, yet one whose essential error was to use his own associations and not first the dreamer's, came from a situation in which *Traumdeutung* was slipping out of his control. The problem was not just the attractive facility of Stekel's approach; it also kept resurfacing the question of cultural symbolism in the psyche at a time when Freud's interests in the phylogenetic component of social and individual psychology were finding their expression in his researches for *Totem and Taboo*. This shift in focus led to the most extensive reworking of the *Traumdeutung* as the section on dream symbolism began to take on a life of its own. Originally chapter 5, section D "Typical Dreams" took on additions between 1909 and 1911, but later that material was reorganized in the 1914 edition with further additions as section E of chapter 6 on the dream work, titled "Representation by Symbols in Dreams – Some Further Typical Dreams."[11] A paragraph from 1909 became the opening paragraph of the new section in 1914, in which he immediately suggests the quest for permanently fixed sexual symbolism might tempt one "to draw up a new 'dream book' on the decoding principle." But he adds that such symbolism is not specific to dreams; rather, it is held in common with other forms of unconscious ideation, such as folklore, myths, legends, linguistic idioms and jokes (SE 5:351), outlining the wide area of research applied psychoanalysis considered fair game and would be investigating through the new journal *Imago* from 1912 onward.

But in a paragraph added in 1914, by which time Freud's break with Stekel was definitive, Freud mentions how the free associative technique comes up short on symbolic content, and yet "regard for scientific criticism forbids our returning to the arbitrary judgement of the dream-interpreter, as it was employed in ancient times and seems to have been revived again in the reckless interpretations of Stekel" (SE 5:353). Freud's concession was ultimately to agree to a "combined technique" that works primarily with the dreamer's associations but filling in the gaps with the analyst's knowledge of symbols. If Stekel had thus pushed Freud into taking dream symbolism seriously, Freud by no means followed him all the way. Stekel, and by association Artemidorus, seemed always to haunt him as virtuosi of wild dream analysis.[12]

Artemidorus' Sex Dreams: The Repression of the Returned

There is, however, more to this story of Artemidorus in the psychoanalytic movement, and this will bring us back to Foucault. I stated earlier that the first edition of the *Traumdeutung* had only two mentions of Artemidorus, one of which was indirect. This second mention was really a complaint against the translator Friedrich Krauss, whom Freud may not have known at the time. At a point in chapter 7, Freud's ambitious attempt to map out the psychology of dream processes, he mentions his theory of the sexual etiology of the neuroses, leaving it an open question whether latent sexual wishes from childhood are a factor in unconscious dream-wishes. A long footnote then mentions other things that Freud knows he has not explained fully in the book and claims there are special reasons why he has not dealt with the role of sexual ideas in dreams or analyzed dreams containing obvious sexual content. It seems at this juncture Freud was worried about being accused of prudery, and he rather incongruously throws Krauss under the bus to cover for his own omissions.

> Nothing could be further from my own views or from the theoretical opinions which I hold in neuropathology than to regard sexual life as something shameful, with which neither a physician nor a scientific research worker has any concern. Moreover, the moral indignation by which the translator of the *Oneirocritica* of Artemidorus of Daldis allowed himself to be led into withholding the chapter on sexual dreams from the knowledge of his readers strikes me as laughable.
> (SE 5:606-607, fn. 2)

In a book where Freud had already risked much in analyzing his own dreams, it is understandable that he withheld his erotic dreams from public discussion. Freud's reference to Krauss's translation, in turn, refers to Krauss's own lengthy footnote on *Oneirokritika* 1.78, in which he explains his omission of most of 1.79-80. *Pace* Freud, Krauss's words here convey something more complicated than simple moral indignation.

> Only the Latin translator ought to have permitted himself to render the further discussion on sex with the mother and unnatural intercourse; the Italian

translator was possessed of enough shamelessness and tastelessness to follow him in this. Seen by and for itself, the discussion I have omitted is of the greatest importance to cultural historians, since it allows us such a clear view into the mores of the later empire. Artemidorus discusses all possible details of sexual behavior in the naïvest fashion, and he always has a fitting example to hand in order to corroborate what he says. It is interesting that precisely these two chapters are the longest in the whole book; they comprise nine full pages. To reproach Artemidorus for this would be biased and unjustified; he just writes in the spirit of his age. The idea of morality is always relative, as it is influenced by climate, lifestyle, and fashion. What to one people or age appeared to give no offense against morality, counts for another people and age as improper and immoral. Of course, the sensual-sexual side appeared in the better period of Greek literature in a more beautiful form and idealized through the noble feeling of love, while in this time of decline we can observe ever more the corrupt overgrowth of crude sensuality. The name of many of these vices is largely unknown to our own age, but not – let it be said to the shame of civilized humanity – the vices themselves.

(Krauss 1881: 93–4 fn. 3)

Here the twenty-two-year-old Krauss fully appreciates the need for a history of sexuality, something to which he would later give great attention in his folkloric research. In fact, he ends the footnote by sending the reader to the relevant bibliography on sex in the ancient world. By advertising Artemidorus' "naïve" and detailed description of sexual dreams, however, he clearly awakened Freud's interest while also arousing his indignation.

As mentioned above, Krauss came to join Freud's circle at the Wednesday night meetings in 1910, and in 1912 he published in his special journal *Anthropophyteia* the missing chapters of the *Oneirokritika* in a translation done by the classical scholar Paul Brandt, a pioneer in the history of ancient sexuality, who published under the pseudonym Hans Licht.[13] Brandt openly credits Freud with the impetus for publishing the suppressed material.

> However, today the significance of the dream for psychological research, particularly of erotic dreams for sexual analysis, has been recognized especially through the very important works of the well-known Viennese psychoanalyst Prof. Freud and his students, and the scientific use of the dream life has become so widely promoted that it seems desirable – even necessary – to present in German translation the erotic dreams of Artemidorus omitted by Krauss in his day to the readers of *Anthropophyteia*.
>
> (Brandt 1912: 317)

In due course, then, Freud's carping footnote in the *Traumdeutung* was emended beginning in the 1914 edition to state, "Incidentally, this chapter has since appeared in German in vol. 9 of *Anthropophyteia*" and it is listed along with Krauss's translation in his bibliographies from then on.

It would seem, then, that psychoanalysis liberated Artemidorus for the modern reader, creating an intellectual environment suitable to foster frank and open access to sexual details which the *fin de siècle* still passed over in silence. Only the strange truth is that Freud *never* actually discusses the famously repressed passages of Artemidorus *anywhere*. In fact, the last reference to Artemidorus added to the *Traumdeutung* is made in 1919, where Freud mentions *Oneirokritika* 2.10, which suggests that a bedchamber (*thalamos*) can represent a wife if one has one (SE 5:354). This is mentioned in the section on dream symbols, in part because of the German word *Frauenzimmer* ("woman-room" literally but designating "woman") suggests the image so strongly. But in the whole reworked section on dream symbols, *nothing* appears from Artemidorus' repressed sex chapters.

The reason for this is not hard to fathom. Freud's theory of symbolism held that sexual ideas are at their root symbolic through civilizational repression; this idea is openly challenged by *undisguised* sexual content. Artemidorus' "naïve" description of sexual acts does not fit into Freud's scheme of the dream as a compromise formation precipitated by the dueling forces of the wish and the censor. So, Freud's *Traumdeutung* continued to investigate the *koinos kosmos* of phallic symbols but proved uninterested in accommodating the phallus *as symbol*. Freud's lack of interest in the censored part of Artemidorus seems to have been replicated by his followers, such that paradoxically a scotoma arose around the very same sexual dream imagery his movement had brought to light by creating the discursive conditions needed to publish the suppressed chapters.

The truth is, Freud had little interest in openly obscene dreams at the time *precisely* on account of his turn to ethnography and folklore, and he made use of other explicit materials Krauss diligently published in *Anthropophyteia*, a journal Freud openly supported.[14] While Krauss was fighting off charges of pornography in Germany that eventually led to his bankruptcy (Burt 1990: 90–101), Freud was doubling down in the years 1911–13 on the nature of repression and society, chasing the origins of civilization itself to the primal horde and trauma over the murder of the *Urvater* in *Totem and Taboo*. The idea of a "naïve" period of unrepressed sexual dream imagery did not fit into a scheme where a truly Freudian archaeology was setting a new agenda for the dreamlife, one linked phylogenetically to the infancy of human culture installed through oedipal trauma as a repressive apparatus first evident in the totem clan.[15] Hence the rather strident statement added to the *Traumdeutung* after the publication of *Totem and Taboo* to the section on regression. Fully deploying Ernst Haeckel's biogenetic law, Freud links individual regression in dreaming to "a picture of a phylogenetic childhood – a picture of the development of the human race, of which the individual's development is in fact an abbreviated recapitulation influenced by the chance circumstances of life" (SE 5:548). This puts *Traumdeutung* on a new track in the research into the "archaic heritage" of "mental antiquities" we inherit as a species. The new configuration of ontogenetic and phylogenetic factors underwrote the Freudian subject twice over as a being whose sexuality was riven and driven by occult forces, the truth of which could only be known by the psycho-archaeological dig of therapy and cultural analysis.

There is a genuine irony in the fact that Freud lost interest in vivid sex dreams so early on. The very notion that originally connected the Oedipus complex to the dreamworld in 1899 was Jocasta's seemingly offhand comment on incest dreams of the kind one might find in Artemidorus (*Oedipus Tyrannus* 981-983).

πολλοὶ γὰρ ἤδη κἀν ὀνείρασιν βροτῶν
μητρὶ ξυνηυνάσθησαν. ἀλλὰ ταῦθ' ὅτῳ
παρ' οὐδέν ἐστι, ῥᾷστα τὸν βίον φέρει.

"for many a mortal has lain with his
mother in his dreams; but he gets on
best in life who makes nothing of it."

In *Oedipus Tyrannus* this is said with devastating irony given what is about to be revealed, and Freud certainly saw the comment as a defensive denial of a psychological truth. But he construed this in 1899 as "an unmistakable indication" that the myth derived from "primaeval dream material," and was quick to add men today "just as then" dream of having sex with their mothers with astonishment (SE 4:264). And yet, the undisguised sex dream was otherwise never at the heart of *Traumdeutung*. In the first edition, Freud already declared there are no innocent dreams, since "Dreams are never concerned with trivialities," a rewording of the maxim *de minimis non curat lex* (SE 4:182). We find he has only deepened in this conviction in the 1925 essay, "Moral Responsibility for the Content of Dreams," where he admits the psychoanalytic interest in manifestly immoral dreams flags in the face of all the depravity revealed upon analysis of common and "innocent" dreams.

> As in the world of waking life, these masked criminals are far commoner than those with their visors raised. The straightforward dream of sexual relations with one's mother, which Jocasta alludes to in the *Oedipus Rex*, is a *rarity* in comparison with all the *multiplicity* of dreams which psychoanalysis must interpret in the same sense.
>
> (SE 19:132, my emphasis)

The *only* real use Freud had for Artemidorus' notorious sex dreams was *the drama of their suppression* by Krauss. It should be noted that while Freud mentioned the subsequent publication of the material by Brandt, he never altered his initial complaint against Krauss in subsequent editions, even after Krauss had been brought to trial and ruined for doing the very kind of thing Freud demanded.

Foucault's Artemidorus: The Return of the Non-repressed

In the light of this complicated history of Artemidorus among the early psychoanalysts, one might assume I have delivered a kind of QED to Foucault's thesis in Volume 1 of the *The History of Sexuality*; namely, that *Sexualwissenschaft* participates in the West's truth game whereby "it is up to us to extract the truth of sex, since this truth is beyond its grasp; it is up to sex to tell us our truth, since sex is what holds it in darkness" (Foucault 1990: 77). When Artemidorus' sex dreams finally arrived on the scene of analysis, the psychoanalysts had no place for them in their repressive apparatus. Yet they still serve a kind of purpose; Freud's rhetorical indignation over their suppression reveals what Foucault called the "speaker's benefit."

> If sex is repressed, that is, condemned to prohibition, nonexistence, and silence, then the mere fact that one is speaking about it has the appearance of a deliberate transgression. A person who holds forth in such language places himself to a certain extent outside the reach of power; he upsets established law; he somehow anticipates the coming freedom.
>
> (Foucault 1990: 6)

Freud, as we saw, railed against Krauss's omission in a context where he was excusing himself for the *lack* of any significant treatment of sexually explicit dreams in the *Traumdeutung*, a diversion from his own self-censorship. Foucault points out the "sterile paradox" of denying the reality of sexual repression in the age of *Sexualwissenschaft*: "It not only runs counter to a well-accepted argument," which we see *in statu nascendi* in the *Traumdeutung*, "it goes against the whole economy and all the discursive 'interests' that underlie this argument" (Foucault 1990: 8).

Freud was capable of exchanging uncensored sexual explicitness for whatever better served his discursive interest, a phenomenon that appeared quite early on. Writing to Wilhelm Fliess (May 31, 1897) he relates an incestuous dream he had about this ten-year old daughter, Mathilde, immediately interpreting it as *discursive wish fulfillment*. At a time when Freud was struggling over the reality of parental seduction, the dream was an attempt, "to catch a *Pater* as the originator of neurosis" and thus prove him right (Masson 1985: 249). His own incest was thus an *allegory* of his desire to establish incest as a common occurrence. By October 1897, Freud would face his incestuous wishes head on, but as the son caught in the tragic oedipal triangle, i.e. the boy in love with his mother, not the man seducing his daughter.[16] But this newly paradigmatic incest is expressed in the tragic disguise of *Oedipus Tyrannus* and *Hamlet*, both plays interrogating secrets of desire and sex as Freud reads them, not explorations of pleasure and erotic experience.

In the face of Freud's maneuvers around Artemidorus, Foucault's deployment of the *Oneirokritika* in chapter 2 of *The Care of the Self* has the quality of a vindication: the stone rejected has become the corner stone. Sandra Boehringer (above in this volume) has detailed the history of Foucault's interest in the *Oneirokritika*, so I wish only to state what is most relevant to my point. When Foucault sees the isomorphism of sexual acts in dreams and social positions in society as the determinative factor in reading the dream omen, it would seem he has found the perfect coin of vantage to expose Freud's historical limitations. "The sexual dream uses the little drama of penetration and passivity, pleasure and expenditure, to tell the subject's mode of being as destiny has arranged it," with the penis "at the intersection of all these games of mastery" (Foucault 1986: 33–4). What better way to refute the repressive hypothesis, Freud's oedipal mythology with its drama of self-alienation and guilt, and the submergence of the penis into a forest of phallic symbols? Artemidorus can deliver for Foucault just the kind of witness he needs to show "the endurance and solidity" of the classical age's characteristics of *aphrodisia*, bodies and pleasures detached from the desiring subject of psychoanalysis (Foucault 1986: 36). Nothing could better show the gulf that separates the Greek oneirocritic from the psychoanalysts, no matter how much they identified with him. And perhaps nothing can show better the distance of the later Foucault from his earliest writing on dreams, where he championed the *idios kosmos* of the dreamer, than this new interest in the *koinos kosmos* of sex and social position chronicled by Artemidorus.

But as Derrida said, Freud is the hinge, the doorkeeper for Foucault. We see traces of this better in his lectures than in *The Care of the Self* (especially the lecture of January 21, 1981). Once Foucault frames Artemidorus as the key pivot, the last moment when the *aphrodisia*—all sex acts that can be done or imagined— still exist on a continuum with the social world, he begins in his lecture to talk of "*our* oneirocriticism" by way of contrast. While Artemidorus projects the sexual onto the social in his analysis, "of any dream with a social content, speaking of a reverse of fortune, of political success *we ask* what sexual truth it conceals. It is the exact opposite in the oneirocriticism of Artemidorus" (Foucault 2017a: 58; my emphasis). He continues,

> In *our* oneirocriticism [*Dans notre onirocritique à nous*], the possibility of decoding social contents of the dream in sexual terms rests on the postulate that there is a natural discontinuity between the sexual, or anyway, desire, and the social. It needed a barrier between [dreams] and their content, it needed heterogeneity of principles and all the mechanisms of repression and conversion for it to be possible to make one speak the truth of the other. On the contrary, in Greek oneirocriticism one is dealing with a sort of continuum of the social and the sexual.
>
> (Foucault 2017a: 58; my emphasis)

Foucault manages here to describe psychoanalytic *Traumdeutung* as the modern correlate, *our oneirocriticism*, to Artemidorus, as if by lining the two up one can see just how far the modern subject has been subjected to the confessional drama of truth. But in doing so, Foucault is clearly speaking Freud's truth; he has just repressed the name of the father. So, is the project to get *beyond* Freud by going back in history, or to get *back to* Freud, to "our" discursive world, so much ours apparently that we do not need to credit Freud for it? Derrida said it best: "This double articulation, this double movement or alternation between opening and closing that is assured by the workings of a hinge, this coming and going, indeed this *fort/da* of a pendulum [*pendule*] or balance [*balancier*]—that is what Freud means to Foucault" (Derrida 1994: 234). Freud is Foucault's pendulum.

8

The Desiring Subject Seeks Pleasure in History

Li Yinhe's Sadomasochistic Fictions and the Cultural Revolution

Leihua Weng
Kalamazoo College

Li Yinhe, born in 1952, is a Chinese sociologist and scholar specializing in Foucaultian studies. Upon retirement, she turned to literary writing, with a particular focus on sadomasochistic fiction. One of her stories, titled "2084," is included in her collection *Dark Knight's Kingdom* (*Hei qi shi de wang guo*). It opens as follows:

> Freedom is the freedom to say that two plus two make four. If that is granted, all else follows.—George Orwell
>
> It's been a century since George Orwell penned *1984*, and I can't forget the initial shock that gripped me when I read it. Orwell crafted this remarkable narrative after his journey through the then-Soviet Union. In contrast, despite living for years in a society resembling the one he described, I've found myself unable to write even a single word.
>
> Yet, the world has evolved considerably over the last hundred years, even if the essence of the present closely mirrors that past era. What can I say about such transformation? Simply put, there is nothing new under the sun. The early twentieth-century French philosopher, Queneau, proclaimed that history had reached its end and time had come to a standstill, suggesting the world had achieved its final form and would change no further.
>
> In line with Freud's brilliant theory, when one can't find a way out of torture, they come to accept, even embrace it. This is our reality today. Torture has become an everyday norm, and we have grown to appreciate this order. It brings us pleasure because the acts involve both sadistic and masochistic elements related to sex. It offers more than the sheer violence depicted in *1984*.
>
> (Li 2016, 3: 250–1)[1]

The opening of Li's "2084" is a tapestry of contrasts. It is at once historical and futuristic, invoking both the past Soviet Union and Orwell's *1984* while setting the scene in the year 2084. This juxtaposition creates a distance between historical and current realities. Though the story is overtly political, drawing from Orwell's themes of freedom within authoritarian regimes, it also exudes a playful and aesthetic quality. This duality is exemplified by a quote from Raymond Queneau (1903–76), known for his narrative versatility in *Exercise of Styles*, a collection featuring ninety-nine different narratives of the same story. Building upon these layered themes, Li converts the historical and political into an aesthetic experience. To tie it all together, she concludes that the story's physical pleasure derived from torture is an exercise in sadism and masochism, thereby transcending the simple violence depicted in Orwell's *1984*.

The initial portrayal of history in "2084" is somewhat nebulous, alluding to an "authoritarian historical reality." However, as the narrative unfolds, it incorporates more explicit historical references such as the public corporal punishment of intellectuals and officials, either directed by an "authoritative leader" or carried out by Red Guards. These elements specifically evoke the Maoist era and, in particular, the Cultural Revolution.

"2084" is not an isolated example in Li's *Dark Knight's Kingdom*, a three-volume anthology of sadomasochistic novellas. Instead, the Cultural Revolution features prominently in multiple stories, shaping character identities and serving as a backdrop for sadomasochistic elements. Specifically, the era is consistently woven into narratives that explore aesthetic exercises in pleasure-seeking.

This chapter looks into the literary use of Maoist history in Yinhe's *Dark Knight's Kingdom* in the perspective of the late Foucaultian notion and practices of the art of existence, *technē tou biou*. In stories like "2084" collected in *Dark Knight's Kingdom*, aesthetic experiences take sadomasochistic (SM) forms, through which the subject turns its desires into "events" of pleasure-seeking. This chapter argues that in these SM narratives, the subject strategically uses Maoist history, specifically the Cultural Revolution, for its sole purpose of pleasure-seeking, and thus renders desire and history into an aesthetic invention in the form of the art of existence. By doing so, the subject constantly renews itself at the very core of its existence.

The chapter starts with an overview of Li Yinhe, focusing on her Foucauldian studies, sexuality research, sadomasochistic writings, and experiences during the Maoist era. It then provides a detailed analysis of historical references in various stories from her *Dark Knight's Kingdom* collection. The third section turns to Foucault's concept of the art of existence, exploring the dynamics between identity and pleasure that Foucault frequently discussed in different interviews and are rendered in Li's SM novellas as the tension and interactions between identity and pleasure, as well as between history and "events" (Foucault 1994e; 1994f). The conclusion places Li's works on sadomasochism in Chinese intellectuals' changing views on Chinese modern history.

Li Yinhe's Writings on Foucault, Sexuality in China, and Sadomasochism

Li Yinhe was born in Beijing in 1952 into an intellectual family. Her parents were early founders of the *China Daily* newspaper. She and her older brother adopted their mother's surname, reflecting the era's communist ideals of gender equality. Living through the Cultural Revolution as a teen and young adult, Li graduated from Shanxi University in 1977. She began her career at *Guangming Daily* before moving to the Chinese Academy of Social Sciences as a researcher on marriage and family. In 1980, she married Wang Xiaobo, who later gained fame as a novelist. Li studied sociology at the University of Pittsburgh in the United States, then returned to China and worked at the Institute of Sociology at the Chinese Academy of Social Science until her retirement in 2012 (Li 2015b).

Mao and the Cultural Revolution deeply influenced Li's adolescence and shaped her views on gender equality, social justice, and the role of intellectuals. These themes recur in her scholarly and literary works. Scenes of young girls wielding power over male authority figures often appear in her SM stories, including "2084" and "Like Father, Like Daughter" (*You qi fu bi you qi nv*). Li acknowledges that her academic and literary contributions are deeply influenced by her SM preferences and experiences, which she describes as a "subtle and delicate" sense of "ecstasy" (Li 2015b: 37).

As a prominent social activist, Li passionately advocates for women's equality, LGBTQ rights, gay marriage, and the decriminalization of prostitution. While often linked to her late husband, Wang Xiaobo, a well-known fiction writer, their political stances differed. In her memoir, Li notes that Wang's friends were shocked he would marry a female "Communist." However, Li asserts that within their marriage, each served as the "conscience" for the other. Wang's family's suffering during Maoist political movements reminded Li of the social injustice they endured. On the other hand, Li reminded Wang of the achievements made on social equality during the Mao era (Li 2015b: 99–100). The couple's differences and shared views largely centered on their interpretations of social justice. This theme permeates Li's SM novellas, which often highlight a utopian vision of equitable resource distribution in society.

Li is a prolific sociologist whose research extensively spans issues in women's studies, contemporary Chinese sexual norms, homosexuality, and queer theory. She has also translated seminal texts on sexuality and queer theory into Chinese, featuring works by Gayle Rubin and Judith Butler among others (Tellis 2015). Of all Western theorists, Foucault stands as the most significant influence on both her scholarly and literary endeavors. Li openly expresses her profound admiration for Foucault and his *History of Sexuality*. In a 2014 interview, she highlighted how Foucault's subversive views on freedom had radically reshaped her own perspectives, stating, "the guidelines he [Foucault] offers illuminate the magnificent possibilities of a future freedom. This is precisely why everyone loves Foucault!" (Li 2015a).

Li's work on Foucault can be categorized into three interconnected areas, each focusing on the practices of the ethical subject as the art of existence, or *technē tou biou*: her interpretation of Foucault's *History of Sexuality*, her application of Foucault's ideas in a Chinese context, and her exploration of the Foucaultian concept of the art of life within the realm of sadomasochism, both in academic research and in her literary creations of SM fiction.

Foucault's philosophy, which focuses on the subject's agency in bodily exercises, serves as the theoretical foundation for Li's work. Contrary to the idea that sexual pleasure is invariably repressed by mechanisms of power, Li posits that individuals actively seek and derive pleasure through their engagement and interaction with power systems (Li 2021: 240–71). Her monograph, *Foucault and Sexuality: A Reading of Foucault's History of Sexuality*, zeroes in on the formation of subjectivity within historical contexts, an element she regards as central to Foucault's *History of Sexuality*.

Li's interpretation of Foucault situates the formation and exertion of subjectivity within the scope of modern Chinese history. Her book, *Discourses of Sexuality in Post-1949 China*, analyzes articles on sexuality published in the major state-run newspaper, *China Daily*, over a span of six decades. It offers a sociological perspective on the interaction between China's official mainstream discourses and the public's understanding and practices of sexuality (Li 2014: "Preface," 1–2). Echoing Foucault's approach in *The History of Sexuality*, which examines texts from the Hellenic period through early medieval Europe, Li's work provides a comprehensive view of how collective subjects have sought pleasure within China's official power structures since 1949. The book conceptualizes power as a pervasive, interactive mechanism in which the subject is actively involved, utilizing systems, discourses, and practices both for physical pleasure and ethical self-governance.

Li's scholarly and creative works on sadomasochism serve as a unique exploration of the individual's quest for self-control and ethical pleasure through the transformation of existence into a form of art. Further, she draws from Foucault's notions that sadomasochism acts as "the use of a strategic relationship as a source of pleasure (physical pleasure)" and can pave the way for new forms of communities (Foucault 1994b: 170; 1994a). For Li, sadomasochism is also a form of political experimentation (Li 2015b: 185–9). In her retirement, she began writing sadomasochistic novellas, which are compiled in her three-volume collection, *Dark Knight's Kingdom*. She advises readers to consider these SM novellas as literary extensions of her theoretical explorations into sadomasochism (Li 2016, 1: 10).

In both the preface and the epilogue to *Dark Knight's Kingdom*, Li cites Foucault to argue that sadomasochism is an art of existence, accessible only to an elite class cultivated through proper upbringing, nurture, and education. She likens this form of art to other classical forms such as poetry and painting, which were once daily pastimes for China's educated leisure class. Li declares that she will continue to engage in her SM pursuits through her writing, choosing it as her preferred form of aesthetic lifestyle, and that she is committed to transforming her existence into a work of art, especially as she enters the later stages of her life, when the specter of death draws near.

The Maoist Era and the Cultural Revolution in Li's *Dark Knight's Kingdom*

The Maoist era, specifically the Cultural Revolution, infuses the stories in *Dark Knight's Kingdom*. This historical period is not merely a backdrop but is intricately woven into the characters, the sadomasochistic scenes, and other elements of the narrative. Moreover, the stories uniquely imbue features of the Maoist era with sadomasochistic qualities. Within this literary landscape, history becomes a medium through which the subject embarks on inventive quests for pure physical pleasure. These novellas also provoke some lingering questions, particularly about the accessibility of the art of existence—expressed through SM pleasure-seeking. For instance, these stories ask whether this form of pleasure is an exclusive right of the educated and cultural elite or a universal right accessible to all members of society.

In addition to the first-person narrator, several recurring characters appear in many of Li's stories in *Dark Knight's Kingdom*, each bringing a stable identity and social status that persist across different narratives. These characters often embody socio-political power structures and elements reminiscent of the Maoist era.

Dongdong, the protagonist in many stories, is a well-read, educated, and intelligent woman. Depending on the story, she occupies different roles. In "An Experimentation of Communism," she is the daughter of a billionaire who sets up a utopian communist SM society on her own island. In other stories like "Like Father, Like Daughter," she is a state-owned newspaper journalist, or a sociologist in as "Love in the 31st Century." Dongdong's character often parallels the author's own background, education, and professional life. In these narratives, similar to the author Li Yinhe in reality, Dongdong serves as an intellectual observer and commentator on class, gender equality, and social justice. Jianshan, who is always portrayed as Dongdong's lover, shares the name of the author's classmate, whose image in bondage influenced the author's adolescent SM awareness during the Cultural Revolution.

Another recurring character is Lao Liang, or the "Old Pillar," who appears as an authoritative male figure. Depending on the story, he may be the head of a research institute or a billionaire mimicking Mao's power. His name itself carries metaphorical weight in Chinese, alluding to an important social and political figure. In some stories, Lao Liang's links to the Maoist era are pronounced, such as in "Island of Eros," where he mimics Maoist practices and enforces SM corporal punishment on the residents of the island that he owns.

Xiao Hong, or "Little Red," is another staple character. She is a youthful, energetic woman who, although not highly educated, loyally serves Lao Liang and carries out public floggings. Her attributes echo those of the Red Guard: young, loyal to the top leader, and willing to inflict physical punishment. She bears resemblance to the Red Guard students who administered punishments to teachers, scholars, and other elites during the Cultural Revolution.

Scenes reminiscent of "denunciation meetings" from the Cultural Revolution—where intellectuals and other elites faced public corporal punishment—frequently appear in various stories within *Dark Knight's Kingdom*. These scenes serve either as characters' memories of Maoist times or as settings for contemporary SM activities.

In some novellas, Jianshan undergoes public flagellation for his "incorrect" speeches, as seen in "Love in the 31st Century." A similar theme of flagellation as punishment for intellectual speech appears in "Like Father, Like Daughter." The story recounts incidents from both the Cultural Revolution and the post-Mao era involving Dongdong and her father. In the first part, a young Dongdong disrupts a "denunciation meeting" where her father is about to be flogged on stage along with other journalist "criminals" for his truthful reporting. In the second part of "Like Father, Like Daughter," Dongdong has become an accomplished journalist enjoying considerable freedom and recognition. Despite this, she still faces public flagellation for her newspaper coverage advocating the decriminalization of pornography.

Several features of corporal punishment during the Cultural Revolution are highlighted in the depiction of SM activities in *Dark Knight's Kingdom*, including a subversion of existing hierarchies—be they socioeconomic, political, or gender-based. Those who are flogged often hold some form of cultural, social, or political capital. For example, in "2084," Lao Liang, the head of a state-owned research institute, is the sole individual subjected to weekly public whipping, while others are exempt from such routine punishment.

Additionally, the act of whipping is usually carried out by a subordinate or junior, often female. In "2084," Xiao Hong (Little Red), whose name alludes to Red Guards, performs the weekly flogging of director Lao Liang, an event that has become a recurring public spectacle. In "Like Father, Like Daughter," Dongdong's father faces flogging from former subordinates, while the adult Dongdong, now a department head and respected journalist, is flogged by a younger female colleague.

Moreover, the public plays a significant role in these scenes, both during the Cultural Revolution and in the contemporary SM settings depicted in the novellas. Detailed descriptions are provided of public spectacles where crowds gather to watch intellectuals being flogged during the Maoist era. Similarly, a jubilant crowd is described as celebrating when Dongdong receives flagellation in "Like Father, Like Daughter." In "2084," the entire staff takes part in and enjoys the weekly flogging of Lao Liang, performed by Xiao Hong. The act of public participation, whether as spectators or as an audience, dilutes the concentration of power and subverts established hierarchical orders. These features, which characterized the Cultural Revolution, are frequently echoed and accentuated in Li's post-Maoist SM-themed novellas.

Meanwhile, the stories draw clear and unambiguous distinctions between corporal punishment during the Cultural Revolution and the SM scenes that replicate aspects of that part of history. These distinctions are further emphasized through ritualization. One particular focus is on the differences in economic and social environments between historical times and the "fictional" present. For instance, many of the SM scenes in the stories are set against a backdrop of material abundance, where the characters have no concerns about fulfilling basic needs. Additionally, the characters in these stories enjoy greater sexual freedom than previous generations and live in a society where marriage is no longer the fundamental social structure.

The opening novella of the Volume 1 of *Dark Knight's Kingdom*, "My Happy Life," begins with the narrator reflecting on the existential void he feels despite his material wealth. This narrator contrasts his life with that of his grandparents, who lived through food scarcity during the Cultural Revolution, and his parents, who faced sexual restrictions in their own era. Inherited wealth now allows the first-person narrator to pursue unprecedented freedoms, leading him to explore sadomasochistic pursuits as a form of stimulation in an otherwise mundane existence. Through these quests, he finds unending satisfaction in life. The attention to such economic and social contrasts serves to underscore Li's argument: the pursuit of SM as a means for sheer pleasure-seeking is an artistic and aesthetic lifestyle, possible only in a society characterized by material abundance and social tolerance.

Moreover, Li's SM novellas highlight the volitional aspect of the participants and the mutual consent in SM scenarios, elements largely missing in her portrayal of the history of the Cultural Revolution. The story "Like Father, Like Daughter" illuminates the difference in public perception between the era when Dongdong's father faces physical punishment and when she herself undergoes public flagellation for a similar offense. In her father's time, people avoided contact with the family and even close friends distanced themselves. In contrast, Dongdong finds a community that not only understands but also supports her. There is a tangible mutual understanding between Dongdong and the woman assigned to carry out the flogging. They both adorn elaborate SM attire for the public event. By the conclusion of the performance, the young sadist and Dongdong's colleagues applaud, expressing gratitude and respect for her participation and her speech about the socio-political transformations in the past Revolution era. With the distribution of power becoming more multilateral and dynamic, all parties engage willingly in the SM scenes, adhering to a shared understanding and consent.

The intricate dynamics between power and subordination in the SM settings differ from the power structures during the Cultural Revolution. Such contrasts add complexity to the story's narrative, further enriching the nuanced relationship between authority, history, and the pursuit of physical pleasure in the novellas. In the realm of SM, the author introduces a fluid and negotiable power dynamic where consent is foregrounded. In contrast, during the Cultural Revolution, power was often wielded in a manner that left little room for negotiation or dissent. This nuanced difference offers an additional lens through which the author illustrates societal evolution and human relationships.

Aesthetic and erotic allure form the core of the SM scenes in Li's works. For instance, in "Like Father, Like Daughter," Dongdong goes to great lengths to prepare her appearance for her public flagellation. The splendor of her carefully curated SM attire captivates everyone present. In contrast, the first-person narrator in the story "Vacation" (*Jia ri*) expresses nostalgia for her past as a "sent-down youth" during the Cultural Revolution, finding modern industrial and urban settings "vulgar." She poses the question, "How does one maintain distance from the mundane, the sleazy, and the pedestrian?" (Li 2016, 1: 78). She discovers her answer in the world of SM, seeing it as a realm of creative originality closely tied to various forms of art like music, literature, and painting. By the end of the story, she asserts that she chooses SM as the aesthetic framework of her lifestyle specifically because it eschews the mediocrity she associates with modern urban existence.

In Li's work, SM is not merely an individual choice of lifestyle focused on aesthetic beauty; it is also portrayed as an act of resistance against capitalism and commercial culture, and as an exploration of potential societal structures (Li 2016, 3: 111). The novella "An Experimentation of Communism," the first and longest story in Volume 3 of *Dark Knight's Kingdom*, serves as a compelling example. The story follows Dongdong and her friends as they, along with other well educated young individuals, opt for a self-sufficient communal lifestyle on an island. This community is characterized not just by shared labor and equal resource distribution, but also by artistic pursuits, SM activities, and Chan Buddhist meditation.

Lao Liang, a recurring character in Li's works who often serves as an authority figure, assumes a different role here. He leads the community in Chan meditation and serves as a Buddhist priest. The novella concludes that SM, with its focus on the pursuit of sexual and other forms of pleasure, serves as a lifestyle that resists the profit-driven forces of capitalism (Li 2016, 3: 111). While the story itself avoids making explicit references to the Cultural Revolution, it does, in an indirect manner, confirm the values of the Maoist era by exploring the possibilities of alternative communal lifestyles and critiquing capitalist ideologies.

Li's novellas present an intriguing tension between the aesthetics of an SM lifestyle and the socio-economic egalitarianism that characterized the Cultural

Revolution. The latter was grounded in an ideology of egalitarianism aimed at dismantling existing social, economic, cultural, and political hierarchies. As a Communist Party member who grew up in an intellectual family supportive of the Party's ideals, Li reaffirms the achievements of the Chinese Communist Party in establishing class and gender equality during the Maoist era (Li 2016: 229).

In Li's portrayals, SM is framed as an aristocratic and refined lifestyle that can only be fully appreciated by cultural elites who possess abundant material resources and freedom (Li 2016, 1: 8). For instance, in "An Experimentation of Communism," most residents of the island community are well-educated individuals capable of engaging in complex discussions on culture, politics, and philosophy (Li 2016, 3: 7). Characters adept at navigating the SM lifestyle are typically cultural elites, in contrast to those who are less educated or financially disadvantaged.

Unlike the elite figures, characters lacking in educational and financial resources often meet grim outcomes in Li's work. For example, individuals like Xiuxiu in "Nightmare" (*E meng*) and the characters in "A Trial Marriage" (*Shi hun*) become victims of domestic violence due to their ignorance or financial desperation. Similarly, the protagonist of "This Is How I Died" (*Wo shi zen me si de*) succumbs to a sadistic killer due to a lack of precaution.

The elitist undertones in Li's portrayal of SM experiences raise pertinent questions in relation to Maoist ideology and the broader aspirations of social equality. Specifically, it brings into focus whether the aesthetic and sexual freedom associated with SM practices should remain exclusive to cultural elites. If so, does this exclusivity contradict the egalitarian principles of Maoist proletarian ideology, which were foundational to the Cultural Revolution? Furthermore, should safeguards be instituted in the realm of sadomasochism to protect vulnerable populations, such as the lesser educated, from potential crimes or harm? In her novellas, Li does not directly address this tension between the social inclusivity championed by the Cultural Revolution and the cultural exclusivity often ascribed to sadomasochism. Instead, she consistently suggests that the enjoyment of SM is contingent on a person's refined tastes, which are acquired rather than innate.

While Foucault dismisses the idea that homosexuals already form a distinct social class within existing socio-economic structures, he leaves room for this possibility in the future. In contrast, Li seems more optimistic about the potential for SM to effect meaningful changes in society and the economy. However, her optimism even in "An Experimentation of Communism" is largely theoretical. She stops short of detailing a more concrete vision for a utopian SM community.

The Desiring Subject Seeking Pleasure in History and in "Events"

At the heart of Li's SM writings is Foucault's concept of the art of existence, which he elaborates in his later works, particularly in the *History of Sexuality*. This ancient principle, termed "the care of the self" or *heautou epimeleisthai*, emphasizes self-cultivation and individual autonomy. In the Greco-Roman context, subjects intentionally shape themselves through actions designed to transform their existence into a work of art. According to Foucault, this art of self-care engages the individual in quests of dependency, autonomy, and interpersonal relationships. It involves an ongoing process by which the subject exercises control over itself, aiming for mastery over self-imposed limitations and transformations (Foucault 1986a: 238–9).

> I am referring to what might be called the "arts of existence." What I mean by the phrase are those intentional and voluntary actions by which men not only set themselves rules of conduct, but also seek to transform themselves, to change themselves in their singular being, and to make their life into an *oeuvre* that carries certain aesthetic values and meets certain stylistic criteria.
> (Foucault 1986a: 10–11)

This development is a process of autonomous and voluntary shaping of one's own subjectivity. In this process, the individual engages in ethical work (*travail éthique*) on themselves. The aim is not merely to align one's actions with existing norms but to fundamentally transform oneself into the ethical subject of those actions (Foucault 1985: 27). Such ethical work might manifest in various forms, ranging from a regulated regimen of sexual activities to a balanced approach that integrates austerity with the pursuit of pleasure.

Li draws heavily upon Foucault's concepts of intentional and voluntary transformation of the self. She dismisses Freudian theories that posit sexual identity as shaped primarily by external repression and circumstance. Instead, Li advocates that the self is an active subject, consistently shaping and reshaping itself through various discourses, social practices, and power mechanisms, all while deriving pleasure from these engagements (Li 2001: 77). Her work, *Discourses of Sexuality in Post-1949 China*, serves as a theoretical extension of Foucault's ideas about autonomous and ethical subjects within the specific socio-cultural context of post-1949 China. Similarly, her SM novellas in *Dark Knight's Kingdom* act as a literary embodiment of Foucault's views on subject autonomy.

In the practice of the art of existence, the ethical labor (*travail éthique*) performed by the subject on itself is designed to meet specific aesthetic criteria. The pleasure derived from this process is multi-faceted, varying both in origin and form. Foucault differentiates between two types of pleasure: serenity and *voluptas*. The former refers to the pleasure the subject finds within itself, while the latter describes the experience of discovering pleasure beyond one's immediate realm, often in an impersonal self that the subject constructs.

> This pleasure, for which Seneca usually employs the word *gaudium* or *laetitia*, is a state that is neither accompanied nor followed by any form of disturbance in the body or the mind. It is defined by the fact of not being caused by anything that is independent of ourselves and therefore escapes our control.... This sort of pleasure can thus be contrasted point by point with what is meant by the term *voluptas*. The latter denotes a pleasure whose origin is to be placed outside us and in objects whose presence we cannot be sure of: a pleasure, therefore, which is precarious in itself, undermined by the fear of loss, and to which we are drawn by the force of a desire that may or may not find satisfaction. In place of this kind of violent, uncertain, and conditional pleasure, access to self is capable of providing a form of pleasure that comes, in serenity and without fail, of the experience of oneself.
>
> (Foucault 1986b: 66)

The tumultuous and conditional form of pleasure found in sadomasochistic eroticism, termed *voluptas*, plays a crucial role in the stylization and transformation of the subject. This intense physical pleasure, derived from various bodily zones rather than solely from genital localization, serves to destabilize the subject and challenge its existing sexual identity. By testing the limits of bodily understanding, it opens the door for a more impersonal self—a self amenable to ongoing ethical and aesthetic development. "By shattering the subject of sexuality, queer sex opens up the possibility for the cultivation of a more impersonal self, a self that can function as the substance of the ongoing ethical elaboration—and thus as the site of future transformation" (Halperin 1995: 97). This notion aligns with Foucault's somewhat enigmatic comments in the conclusion of *The History of Sexuality*, Volume 1, which link the pursuit of bodily pleasure to a transformative alteration of the self.

> We must not think that by saying yes to sex, one says no to power; on the contrary, one tracks along the course laid out by the general deployment of sexuality. It is the agency of sex that we must break away from, if we aim—through a tactical reversal of the various mechanisms of sexuality—to counter the grips of power with the claims of bodies, pleasures, and knowledges, in their

multiplicity and their possibility of resistance. The rallying point for the counterattack against the deployment of sexuality ought not to be sex-desire, but bodies and pleasures.

(Foucault 1990: 157)

In Foucault's writings, the subject undergoes self-transformation through a dialectic involving desire, identity, and pleasure, which manifests as a form of event. Foucault distinguishes "desire" as a concept rooted in medical and psychoanalytical discourse, often falsely lending stability and intelligibility to the subject. He contrasts this with "pleasure," which he describes as a bodily, ever-evolving, and non-designatory experience that should precede "desire." Foucault notes, "We have to liberate our desire," but corrects this by stating, "No! We have to create new pleasure. And then maybe desire will follow" (Foucault 1994b: 166).

Foucault sees identity as strategically useful in the pursuit of pleasure and the exploration of new relational forms, but not as something that can be "revealed." He argues for a shift from relationships based on identity to those fostering differentiation, creation, and innovation. Foucault posits, "To be the same is really boring. We must not exclude identity if people find their pleasure through this identity, but we must not think of this identity as an ethical universal rule" (Foucault 1994b: 166).

In the "event" of pleasure-seeking—sudden, radical shifts where the subject encounters an impersonal self through intense physical pleasure—conventional constructs such as desire and identity all disintegrate. During these transformative "events," the subject is lifted out of its own identity and distanced from its desires, achieving in the process a profound self-transformation.

> [B]y using the word pleasure, which in the end means nothing, which is still, it seems to me, rather empty of content and unsullied by possible uses—in treating pleasure ultimately as nothing other than an event, an event that happens, that happens, I would say, outside the subject, or at the limit of the subject, or between two subjects, in this something that is neither of the body nor of the soul, neither outside nor inside—don't we have here, in trying to reflect a bit on this notion of pleasure, a means of avoiding the entire psychological and medical armature that was built into the traditional notion of desire? ... The main thing is this notion of an event that is not assigned, and is not assignable, to a subject. Whereas the, let's say, nineteenth-century notion of desire is first and foremost attached to a subject. It's not an event; it's a type of permanent characteristic of the events of a subject, which for this reason leads to an analysis of the subject, a medical analysis of the subject.
>
> (Foucault, Morar, and Smith 2011: 390–1)

Li aligns closely with Foucault's distinctions between desire and pleasure, as well as between identity and transformative "events," placing them at the heart of the subject's journey toward self-transformation in sadomasochistic experiences. Like Foucault, she prioritizes bodily sensations and pleasures over the constructs of desire and identity. Li argues that while desire is affixed to the subject and tied to its past and identity, pleasure disrupts these fixed designations. Specifically, pleasure experienced during transformative "events" de-subjectivizes the individual, breaking down past designations and identity, thereby unlocking boundless possibilities for the subject's alterity, a crucial factor in achieving self-transformation (Li 2009: 273–4).

Li interprets Foucault in a way that emphasizes how the "events" of sadomasochism continuously dismantle and destabilize desire, an element intrinsically linked to the subject's past. This process facilitates ongoing self-reinvention and transformation through intense physical pleasure. Despite her professed disinterest in history, as stated in an interview—"history records distant past events and accounts of people long departed. Therefore, I am not much interested in history" (Cochrane and Wang 2020: 450–1)—Li's SM novellas tell a different story. Characters like Dongdong and other pivotal figures in her works often have their roots in the Cultural Revolution or bear the legacies of their parents' or grandparents' experiences during the Maoist era. In these novellas, the past is not a static concept but rather a living entity that resonates through the experiences and memories of contemporary characters, especially within the recreated SM scenes of the Cultural Revolution. It remains alive in the present collective consciousness. Consistent with Foucault's assertion, identity in the practice of SM serves a strategic purpose in Li's SM novellas. It acts as a source of physical pleasure.

Although Li emphasizes pleasure over desire and "events" over identity, the characters in her SM novellas are not without history, identity, or pre-existing desires. These elements, however, remain fluid, continuously disrupted and reshaped by the quest for intense and situation-specific physical pleasure, especially within SM scenes that echo the Cultural Revolution. In this process, the characters use their history, identity, and desires, strategically and effectively dismantling and reconstructing them. As these designators are continually shattered and reassembled, the characters gain renewed agency and subjectivity. This ongoing cycle of deconstruction and reconstruction allows them to transcend their historical and identity-based confines, diving deep into the core of their own alterity. This is the art of existence at work, as the characters continuously stylize and transform themselves.

The association of the Cultural Revolution with the philosophical concept of an "event," signifying sudden, radical shifts and disruptions, is not a novel idea. Alain Badiou, for instance, views the relentless struggles of Mao's Revolution as "events" essential for progress toward the "real" (Weng 2015: 47–64). In Badiou's unique interpretation of Plato's *Republic*, he portrays Socrates as a post-structuralist Maoist, a contemporary philosopher who echoes Mao's teachings (Badiou 2012).

Many of Li's SM novellas incorporate both public and private memories, as well as collective and individual experiences of the Cultural Revolution. These stories reimagine these elements within sadomasochistic scenes set in a "futuristic" present. In particular, these narratives focus on subjects whose desires are historically rooted yet contemporarily relevant. These subjects continuously seek unadulterated, intense, physical pleasure in sadomasochistic "events." They aim for a transformative experience that goes beyond temporal or political constraints, as part of their ethical endeavor to gain complete mastery over themselves. This relentless pursuit of self-transformation embodies what Foucault calls the art of existence, or *technē tou biou*.

Conclusion

The Cultural Revolution was a grand social experiment in the quest for sociopolitical, cultural, and gender equality, spearheaded by young students. Although it aimed for lofty ideals, it came at a significant human cost, particularly for intellectuals and government functionaries. Over half a century later, those who lived through it continue to reflect. Their perspectives evolve in response to both domestic and global contexts.

Scholarly perspectives on the Cultural Revolution have undergone significant changes over the years. During the 1980s and 1990s, many scholars, influenced by their immediate experiences, primarily characterized the period as a catastrophic political disturbance that stifled individual freedom. More recently, however, a different vein of scholarship reassesses the outcomes and societal vacuum created by the Cultural Revolution, particularly as a precursor to the ideological shifts marked by Deng Xiaoping's Open and Reform policy in the early 1980s. What was once largely deemed a "colossal mistake" has now been reevaluated and is officially regarded as a "socialist development amid twists and turns"—a view increasingly shared by scholars who identify with positions beyond liberalism (Editorial Committee for *A Concise History of the Community Party of China* 2021; Gan 2011).

As a statist feminist and a member of the Communist Party, Li Yinhe adopts a more lenient view of China's post-1949 history. This stance diverges from that of her late husband, Wang Xiaobo, often seen as a luminary of liberal thought. Li incorporates her personal recollections and experiences of the Cultural Revolution into her sadomasochistic novellas. These works are further shaped by her engagement with Foucault's concept of the art of existence, wherein the subject undertakes ethical endeavors for aesthetic pleasure through deliberate choices and actions. Within the framework of her novellas, Li weaves in references to the Cultural Revolution, repurposing practices and rituals from the Maoist era into sadomasochistic scenarios for the explicit aim of intense physical gratification. Guided by their own agency, the subjects in her novellas achieve self-transformation through the pursuit of bodily pleasure.

In Li Yinhe's SM novellas, the subject engages with historical resources and its own historical identity to enact aesthetic and apolitical experiences. Li Yinhe asserts that sadomasochism should not bear any political significance; what unfolds in the private sphere should remain disconnected from external activities (Li 2009: 273–4). She privileges situational and spontaneous pleasure over the prescriptive concept of desire in guiding the subject's sadomasochistic engagements. Accordingly, she posits that it is during distinct "events," rather than through a history-anchored identity, that the subject undergoes formation and transformation. Despite this stance, history inevitably permeates her SM narratives through the lived memories and present experiences of the subject. However, within the framework of these SM activities, history is re-contextualized as part of the subject's ahistorical and apolitical pursuit of its own alterity. Thus, in Li Yinhe's SM narratives, the subject, while deeply rooted in its history, consistently seeks to transcend its past and identity through ethical and aesthetic labors of self-transformation, for its sole purpose of pleasure-seeking.

9

Foucault's Herculine Barbin

A Step in the Genealogy of Psychoanalysis

Laurie Laufer[1]
Université de Paris Cité

Translated by Meryl Altman

> *We demand that sex speak the truth ... and we demand that it tell us our truth.*
> (Michel Foucault 1990: 69; 1976: 93)[2]

"What is invention of the truth? What turn of events made it possible?" asks Michel Foucault, in Volume 1 of his 1970 lectures at the Collège de France (2011: 199; 2013: 207). From *La Volonté de savoir* (*The Will to Knowledge*) through *Les Aveux de la chair* (*Confessions of the Flesh*), Foucault was concerned with the phenomena that led to the articulation between power and truth. As Foucault scholar Arnold Davidson writes, "'We are our sexuality' or at least we have been told so over and over" (Davidson 2005: 9).[3] He continues: "In a sense, there is no doubt that this goes without saying; we would not be able to think of ourselves, of our most fundamental psychological identity, without thinking of our sexuality, of this often deep and secret layer of our desires that reveals the type of individual that we are" (Davidson 2005: 11). However, Foucault states, "psychoanalysts have never taken very seriously the problem of the production of theories of sexuality in Western society" (Foucault 2001a: 555; 1999: 118). When Foucault analyzes the historical appearance of the connection between sexuality, subjectivity, and the injunction to truth, he lays the responsibilty for this triad to the charge of psychoanalysis. In his view, psychoanalysis is heir to that *scientia sexualis* which searches for truth in the depths of sex, which speaks true sex and true identity.[4]

Foucault's genealogy of the practice of confession would confirm this articulation between psychoanalysis and *scientia sexualis*, binding truth and sexuality closely together. In 1976, in *La Volonté de savoir*, Michel Foucault shows how "the history of the deployment of sexuality, as it has evolved since the classical age, can serve as an archaeology of psychoanalysis" (Foucault 1990: 130; 1976: 172). Western civilization gave rise to a *scientia sexualis* which took the form of a specific procedure, the practice of confession. The foundation of this practice was laid by the Church, beginning in 1215 with the general requirement of annual confession by the Fourth Lateran Council. From the standpoint of genealogy, Foucault writes:

> Historically, there have been two great procedures for producing the truth of sex.
> On the one hand, the societies—and they are numerous: China, Japan, India, Rome, the Arabo-Moslem societies—which endowed themselves with an *ars erotica*. In the erotic art, truth is drawn from pleasure itself, understood as a practice and accumulated as experience; pleasure is not considered in relation to an absolute law of the permitted and the forbidden. nor by reference to a criterion of utility, but first and foremost in relation to itself.
> (Foucault 1990: 57; 1976: 76)

His analysis continues:

> [O]ur civilization possesses no *ars erotica*. In return, it is undoubtedly the only civilization to practice a *scientia sexualis*; or rather, the only civilization to have developed over the centuries procedures for telling the truth of sex which are geared to a form of knowledge-power strictly opposed to the art of initiations and the masterful secret: I have in mind the confession.
> (Foucault 1990: 58; 1976: 77–8)

Western man thus became a "confessing animal" (Foucault 1990: 59; 1976: 80). Religion passed the baton to science, as a "confessional science" (*science-aveu*) took shape (Foucault 1990: 64; 1976: 86). The "apparatus of sexuality" is thus located, through the historical deployment of a *scientia sexualis*, between Christian confessional practices and the scientificization of confession. Confession about sex began to be scientized as the Catholic monastic tradition spilled over into economic policy, the police and the law courts, psychiatric hospitals and psychoanalysts' consulting rooms.

So, as Judith Butler writes, "Foucault understands sexuality as saturated with power" (Butler 2006: 127). This saturation has the effect of concealing its own production and the conditions under which it emerges. Power—juridical, medical, social, psychological, psychoanalytic— marches on, masked with the face of truth, and this regime of veridiction gives rise to a unique way of thinking sex.

How then can we think about what is outside the norm, what escapes from this power, what falls outside this univocity? Analyzing these forms of power, Foucault writes in *La Volonté de savoir*:

> this form of power demanded constant, attentive, and curious presences for its exercise; ... it required an exchange of discourses, through questions that extorted admissions, and confidences that went beyond the questions that were asked.... The *medicalization of the sexually peculiar* was both the effect and the instrument of this.... The power which thus took charge of sexuality set about contacting bodies, caressing them with its eyes, intensifying areas, electrifying surfaces, dramatizing troubled moments.
>
> (Foucault 1990: 44; 1976: 60–1, emphasis added)

In *The Birth of the Clinic* (1963), Michel Foucault had already shown how the historical construction of modern medicine was connected to forms of power over the body. According to him, modern medicine was born with the imposition of the "medical gaze" (*regard médical*). "[T]he gaze that sees is a gaze that dominates" he wrote (Foucault 2003: 39; 1963: 38). The object of this gaze is already, according to his analysis, an object constituted on the basis of a norm. The patient is the "object of the gaze" and the doctor the "subject of the gaze"; the medical institution takes charge of socially legitimating the apparatus and the relation between the subject who looks and the object who is seen. As Foucault indicates, the point is not to know what power *is*, but to ask how it operates, what categories of subjects it deploys, according to what values, what interests, what strategies.

In his analyses of the emergence of the gaze and the confession in medicine and the "medicalization of the sexually peculiar"—a task taken up, according to him, by psychoanalysis—Foucault criticizes all the violence of the power apparatus that tries to establish the truth of a body or to characterize the body in truth. For him, psychoanalysis and phenomenology are both mechanisms of veridiction, which aim to dominate and control the body.

Herculine Barbin or the True Sex

Foucault's research on hermaphrodites and their connections to discourses of the "monstrous"[5] led him to problematize the nineteenth-century relation between veridiction, sex, and *scientia sexualis*. My project here is to reexamine Foucault's reading of the "journal of Herculine Barbin called Alexina B,"[6] to take a fresh look at the triad of truth/sexuality/subjectivity and to put the games of truth, sexuality, and confessional science into perspective.

The memoirs of Herculine Barbin were discovered by Ambroise Tardieu, a well-known medical examiner of the day. Tardieu, "a medical luminary if there ever was one" as Gabrielle Houbre reminds us,[7] was already famous for his widely-discussed book *Les Attentats aux moeurs* [Moral Indecencies] ([1857] 1995). In this book, a veritable descriptive guide to anatomy, Tardieu draws a bodily map of violence and sexual crime: for instance, he deduces the practice of fellatio, which at that time was strongly condemned, from the shape of a mouth. The doctor walks hand-in-hand with the judge. From the very beginning, sex is potentially the vector of crime: "In every case, the physical signs are excellent ways to conduct legal research" (Tardieu 1995: 398).

In 1872[8] Ambroise Tardieu published a scientific book entitled *Question médico-légale de l'identité dans ses rapports avec les vices de conformation des organes sexuels* [The medico-legal question of identity as it relates to the vices of conformation in sexual organs], which includes a manuscript discovered in 1868 in a Latin Quarter garret. Lying beside the manuscript was a body: the body of Abel Barbin, eighteen years old, who had just committed suicide. Abel had been born Adélaïde Herculine Barbin (called Alexina by her family and friends) and rebaptized at the age of twenty-one, after an administrative tribunal had declared her/him to be of masculine sex, on account of the "evident predominance of the masculine sex" from a physiological point of view (Chesnet [in Barbin 1980] 2014: 150). In 1868 this "young man," who had been born a woman in 1838, took his own life, leaving on the table, a letter addressed to his/her mother and also a manuscript entitled *Mes souvenirs*[9] [My memories], which recounts a solitary and miserable life.

The doctor sent by the civil status registry office to give the death certificate examined the corpse; he inspected the genital organs to see whether the subject was suffering from a disease which might have explained the act of suicide. In the course of this examination, Dr. Régnier discovered with astonishment "one of the most typical cases of masculine hermaphroditism" (E. Goujon [in Barbin 1980: 129] 2014: 152). Ambroise Tardieu felt able to write:

> The extraordinary case that remains for me to report indeed furnishes the most cruel and painful example of *the fatal consequences that can proceed from an error committed at the time of birth in the establishment of civil status*. We are about to see the victim of such an error, who, after spending twenty years in the clothing of a sex that was not his own, at the mercy of a passion that was unconscious of itself until the explosion of his senses finally alerted him to the

nature of it, *had his true sex recognized and at the same time became really aware of his physical disability*, whereupon, disgusted with his life, he put an end to it by committing suicide... To be sure, the appearances that are typical of the feminine sex were carried very far in his case, but both science and the law were nevertheless obliged to recognize the error and to recognize the true sex of this young man... I do not hesitate to publish [the memoir] almost in full, as I wish to keep the lesson that it contains from being lost. This is doubly precious, on the one hand from the standpoint of *the influence that the malformation of the sexual organs exercises upon the emotional faculties and upon psychological health, and on the other hand from the standpoint of the serious individual and social consequences that may be entailed by an erroneous declaration of the sex of a newborn child.*

(Tardieu [in Barbin 1980: 122–3] 2014: 145–6, emphasis added)

Or as Dr. Goujon also writes, "In fact, at this time [the age of puberty], inclinations and habits of their true sex are revealed in people who have been victims of an error" (Goujon [in Barbin 1980: 138–9] 2014: 159). Thus, it was in order to scientifically demonstrate the tragic effects of a mistake in sex assignment, and also to establish a causal link of "rational" and "scientific" truth between sexual belonging and sexual attraction, that Tardieu published *Mes souvenirs* by Herculine Barbin.

Herculine was raised in religious institutions, a girl among other girls. About her/ his gender trouble, she/ he writes: "What happened was not a revelation to me, but a further torment in my life" (Barbin 1980: 33, translation altered; 2014: 54). And, far from being a revelation that saved her from a "problem" (*mal*) of identity, the later veridiction caused her much more suffering than relief. And Foucault comments:

Alexina wrote her memoirs about that life once her new identity had been discovered and established. Her "true" and "definitive" identity. But it is clear she did not write them from the point of view of that sex which had at last been brought to light. It is not a man who is speaking, trying to recall his sensations and his life as they were at the time when he was not yet "himself." When Alexina composed her memoirs, she was not far from her suicide: for herself, she was still without a definite sex, but she was deprived of the delights she experienced in not having one, or in not entirely having the same sex as the girls among whom she lived and whom she loved and desired so much.

(Foucault [in Barbin 1980: xiii] 2001b: 939)

However, Alexina is not "without a definite sex" when she loves and she desires. Foucault seems to skim over the enunciatory modalities of Alexina's text a little too quickly. Even after her sex reassignment by the State, Alexina writes her memoirs using feminine grammatical gender. In fact, in the language that sustains her, in the body of her writing, Alexina loves as a woman and she loves women. "I was generally well-liked [*aimée*] by my teachers and my companions, and I returned their affection fully.... I was born [*née*] to love" (Barbin 1980: 27; 2014: 29). The underlining of *aimée* and *née*, where the final e indicates feminine gender, is Alexina's own.[10] This desire, these erotic impulses, are also what become suspect in the eyes of the doctor and the judge of that era. It is because as a woman she desires women that Alexina is assigned by the medical establishment to be a man. For Tardieu and the experts of his day, a woman who loves and desires a woman can only be a man.

Brought up as a woman, educated as a woman, "socially constructed as a woman," living in a community of women, she recounts the catastrophic effects that the "medical truth" of her indeterminate sex has upon her body and upon her life. Here sexual practices are reduced to the necessity that one have a true sex, and that sexual attraction correspond to membership in one sex or the other. Alexina is medically hermaphroditic, yet the conclusions of the medical experts' report affirm the "evident predominance of the masculine sex." Here is Dr. Chesnet: "We can now conclude and say: Alexina is a man, hermaphroditic, no doubt, but with an obvious predominance of masculine sexual characteristics" (Barbin 2010: 128; 2014: 150). A bit earlier, he had written:

> What shall we conclude from the above facts? Is Alexina a woman? She has a vulva, labia majora, and a feminine urethra, independent of a sort of imperforate penis, which might be a monstrously developed clitoris. She has a vagina. True, it is very short, very narrow; but after all, what is it if it is not a vagina? These are completely feminine attributes. Yes, but Alexina has never menstruated; the whole outer part of her body is that of a man, and my explorations did not enable me to find. a womb. *Her tastes, her inclinations draw her toward women.* ... We can now conclude and say: Alexina is a man, hermaphroditic, no doubt, but with an obvious predominance of masculine sexual characteristics."
> (Chesnet in Barbin 2010: 127–8; 2014: 150, emphasis added)

The true evidence/ witnesses of sex are thus her feelings of attraction toward women.

But what happens when Alexina has been brought back to "her true sex"? The change of name and sex in the civil status of Herculine Barbin, which could have made it possible for Abel to love her friend Sara with no more need to hide, no need for shame and anguish, instead became the tipping point toward suicide.

The "true sex" of Herculine, established by social and scientific discourse, her/his sexual identity brought back by her "veridiction," leads her/him to take her/his own life. Far from launching her/him toward a destiny under the sign of freedom and truth, the "true sex" of Herculine leads to suffering, to an impasse from which the only "true" way out will be death.

She/he writes:

> So, it was all over. According to my civil status, I was henceforth to belong to that half of the human race which is called the stronger sex. I, who had been raised until the age of twenty-one in religious houses, among shy female companions, was going to leave that whole delightful past far behind me, like Achilles, and enter the lists, armed with my weakness alone and my deep inexperience of men and things.
>
> (Barbin 2010: 103, translation altered 2010: 89; 2014: 126)

This "passage" into the masculine universe, marked by the use of masculine grammatical gender (before this point Alexina had accustomed her readers to a fluctuation between genders, or had emphasized the feminine), does not reconcile her to her "true sex," but in reality engenders only chagrin, isolation, and despair.

These descriptions of suffering are exactly what Tardieu goes to great lengths to censor, leaving just a few pages so as not to break the flow of this style of writing—a style which Foucault considers "a manner of living," a tone which is also a way of being-in-the-world: "that elegant, cultivated, allusive style, a bit grandiloquent and old-fashioned, which for boarding schools of the day was not only a style of writing but a way of life" (in Barbin 2010: xii, translation altered; 2001b: 938). Thus, Alexina writes:

> This incessant struggle of nature against reason exhausts me more and more each day, and drags me with great strides toward the tomb. . . .
>
> When that day comes a few doctors will make a little stir around the remains of my corpse; they will break down all its exhausted workings, plumb its depths for new knowledge, analyze all the mysterious agonies heaped upon a single human being. O princes of science, enlightened chemists, whose names resound throughout the world, analyze then, if you can, all the sorrows that have burned, devoured this heart down to its last fibers; all the scalding tears that have drowned it, squeezed it dry in their savage grasp!"
>
> (Barbin 2010: 103, translation altered; 2014: 126)

Alexina was quite correct to write that she/he would become an object of the gaze of science and the language of science, but not, as she/he thought, in order for the doctors to "analyze [. . .] all the sorrows that have burned, devoured this heart down to its last fibers." Instead, they would cut open, dissect, bring an expert gaze to bear upon the reality of a body, in an effort to attain "the ideal of an exhaustive description." This visibility was so greatly sought after that Felix Nadar, the photographer of the day, took a series of pictures of a hermaphrodite who could have been Herculine Barbin (see Le Mens and Nancy, 2009). This will to exactitude in description of the real rests on the assumption that, as Foucault writes, "all that is *visible* is *expressible*, and that it is *wholly visible* because it is *wholly expressible*" (Foucault 2003: 115; 1963: 116).

Abel's agony countervenes the idea (championed by the doctors) that it is necessary to "give back" the individual's true sex—liberating him from his false sex—which supposedly would *naturally* reconcile him with his true nature. According to Tardieu, Abel's despondency and moral disarray was not connected to the adjustment of his civil status (name and sex) in adulthood, but resulted rather from the mistaken certification of sex at birth. "The struggles and disturbances to which this unfortunate person was prey" are, according to Tardieu, only "the serious individual consequences that may be entailed by an erroneous declaration of the sex of a newborn child" (Barbin 2010: 123; 2014: 146).

Medicine puts right the wrong that has been done to the subject: Tardieu and his expert colleagues never think to question whether the act that "rectified" Herculine's sex was legitimate. As Georges Canguilhem writes:

> The hallmark of a false science is that it never has to face falsity; it does not need to renounce anything and never has to change its terminology. For a false science, pre-scientific states do not exist. Its discourse cannot accept contradiction. In short, false science has no history.
> (Canguilhem 1981: 22, translation altered; 2009: 46)

In his article, "Monstrosity and the Monstrous," he writes that, in a rationalized, and thus weakened, form, we "find the monstrous at the origin of . . . monstrosities" (Canguilhem 1969: 40; 2003: 225). The rational discourse of medical science aims to show how abnormal physical conformations are evidence of monstrous possibilities on the level of society. The monstrous bears in itself the seed of criminality. So, as Canguilhem also writes, "In the presence of a bird with three claws, should one be more aware that it has one too many, or that it has only one too many?" (Canguilhem 1969: 30; 2003: 222).

Foucault writes in his notes that

> the hermaphrodite is not a being who would simply have one sex too many, or would simultaneously have two different sexual organs, but rather a double being . . . sex is not so much a collection of organs intended to have a function,

but it is a "nature" in itself. One does not have a sex, one is a sex, as one is of a nature. [...] The opposition between the sexes which ensures the human race, only has to do with its role in reproduction among many other features, neither more nor less essential; it marks the existence of two "natures." And the hermaphrodite, to be a monster, need only combine in one form two individuals who were supposed to be separated: it is enough to mix in one unique individual the two "natures" that ordinarily distinguish men from women. The hermaphrodite is the improper mixture of these two natures.[11]

We can see, then, that in this context sexuality and sexual practices are the object and the stakes of a scientific discourse that determines the identity and the "nature" of a subject: everything proceeds as if the truth of a subject was reducible to his identity and his sexual "nature." According to Foucault, with the advent of sexuality and its discursive apparatus, the subject became a "psychological man." So, the question which the philosopher poses in his text introducing the edition of *Herculine Barbin dite Alexina B.* is, "Do we *truly* need a *true* sex?" (Foucault 2010: vii; 2001b: 935).

Does not truth operate in service of a categorization of the self which the subject himself interiorizes so as to be identified, recognized, by the gaze of the other? Sexuality has been one of the fields subjected to this regime of veridiction in order to constitute the identity and the personality of a subject; modern medicine enters this field of veridiction which lays claim to "the truth of sex."

Michel Foucault writes: "Indeed it was a very long time before the postulate that a hermaphrodite must have a sex—a single, a true sex—was formulated" (Foucault 2010: vii; 2001b: 935). In the Middle Ages, he explains, "it was the role of the father or the godfather (thus of those who 'named' the child) to determine at the time of baptism which sex was going to be retained" (Foucault 2010: vii; 2001b: 935). But then, beginning in the 18th century,

> Biological theories of sexuality ... led little by little to rejecting the idea of a mixture of the two sexes in a single body, and consequently to limiting the free choice of indeteminate individuals. Henceforth, everybody was to have one and only one sex. Everybody was to have his or her primary, profound, determined and determining sexual identity.
>
> (Foucault 2010: viii; 2001b: 935–6)

From a medical point of view it became, from then on, a question of deciphering which was the true sex that was hidden beneath appearances. Foucault comments:

> I am well aware that medicine in the nineteenth and twentieth centuries corrected many things in this reductive oversimplification. [...] Nonetheless, the

idea that one must indeed finally have a true sex is far from being completely dispelled. Whatever the opinion of biologists on this point, the idea that there exist complex, obscure, and essential relationships between sex and truth is to be found—at least in a diffused state—not only in psychiatry, psychoanalysis, and psychology, but also in current opinion. We are certainly more tolerant in regard to practices that break the law. But we continue to think that some of these are insulting to 'the truth': we may be prepared to admit that … [they] do not seriously impair the established order; but we are ready enough to believe that there is something like an "error" involved in what they do. An 'error' as understood in the most traditionally philosophical sense: a manner of acting that is not accurate to reality. Sexual irregularity is seen as belonging more or less to the realm of chimeras.

(Foucault 2010: ix; 2001b: 935)[2]

It is thus a question of "telling the truth" about sexuality and, as Foucault writes, "sexuality, much more than an element of the individual which could be discarded as external to himself, is constitutive of the bond that requires people to be tied to their identity under the form of subjectivity" (Foucault 1999: 129–30; 2001a: 528).

What Foucault criticizes in medicine—and in psychoanalysis which, according to him, takes up the same task—is all the violence of the apparatuses of power that work to establish the truth of a body, or to characterize a body in truth. For him, the body exceeds and destabilizes the truth by way of pleasure, which cannot be reduced to any fixed resolution or category. *Bodies and pleasures*, as he says in *La Volonté de savoir*, should remind us of the precarious, contestable, potentially violent character of any "true" characterization of the body, by emphasizing what exceeds and destabilizes any such "truth." *Bodies and pleasures* must be preserved, defended, affirmed, against any claim to definitively determine what is going on with the body. Foucault writes:

> And then, we also admit that it is in the area of sex that we must search for the most secret and profound truths about the individual, that it is there that we can best discover what he is and what determines him. And if it was believed for centuries that it was necessary to hide sexual matters because they were shameful, we now know that it is sex itself which hides the most secret parts of the individual: the structure of his fantasies, the roots of his ego, the forms of his relationship to reality. …
>
> It is at the junction of these two ideas—that we must not deceive ourselves concerning our sex, and that our sex harbors what is most true in ourselves—that psychoanalysis has rooted its cultural vigor. It promises us at the same time

our sex, our true sex, and that whole truth about ourselves which secretly keeps vigil in it.

(Foucault 2010: x–xi; 2001b: 937)

The analysis of Herculine's memoir he proposes is marked throughout by an opposition between sexual *difference*, the badge of subjective identity, to which Herculine is assigned, and bodily *differences*, which arise from experience and from its practices.

It is as if the medical, juridical, and normative definition of *the body* was becoming the moral law for a multiplicity of *bodies* older than itself, a multiplicity that makes it impossible to regard the various versions of modern individuality as evident, satisfying, or definitive. And Foucault insists upon the gap that exists between, on one hand, the forms of social or discursive regulation of the body, and on the other hand the disorder that resists them: a reminder not to lose track of the harm that is done when the many are reduced to the one. This Foucauldian refusal to identify an individual by and by means of his/her sexuality, has been expressed by Jean Allouch as a maxim: "There is no truth of sex" (Allouch 2003: 74).

Variation, Truth, "Varité"

Foucault's criticisms of psychoanalysis notwithstanding, Freud, and then Lacan, never tired of demonstrating that the human experience of sexuality includes multiple differences and multiple types, a wide range of sexual behaviors and practices; in short, complex and subtle differentiations make up a sexual diversity that has been subjected, at different times and places, to a variety of norms, which themselves may be more or less insistent and more or less binding. Freud showed us that norms are arbitrary and conventional, that they arise from a fiction and thus from the social imaginary. Lacan picks up this idea in a 1973 interview on France Culture (published in the journal *Le Coq Héron* in 1974). Lacan hit upon this formula: "There are social norms in the absence of any sexual norm, that's what Freud is saying."

As Foucault himself put it, "we must be fair to Freud": even though psychoanalysis, as its discourse developed, drew up boundaries for sexuality that expressed the prevailing norms of the day, we should nonetheless give psychoanalysis credit for having theorized polymorphous perversity, infantile sexuality, and the unconscious which knows nothing of sexual difference, and for developing the concept of the drive, whose object is variable and contingent. This variability, this variety of possible objects, makes any idea of truth a construction, built upon a fiction.

Lacan, differently from Freud to be sure, brings about a relativization of truth. Lacan states that truth has the structure of a fiction: consequently it belongs to the realm of fabrication, and thus ultimately has to do with semblance (*le semblant*). Language as such, the Symbolic, has a fictional structure. Lacan has noted the impact of this variability, by inventing a neologism, *varité*.[13] Taking note of "the variability of Lacan's statements about love," Jean Allouch writes in his book *L'amour Lacan*:

> It took Lacan a long time to recognize the impact of this variability. He then did so by inventing a neologism that subverted his own concept of truth, already a quite muted version of truth (understood as 'half-said'). Thus we see, with 'varité', that variability strikes not only the truth of certain statements, but truth itself.
> (Allouch 2010: 50)

As Lacan says, "One would have to see, to open oneself up to the dimension of truth as variable *varité*, namely, of what, in condensing like that these two words, I would call the *varité*, with the little é swallowed, the varité"[14] (No date: 116, translation slightly altered).

There is something irreducible about the subject in psychoanalysis: it is the subject that does not enter into any normative discourse. The subject with which analytic practice has to do confronts a reality that exceeds it, a reality that exceeds the order of the normative and the biological. The unconscious, the drive, breaks with the "normal" and "natural" course of things. Psychoanalysis proliferates upon the excess, upon the irreducible remainders of the norm. What kind of psychoanalysis thinks by means of categories? "Barricaded" within these lines of demarcation, what would psychoanalysis be? At the May 5, 1965 session of his seminar, *Crucial problems for psychoanalysis*, Lacan gave this analysis:

> A subject is a psychoanalyst, not as a scholar barricaded behind categories in the midst of which he tries his hardest to construct the drawers into which he will be able to put the symptoms that he registers in his patient, psychotic, neurotic or other, but in so far that he enters into the signifying operation.
> (No date: 233–4)

The signifier cannot determine any fixed, absolute truth: the signifier is fundamentally unstable, unable to set in place any definitive meaning. Nor can it determine any fixed truth of sex.

Analytic practice strongly emphasizes the idea that any construction of identity, any truth of sex, any truth of identity can become a problem for the subject. The young white man, active, cisgender and heterosexual, the heterosexual white woman, passive and maternal—that is to say, the putative representatives of universal health—are deconstructed by, and on, the analytic couch. The normative discourses that may have duped them melt away; these identities get lost among many other possible costumes and "props," as Lacan puts it. He indicates in his seminar on the theory of the ego that "the ego is the sum of the subject's identifications, with all that this can include of the radically contingent. If you permit me to give an image, the ego is like the superposition of different coats borrowed from what I would call the bric-à-brac of its props department" (Lacan 1988: 155; 1978: 187). And if, as Lacan puts it, "the sexed being is authorized by himself and a few others" (197314), it is in light of this contingent process of bricolage.

Contingency, bricolage of identifications: this, then, is the Ego, no more than a collection of fictional truth-effects. For this reason Foucault prefers to speak, not of truth, but of the creation and invention of the self, or the aesthetics of existence. As Foucault says: "What we must work on, it seems to me, is not so much to liberate our desires but to make ourselves infinitely more susceptible to pleasure [plaisirs]" (Foucault 1997c: 137; 2001c: 165). Multiplicity, variation, variability, possibilities, experiences, events: these are at the heart of Foucauldian epistemology, which thereby overturns the classic schemas of identity, of fixed and defined categories, along with the classic notion of transcendence.[15]

For Foucault, the concept of desire evokes the idea of a psychological unconscious; the category of "sex," the bearer of the subject's identity as her or his truth, is, according to him, produced by a juridico-medical power. By contrast, what replaces them -- his notion of pleasure -- is de-psychologized, because it does not refer back to any meaning or any explanation. That is how he can ask himself, by way of his reading of Herculine Barbin, "Do we truly need a true sex?" Why not listen, instead, to the ambivalence, the ambiguity, the fluidity of pleasures?

This way of envisioning the multiplicities and the field of possibilities runs counter to any attempt to categorize either identity or sexual practice. To think flux and multiplicity, to think the genealogy of the event, to think displacement and series: if we follow Foucault's method, these must now be the epistemological stakes. Twenty years before Foucault, Lacan had opened the question of variablity, by accentuating Freud's propositions on sexual variation. Today, in light of Foucault's genealogy of psychoanalysis, it is possible to launch anew an epistemology of the subject and of sexuality within the field of psychoanalysis. As Jean Allouch wrote in 1998: 179, "psychoanalysis will be Foucauldian or it will cease to exist."

10

The Foucault Effect

Queer Theory and Its Discontents

David Greven
University of South Carolina

In most early queer theory analyses, Foucault is the gentleman in the dustcoat, waiting, but not for long. Before Foucault's emergence on the sexual scene, gay men found inspiration and sustenance in the work of artists like Byron, Whitman, Melville, Wilde, Proust, Gide, and James Baldwin; Mae West, Marlene Dietrich, Bette Davis, Judy Garland, Eartha Kitt; Michelangelo, Leonardo da Vinci, Caravaggio, and so forth. The list may be familiar, but it is also a tradition of empathy, sympathy, hero-worship, and personal connections. Foucault is a very different kind of gay icon. With his bald dome, glasses, and sustained stoicism, he signals intellectualism, authority, and humorlessness. Whitman sang of the body; Foucault made the body the site of discipline and punishment. What is most extraordinary about Foucault's legacy is that, for a theorist who spoke so influentially of the pernicious effects of the "author-function"—for Foucault the end of the proliferation of meanings rather than their generative site—he has spawned generations of critics who enable and enshrine his own. Modeling themselves on his implacable affect and on his intellectual preoccupations—surveillance, the transformation of sexual practices into discourse, the infinite methods of social control, "bio-politics"—many Foucauldian queer theorists write in dutiful emulation of the master, co-opting his resolute rhetoric. There is often a dystopian view: the grim state of the world justifies our fealty to this legacy.

No critics are more consistently, self-proclaimedly Foucauldian than D. A. Miller and David Halperin, who will be my focus here. Critics of considerable acumen, both hold a rarefied position within the annals of queer theory and demand attention. Miller and Halperin have been shaping forces in the development of queer theory and also in the construction *of* the queer theorist in the guise of the gay male academic. In sum, the result of their work and their early critical positions has been the composite portrait of aca-gays as staunchly political creatures ruthlessly interrogating academic practice and the social order for any sign of investment in the idea of sexual subjectivity. My effort in this chapter is to track the emergence of a "Foucauldian" gay male academic persona and to demonstrate its limitations.

Queer theory emerged from the wreckage of the Reagan-AIDS 1980s, which is to say, the smoldering remains of 1970s Gay Liberation. The timing is significant. During the Reagan and AIDS era, queer people, among others, were a terrifying disease that was a death sentence. As the Reagan administration maintained silence and inaction, the disease gathered in force, rapidly becoming the global pandemic it remains to this day. Silence about the disease and its devastations reigned (hence the famous campaign, "Silence=Death"). But where it did not, there was rhetorical thunder: screeds from politicians against the homosexual "lifestyle" that frequently called for the banishment of gays to quarantined zones reminiscent of leper colonies; cruel invectives ("AIDS is God's way of weeding his garden," and so forth) spouted by fundamentalist religious leaders. The atmosphere was inexpressibly grim.

Only with the mid-1990s emergence of protease inhibitors, which allowed AIDS to become a manageable chronic disease, did homophobia sufficiently loosen its grasp on queer communities that new identities, as well as lifespans, could emerge. Since the mid-nineties, queer life has experienced not only a remarkable resurgence but also, and more importantly, a series of profoundly significant transformations. With the threat of AIDS diminished, though never conquered, queers have achieved a public visibility and acceptance unprecedented in the United States. In recent years, we have seen the legalization of same-sex marriage by the United States Supreme Court in 2015 (Obergefell v. Hodges) and The Respect for Marriage Act, a federal law signed by President Joe Biden in 2022, requiring all states to recognize same-sex marriages performed in other states, even as homophobic and transphobic energies have also surged.

The status of LGBTQ+ rights in the twenty-first century indicate momentous progress and repeated failure; legal victories for gay and trans rights are repealed while others are granted or restored, and opposition to trans rights continues to mobilize the intolerant and worse. Medical evidence for the genetic causes of homosexuality gives joyful reassurance to some while eliciting a fervent enthusiasm that a cure for the dread persuasion will be found. The rise in suicide rates of young gay teens sparked a movement, designed by sex-advice columnist Dan Savage, to reach out to this often bullied, harassed, and generally persecuted population through videos that counsel "It Gets Better." Yet homophobia has hardly abated; what child does not dread having the word "Fag" or "Dyke" hurled at them in the schoolyard? Homophobic and anti-trans violence has occurred not only in individual incidents but in mass shootings, such as the massacres at Pulse, a gay nightclub in Orlando, Florida, in 2016 and at Club Q, an LGBTQ nightclub in Colorado Springs, Colorado, in 2022.

The situation, for all the gains queers have made, remains incoherent and troubling, if indubitably more hopeful. Perhaps the most encouraging development is that *gay* itself has become so denatured a term. With the rise of new visibility for an astonishing array of sexualities—as gay or lesbian has transformed into "queer," and as the queer movement has enlarged to include the fight for trans rights as well, and as normative heterosexuality's own definitions have enlarged in response—we have moved ever more into a new era of sexual openness, in which the old, two-sexuality system of hetero- and homo- seems to be giving way to a much more expansive set of gendered and sexual possibilities.

I began this chapter with an evocation of the AIDS crisis of the 1980s because I believe it is important to establish the atmosphere of terror and sorrow from which queer theory emerged. We must remember the pain, loss, and sheer bewilderment of that era. I write from a position of gratitude toward the theorists who have shaped the field. In solidarity with my queer brethren past and present, let me state that I do not want this chapter to be used for anti-queer theory purposes. My effort here is not to condemn or to demean queer theory applications of Foucauldian thought, or Foucault's own work, whose brilliance and incisiveness hardly need testimonials. The last enterprise I wish to undertake is the "attack queer" diatribe of gay neo-cons such as Camille Paglia and Andrew Sullivan. What I do want to argue, however, is that the widespread adoption, by both queer theory and those who have been influenced by it, of a certain Amercian reading of Foucault has created an often misleading critical and theoretical straitjacket. The trajectory of this chapter is as follows. I begin with an overview of queer theory's Foucauldian roots and its investment in a certain reading of this theorist. I then turn to a discussion of Miller and Halperin as critics whose positions emblematize this approach.

Foucault's Pendulum: Queer Theory and Homosexuality's Histories

For quite some time, the identity of American queer theory has remained fixed—solidified as a Foucauldian orthodoxy with clear and consistent positions and motives. Works such as D. A. Miller's *The Novel and the Police* (1988), Jeffrey Weeks's *Sex, Politics, and Society: The Regulation of Sexuality Since 1800* (1981), David M. Halperin's *One Hundred Years of Homosexuality: and Other Essays on Greek Love* (1990), and Michael Warner's *The Trouble with Normal* (1999) remain defining titles.

The chief intersection among these works is the view of sexuality as a recent invention, one that emerged from the taxonomical zeal and efforts of the massive "juridico-medico" movements of the latter half of the nineteenth-century. In *The History of Sexuality*, Volume 1, Foucault revolutionized sexual history. In 1870, Foucault argued, homosexuality emerged as a psychological, psychiatric, and medical category, "a certain way of inverting the masculine and feminine in oneself. Homosexuality appeared as one of the forms of sexuality when it was transposed from the practice of sodomy onto a kind of interior androgyny, a hermaphrodism of the soul. The sodomite had been a temporary aberration; the homosexual was now a species." This new entity was a person whose sexual acts were now tied to subjectivity. This homosexual replaced the earlier pariah the "sodomite" (Foucault 1990: 43).

The terms that decisively shape our lived identities—most prominently, homosexuality and heterosexuality—emerged from the late-Victorian era. Foucault's argument that modern sexuality sprang from the introduction of late nineteenth-century taxonomies of sexual identity proved pervasively influential. Not very gradually, these innovative paradigms flamed into new truths that spread throughout academe. The writings and identificatory celebrations of only a few years earlier were consumed by this new Foucault-inflected approach. There were no homosexuals in history; there was no homosexual *history* save for the one that could be shaved off from the past century and a half. Expressions of same-sex desire found from classical antiquity to the present could never be interpreted as exhibitions or indications of an orientation. No desires, no sensibility, and certainly no sexuality, but only same-sex practices—only sexual *acts*. Social actors lived their lives as extras in an endless drama of sexual repetition, citing performances only the imitations of which preserved their incessant, mechanized life. As Graham Robb observes, while Foucault's influential social constructionist views "allowed sexuality to be studied in the light of history and sociology," they also "popularized the view that queer people have no real heritage before the 1870s" (Robb 2003: 11).

In the course of queer theory's development, indelible insights have been offered—Eve Kosofsky Sedgwick's theories of homosociality and the Girardian concept of triangulated desire; Judith Butler's theory of gendered identity as a performance; D. A. Miller's concept of homosexuality as the "open secret," further developed by Sedgwick; David Halperin's reminder that ancient Greco-Roman sexualities were not our own; Jeffrey Weeks's thorough analysis of the social construction of homosexuality.

Yet with these insights have come a set of presumptions hardening into accepted fact and, perhaps more pressingly, a consistent tone. This tone—ominous, machine-tooled, bleak—has so resolutely shaped our understanding of sexual life from early times to the present that it seems doubtful that anything short of an intellectual revolution will dispel it. Even Sedgwick began to weary of this ominous atmosphere, lamenting the "paranoia" rife within queer theory and urging "reparative" readings of literary texts. The received Foucauldian image of sex throughout the ages came to resemble the postapocalyptic landscapes of *The Matrix* films, where massive insect-like machines drain human matter of its vitality.

Any reader who has been keeping up with developments in queer theory over the decades knows that numerous emendations to this orthodoxy have been offered. Halperin has offered a series of self-revisionary essays in which he has qualified and redefined his previous positions. This self-revisionary reframing of his earlier positions begins, to my understanding, with his 2003 "Introduction: Among Men—History, Sexuality, and the Return of Affect," in *Love, Sex, Intimacy, and Friendship Between Men*. It continues with his book *How To Be Gay*.

One might reasonably ask why we should return to earlier interpretations of the Foucauldian view of sexual history, as I am asking us to do here, when, clearly, these views have been modified by the early practitioners themselves. One of the main reasons we should reconsider the history of Foucauldian queer theory is its enduring influence. Ironically, this influence is felt less, perhaps, in queer theory today than in the *wider* realms of critical practice and even mainstream discourse. Specifically in terms of the history of homosexuality, Foucauldian queer theory has become accepted popular dogma. The other main reason, related to the first, is that Foucauldian queer theory has profoundly shaped—by thoroughly revising—our understandings of homosexual/queer subjectivity, or, more specifically, this subjectivity in an academic context. (Even the archetype of the queer male, academic male, is modeled after a mythic Foucault: bespectacled, shaven-headed, humorless.)

A complex series of revulsions against previous modes of gay life informed the queer movement that began in the 1980s. Knowingly or not, the formation of queer theory paradigms intersected at key points with Reaganite rhetoric in the first AIDS decade. If the Gay Liberation of the 1970s seemed grotesquely florid, irredeemably irresponsible, and sadly unaware of its impending demise to many commentators on the right, American Foucauldian queer theory also cast the gay 1970s in a pejorative light. Both directly and indirectly, it framed the intellectual efforts of Gay Liberation as naive and endlessly correctable. Where the right named the bathhouses, discos, leather bars, and brazen promiscuity of the 1970s as the causes for AIDS, American Foucauldianism cast 1970s attempts to claim historical figures as gay and/or as gay icons, to write accounts of homosexuals in history, or to draw lines of solidarity across historical periods, as simplistic, misguided, and factually, scientifically, discursively, wrong. Unlike those earlier efforts, queer theory would lead with its theoretical sophistication and innumerable levels of qualification and complexity, a gay science for a queer future.

What I am referring to is the anti-social thesis that emerged within queer theory writings of this era. Leo Bersani's *Homos* preceded Lee Edelman's *No Future: Queer Theory and the Death Drive*. Bersani anticipates Edelman's argument in *No Future* in Bersani's affirmation of Jean Genet's positions in *Funeral Rites*. In Genet, Bersani writes in chapter four, "The Gay Outlaw," of *Homos*, "homosexuality is enlisted as the prototype of relations that break with humanity, that elevate infecundity, waste, and sameness to requirements for the production of pleasure." While conceding this as a "noxious" view of homosexuality, Bersani makes a case for Genet's "rejection of relationality," writing that "without such a rejection, social revolt is doomed to repeat the oppressive conditions that provoked the revolt." Bersani, channeling Genet, frames homosexuality as achieving its most politically efficacious form when it embraces its essential wastefulness and refuses normative efforts to frame homosexuality as progressive (Bersani 1995: 172).

Of course there were dissenters, and often these dissenters, while making some admirable points, positioned themselves against the new orthodoxy in ways that gave it more credence. Substituting scorn and invective for carefully argued theory, anti-queer theory critics often perpetuated the sense that, before queer theory, homosexual intellectualism relied on passions and pleading. Yet it is also true that these efforts to challenge queer theory, which indeed led to inflexible positions themselves, were uniformly classified as not only simplistic but also inherently conservative, capitulations to the normative social order. In other words, it became unimaginable that a really engaged, leftist queer thought that was *not* allied to a presumed Foucauldian orthodoxy was possible. And with this view came related ones; in the academic perception of queer theory, allegiance to Foucault was taken as a given, with myriad implications for how queer theory insights were deployed through intellectual cross-fertilization and through the widespread application of Foucauldian thought in numerous disciplines. And here is the clearest point where these ideas have become injurious to histories of sexuality, homosexual and otherwise: they have facilitated a broad and consistent desire to ignore, obfuscate, and diminish the importance of same-sex love.

Sex Versus Love

Indicative of the self-revisionary project that he has undertaken since the 2000s, Halperin offers a compendium of information about the shifting cultural understandings of gay culture from the postwar era to the present in *How To Be Gay*. Halperin offers his own evolving stances to gay culture as an index to these shifts. Recalling his views when an out young gay man in 1970s San Francisco, Halperin reports that he felt alienated from tribal experiences such as gay male-dominated screenings of female-centered Hollywood films such as *The Women* (George Cukor, 1939) at the Castro movie theater. These events left him feeling "like I had nothing in common with gay men. At least, nothing in common with *those* gay men." The young Halperin joined a new, post-Stonewall generation of men who were masculine, who had discovered that "it was possible to be gay without being effeminate," and who defined themselves specifically by "rejecting gay culture itself" and the sad, loud, effeminate old queens associated with it (Halperin 2012: 40–1).

Certainly, no one could accuse Halperin, Miller, and others of softness and frivolity. A hard, precise, unrelentingly logical rhetoric emerged, one that consistently presented sexual matters as inextricable from the interlocking gears of the social order. The sexual was treated as the chief means whereby power constricts, shapes, mobilizes, and possesses human bodies. Be it ancient Greece or Victorian America, sex is a device for the control of human beings. In the works of prominent theorists such as Halperin, Warner, Bersani, and Edelman, the erotic was reframed as an icy, precisely structured performance of a social self.

One of queer theory's first strikes against the 1970s attempts to draw inspiration from a long history of homosexual desire and love was a massive re-reading of ancient Greco-Roman homosexuality. The chief object of scorn was the idea of *love* between members of the same sex—a love that shaped personhood, a desire that informed the self. Disabusing anyone of their romantic notions of this era, queer theorists spent no time celebrating the loves of Achilles and Patroclus, Nisus and Euryalus, or Sappho; the focus was on the ways in which "free, adult" male "citizens" used sex as a means of establishing their power over others. Stripped of any mythological and affectional glamour, ancient sex became emblematic of the inescapable and all-pervasive normalizing efforts of the social order to organize bodies through the fused ideologies of eros and the self. No passion, no tenderness, and no personal expressions of feeling or desire, not even lust, inhered in ancient sexual arrangements; rather, its actors performed ritualized versions of dominance and submission in an atmosphere of Kubrickian impersonality.

Qualifying and in some cases reversing his earlier positions, especially in *Saint Foucault,* Halperin in *How to Do the History of Homosexuality* today locates friendship and male love as possible sites of same-sex (male) desire in history, along with, as George E. Haggerty parses, the categories of "effeminacy; pederasty or active sodomy; passivity or inversion; and the twentieth century portmanteau concept of homosexuality" (Haggerty 2003: 76). Halperin writes that nothing Foucault says about the "historical and political specificity of 'sexuality'.... prohibits us from inquiring into the connections that pre-modern people may have made between specific sexual acts and the particular ethos, or sexual style, or sexual subjectivity, of those who performed them." This declaration may come as a surprise to those who read Halperin's earlier work, but it is ample evidence that a new understanding of how we ought to "do the history of homosexuality" needs to be found. As Halperin observes, John J. Winkler was already advancing this argument in the late 1980s, less in opposition to Foucault than to "dogmatic misreadings of Foucault" (Halperin 2002: 32).

In his 1990 book *The Constraints of Desire,* Winkler examined a figure that was highly promising for the consideration of links between same-sex sexual acts as well as desire and subjectivity in the ancient world. The *kinaidos*—a male whose desire was the conventionally feminine one to be sexually penetrated by other men—was a "scare-image" that represented a phobic construction of a sexually deviant as well as gender-deviant male. Winkler's thesis was that the *kinaidos* was a category for a kind of person as well as for sexual acts. As Halperin parses Winkler, the figure of the *kinaidos* "arose in the context of a belief system in which, first of all, the two genders are conceived as opposite ends of a much-travelled continuum, and, second, masculinity is thought to be a difficult accomplishment" (Halperin 2002: 33). The *kinaidos* forfeits not only his claim to a normative masculinity but his obligation to struggle towards the embodiment of it.

Halperin ultimately places more emphasis on what distinguishes the *kinaidos* from the modern homosexual. He makes some points that are of great importance for the present essay, so I will quote at length:

> One significant difference between the *kinaidos* and the "homosexual" is that the *kinaidos* was defined more in terms of gender than in terms of desire. For whether he was imagined in universalizing or minoritizing terms, the *kinaidos* in any case offended principally against the order of masculinity, not against the order of heterosexuality. As such, the *kinaidos* does not represent a salient example of deviant sexual subjectivity. Although he was distinguished from normal men in part by the pleasure he took in being sexually penetrated, his peculiar taste was not sufficient, in and of itself, to individuate him as a sexual subject. Rather, it was a generic sign of femininity.... To be "womanly"... is of course a sexual as well as a gendered trait, and "gender deviance" should not be conceptualized as hermetically sealed off from matters of desire. Nonetheless, the *kinaidos*'s desire did not distinguish him as the bearer of a unique or distinct sexuality as such. Neither did his lust for bodily pleasure...such lust was thought common to all men. Nor was there anything peculiar about the *kinaidos*'s sexual object-choice:... [as long as the male was the penetrator], it was quite possible in the ancient Mediterranean world for a male to desire and pursue sexual contact with other males without impugning in the slightest his own masculinity or normative identity as a man.... Unlike the modern homosexual, then, the *kinaidos* was not defined principally by his "sexuality." Even without a sexuality of his own, however, the *kinaidos*'s betrayal of his masculine gender identity was so spectacular as to brand him a deviant type of person and to inscribe his own deviant identity on his face and body. To put it very schematically, the *kinaidos* represents an instance of deviant sexual morphology without deviant sexual subjectivity.
>
> (Halperin 2002; 37–8)

In other words, suggestive and provocative though the figure of the *kinaidos* is for a new understanding of the presence of a pre-taxonomical queer subjectivity, ultimately the figure cannot advance our understanding of sexual identities that fuse acts, desires, and feelings. Customarily exact and comprehensive, Halperin errs, in my view, in relegating gender deviance to irrelevancy. One can make the case that figures like the *kinaidos* render problematic, not merely gendered identity and sexuality-based identity, but also the possibility that we can draw a bright line between them.

As George Haggerty argues, "by insisting on the same classical model of male relations that he articulated throughout *One Hundred Years of Homosexuality*, relations based on hierarchy and status, Halperin reifies male-male relations and makes it impossible for men who see themselves as equal to express their love for one another" (Haggerty 2003: 74). Halperin's approach has had the effect of installing an idiosyncratic view of eros and gender in the classical world as the fixed, unchanging model of all pre-terminological same-sex desire, which obviously has implications for female–female desire as well.

Perhaps the chief problem with this approach is, surprisingly enough, its transhistorical practice. Given the way the debates over sexual acts and identities have been conducted, the *kinaidos* can easily come to seem as relevant to antebellum American sexual politics as the figure of the onanist, or masturbator, that target of so much Victorian health reform-rhetoric. In other words, so profoundly powerful has been the view that no sexual identities were tied to acts before terminologies soldered them together that all discussions of any historical moment and its sexual actors have come to seem indistinguishable.

The line of argument that most readily emerges from this approach is one like this: If the *kinaidos* was not, in the end, a type of sexual identity like the homosexual, then the Victorian onanist or the sodomite were not either. It is deeply ironic that Foucault, who argued for the *specificity* of each historical era's construction of sexual discourse, has been so crucial to a broad, homogenizing view of sex in history as radically distinct from its modern terminological character. This is a point that the later Halperin makes, but the legacies of the his earlier approach inform his new sensibility to the degree that it comes to seem a re-entrenchment, rather than a revision. Channeling Halperin's early Foucauldian stances, the nineteenth-century Americanist Christopher Looby makes a pronouncement that audibly evinces Halperin's continuing influence:

> Sexuality as such (featuring sexually identified persons) may have been emerging from the looser milieu of "sensual tendencies" in Great Britain in the eighteenth century but this emergence happened only much later, in the late nineteenth-century, in America. Until then, there was no "sexuality" in the United States; there were bodies, those bodies had pleasures, and those pleasures could be fairly described as erotic, or sensual—or aesthetic.
>
> (Looby 2011; 69–70)

This is not to suggest that simplistic and ahistorical celebrations of homo-classicism could be maintained. It is to suggest that Foucauldian queer theory's tracing of how homosexuality assumed its contemporary meaning ironically became a campaign to determine what homosexuality *should* mean.

These foundational theoretical efforts adamantly stripped bare of their emotional textures all episodes of homo-desire throughout the Western tradition even as they demanded social recognition and a sanctioned place for present day same-sex relationships. The famous friendships, with their erotic and emotional intensities, and other kinds of male relationships in the classical world underwent a radical denaturing. At the same time, AIDS-era and post-AIDS-era friendships and loving relations, polyamorous ones in particular, and even more so encounters facilitated by and emblematic of cruising took on ever-greater, utopian significance. As the argument that homosexuality was a social invention, and a pernicious one at that, gathered definition and force, the loving relationships, however transitory, spontaneously born of the cruising encounter and just as quickly filed away in the archives of the cruising memory palace, amongst contemporary queers became extolled and enshrined, as well as the fierce, intransigent, identity-dissolving sex. ACT-UP, the most well-known organization to demand for an end to the AIDS crisis and for equal rights for gays, embodied the image of gay men as comrades in arms, as passionate friends as well as lovers. But more and more, this image of loving brotherhood ceded to something else—an equally passionately upheld but now quite distinct focus, promoted by protest movements like "Gay Panic" of the mid-1990s, on the freedom to pursue sexual experiences as randomly and anonymously as one wished. This was a spirited return to the hedonism of the 1970s, but, unlike its 1970s form, this new sexual utopianism emphasized the idea of sex as social intransigence and political critique, eschewing both emotional ties and a sense of sexuality—as opposed to sex—as liberation.

The sex that this queer theory championed was a sex freed from the self and from the social—identity, ideologies of selfhood, especially the idea that sex was an expression of one's personhood or feelings for someone else. This was a depersonalized sex squarely centered in the body, getting away from what sex had been forced to mean in pietistic liberal fantasies. Foucault's call to go back to bodies and pleasure became code for a different message: decouple sex from love. Foucauldian critics praised each other for not allowing "sex to degenerate into love," as Halperin extolled Paul Morrison's queer theory text *The Explanation for Everything* (2002) in a blurb for the book. Sex, that prime site of social control, emerged as the endless frontier of personal liberation, even as personhood and liberty were being exhaustively evacuated of positive or presumptive value.

The Novel Policed

The widespread influence of these Foucauldian paradigms—and again, I emphasize "Foucauldian" rather than saying they emanate from Foucault—that flourished in the 1980s finds its fullest expression in D. A. Miller's seminal 1988 study *The Novel and the Police*. *The Novel and the Police*, writes Miller, "centers not on the police, in the modern institutional shape they acquire in Western liberal culture during the nineteenth century, but on the ramification within the same culture of less visible, less visibly violent modes of 'social control.'" Arguing that "discipline provides the novel with its essential "content," Miller depicts authorial/narrative empathy or even concern as a masking device for the novel's real purpose, the dissemination of societal "knowledge" (*savoir*) (Miller 1988, viii).

Drawing on Flaubert's aphorism that the author should be like God, everywhere present but nowhere visible, Miller opines thusly about George Eliot's *Middlemarch* (1871–2), widely considered the definitive nineteenth-century novel:

> Power, of course, might seem precisely what the convention of omniscient narration foregoes. Omniscient narration may typically know all, but it can hardly *do* all. "Poor Doreathea," "poor Lydgate," "poor Rosamond," the narrator of *Middlemarch* frequently exclaims, and the lament is credible only in an arrangement that keeps the function of narration separate from the causalities operating in the narrative. The knowledge commanded in omniscient narration is thus opposed to the power that inheres in the circumstances of the novelistic world. Yet by now the gesture of disowning power should seem to define the basic move of a familiar power play, in which the name of power is given over to one agency in order that the function of power may be less visibly retained by another. Impotent to intervene in the "facts," the narration nevertheless controls the discursive framework in which they are perceived as such.
>
> (Miller 1988: 24–5)

For Miller, the narrator—which Miller genders as a "he"—projects powerlessness over the course of the narrative while covertly controlling it. Superhuman tacticians, the author and the narrator are able to engage the reader's sympathies while manipulating every facet of the reader's response. The Narrator in *Middlemarch* is the supreme example of Bakhtin's "monologism," which, as Miller distills Bakhtin's term for us, is

> the working of an implied master-voice whose accents have already unified the world in a single interpretive center.... The master-voice of monologism never simply soliloquizes. It continually needs to confirm its authority by qualifying, canceling, endorsing, subsuming all the other voices it lets speak. No doubt the need stands behind the great prominence the nineteenth-century novel gives to

style indirect libre, in which, respeaking a character's thoughts or speeches, the narration simultaneously subverts their authority and secures its own.
(Miller 1988: 25)

The tergiversation, the moments of stylistic confusion, the moral incoherence, the varieties of tone, the conflicts in authorial intentionality, the gaps in narrative rhetoric: all these disparate complications in Eliot's work produce, for Miller, one effect: the inscription of power on us, its subjects.

Miller had already begun to develop this view of Eliot in his earlier work, *Narrative and Its Discontents*, in which he exposed *Middlemarch*'s seeming celebration of the heroic individuality of the main characters whose epic ambitions seemingly drive the novel—especially the benevolent heroine Dorothea and the physician Lydgate—as a screen for its chief objective: to reconcile these vivid personae to the needs of the community, to make them finally indistinguishable from the larger, more anonymous community as a whole. Dorothea's desire to make the world kinder, Lydgate's quest for the "primitive tissue" with which he may innovate medicine, Fred's desire to be a successful gentleman through the inheritance of Stone Court, Casaubon's search for the *Key to All Mythologies*: all participate in the elaboration of one of "the nineteenth-century novel's favorite themes: the impossibility of transcendence." In other words, the very impossibility of transcendence enables the novel to stall strategically, remaining in a precisely calibrated limbo. It allows the narrative to strive for radical change while it secures, maintains, and enshrines the status quo, the seemingly threatened yet perpetual sameness of community.

Miller's depiction of *Middlemarch*'s narrator as "He" seems the most telling indication of his critical position. The force of containment in *Middlemarch*, as Miller would have it, is embodied by the tyrannical unity of the narrator's "superior retelling." In his gendering of Eliot's narrator as "He," Miller depicts the narrator as an arm of power, or power itself. In a footnote aside, Miller contends that, while "One might say that…the narrator's discourse is merely *in* the novel, the novelist's discourse quite simply *is* the novel" (Miller 1981: 158–9). The crucial nuggets of Miller's Foucault-inspired schema—collaboration and resistance—inform our unwitting union with the narrator's mission, a *collaboration* with the narrator, or, with power itself, that we can only reject by *resisting* the narrator's totalizing though hypocritically generous voice.

Miller's Ozymandian figure of the all-powerful, masculinist narrator is in stark contrast to the one I encounter in *Middlemarch*: the Wise Woman, the voice of Athena guiding our passage through the Wandering Rocks of the narrative, with powers of empathy and engagement, who enables us to perceive a multiplicity of alternatives. As Quentin Anderson put it:

> the light which illumines all these things in their mutual relations…[is] the voice of the wise woman. That voice is often heard speaking directly with an authority which makes use of the Victorian reader's involvement with the characters to make him look up and look about, to see how human relations are established within the world of the story.
>
> (Anderson 1970: 147)

Miller's insistence on gendering Eliot's Narrator as "He" sharply contrasts with feminist criticism. As Virginia Woolf observes, "In *Middlemarch* and *Jane Eyre*… we are conscious of a woman's presence—of someone resenting the treatment of her sex and pleading for its rights" (Woolf 1975: 79–80).

David Carroll observes that Eliot never allows us one conclusion to the dilemma at hand; she never allows us "to evade that uncomfortably fine balance between sameness and difference, credulity and skepticism, which seems to reflect ironically and step by step [our] own reading process" (Carroll 1992: 234–5). The multivalent, abundant generosity in this voice illuminates even the dim reaches of minds like that of the pedant Casaubon, on whose behalf we are urged to open up our guarded sympathies. The narrator is the most heightened version of a fellow reader. But where some of us may experience pleasurable intimacy, a pleasure that lies to a certain extent in our moral education, the heightening and refining of our sympathetic faculties, with the Wise Woman, Miller finds an Iron Maiden.

Eliot's novel enjoins us in a sustained dialogue with the distilled essence of another mind. Even while he expresses numerous complaints about the novel, Henry James clarifies what is central in *Middlemarch*: "The author has commissioned herself to be real, her native tendency being that of an idealist, and the intellectual result is a very fertilizing mixture. The constant presence of thought, of generalizing instinct, of *brain*, in a word, behind her observation, gives the latter its great value" (James 1986: 54). In her engaging collection of essays and reviews *Passions of the Mind*, A. S. Byatt contends that "Eliot… demonstrates and argues the case for independent thought, in reader as in writer.… [We are granted the] freedom…of the moral daydreamer who temporarily inhabits the world of *Middlemarch*" (Byatt 1991: xvi). Miller's Foucauldian project renders Byatt's view of literature as "moral daydreaming" unintelligible. But Byatt's view is much closer to my experience than Miller's; there is little sense in his analysis that that the reader might enter a realm of pleasure rather than complex social discipline. Or, to put it another way, the only way to enjoy these readerly pleasures is to submit to the pernicious discipline. The sheer spectacular bulk of *Middlemarch* allows one the feeling of time spent in a created world, reading it, living inside of it. Freed from the constraints of quotidian everyday experience, we are given the opportunity to roam through the "landscape of opinion," as Anderson wrote. So unfettered, we are free agents in ways we can never be in life. What is closed off to us through the sheer strangeness of other people—those beings so eerily like ourselves and so resolutely remote from us—the novel gives us a certain access to, or at least the illusion of access.

Such committed connections to literature are alien to Miller, the message of whose works is that *Middlemarch* and cultural behemoths like it seduce us into volitional submission to their mazy tyrannies. This approach is so familiar now that it hardly needs further elaboration, but the relevance of revisiting the argument is that its influence has been profound, on generations of queer scholars that have followed Miller, Halperin, and their queer theory, and on those in other disciplines who have assumed that this orthodoxy is the defining Foucauldian critical position. Miller and other key (mostly American) Foucauldian critics have institutionalized the view that a queer reader is determinedly hostile to anything other than an antagonistic, oppositional relationship with an artist or a text. Representation is inherently untrustworthy and deeply hypocritical in its efforts to befriend us while betraying us to the authorities.

Those familiar "gay" names listed at the start remind us that, at one point, we felt that such artists spoke for us and to us, that they communicated with us in ways no one else had—in our families, social interactions, culture—often at great risk to themselves. Certainly, the view that literature and the artist are removed from the structures of power, an alternative to them, is an outdated, naive one. Yet this version of queer theory maintains an equally absolutist stance toward representation as the enemy to fight rather than a potential refuge.

The transformation of gay attitudes—the process whereby we went from feeling kinship to sustained suspicion—has been infrequently addressed. Eve Kosofsky Sedgwick, one of queer theory's foundational figures, has critiqued the hermeneutics of suspicion prevalent in this Foucault-inflected queer theory, making a special point of Miller's work (Sedgwick 1997). Arguing from a revisionist-Kleinian position, Sedgwick argues that to "read from a reparative position is to surrender the knowing, anxious paranoid determination that no horror, however apparently unthinkable, shall ever come to the reader as new; to a reparatively positioned reader, it can seem realistic and necessary to experience surprise. Because there can be terrible surprises, however, there can also be good ones." She continues, "The desire of a reparative impulse...is additive and accretive. Its fear, a realistic one, is that the culture surrounding it is inadequate or inimical to its nurture; it wants to assemble and confer plenitude on an object that will then have resources to offer to an inchoate self" (Sedgwick 1997: 27–8). Sedgwick offers an alternative to a queer theory stance steadfast in its view of cultural productions as pernicious. To be clear, I am in no way arguing for being less than vigilant about the politics of representation. What I am disputing is that representation is *always* pernicious.

Becoming Reverential

Given the connotations of faith and reverence in its title, *Saint Foucault* by David Halperin can be taken as the bible of this Foucauldian queer theory, both because of its rhetorical forcefulness and its synthesis of the critical tenets of the Foucauldian critical movement. A classicist by training, Halperin emerged as one of the major queer theorists with the publication of his 1990 book *One Hundred Years of Homosexuality*, which, while a study of sexual practices in ancient Greece, is most memorable today for the effectiveness with which it entrenched the Foucauldian idea of homosexuality as a modern invention of the late-Victorian era. It was one of a number of classicist works by LGBT scholars of the time that, as Allen Miller puts it in his astute overview, "fundamentally changed the way ancient sexuality was studied" (Miller 2021a: 13).

In *Saint Foucault*, Halperin provocatively takes as his title the derisive phrase used by one of his most outspoken critics, Richard Mohr, who accuses Halperin and other social constructionist critics of worshipping "Saint Foucault" (Mohr 1992). Appropriating, in a classic queer manner, the language of abuse for his own purposes, Halperin writes, "let me make it official. I may not have worshipped Foucault at the time I wrote *One Hundred Years of Homosexuality*, but I do worship him now. As far as I am concerned, the guy was a fucking saint" (Halperin 1995: 6).

Foucault is an odd candidate for canonization. The Church was the subject of some his most stringent critiques, particularly in its enshrinement of confession, which for Foucault was the template for the forms of social control that would be most acutely developed in the modern liberal state. By conscripting the penitent into confessing his or her sins, confession paved the way for psychoanalysis, the chief face of modern liberal power and its program of self-disclosure. For Foucault, the talking cure, like confession, gets us to confess our own failures to be properly socialized, and to seek out assistance, through a properly penitent attitude and from the psychoanalyst, the modern priest, in becoming better socialized. Halperin tweaks the irony in his title by calling Foucault the *fucking* saint—implicitly, Foucault is saintly precisely because he fucks, unlike the conventional, ascetic saint. Yet, as Halperin will make clear, it is Foucault's ascetics of sexuality that is the most valuable aspect of his work. Halperin's treatment of Foucault vividly reveals the central incoherencies in the queer theory valorization of the theorist. Both for sex and ruthlessly opposed to it, both the proponent of sexual experiences the more inventive the better and the critic of positively valued sex, "Foucault" for Halperin persists as an essentially untenable figure for a politics of sexual liberation—for, despite the myriad qualifications, that is the goal of Halperin's work, among others—nevertheless elevated into saint-like status for its cause. All of this is to say that his Foucault has much more in common, in some significant ways, with the ascetic saint of Catholicism than with the liberationist sexual radicalism of queer theory.

For Halperin, of chief importance in Foucault's theory of sexuality is the concept of *askēsis*. While the concept has many specific meanings in both a classical and early Christian context, in queer theory it has been deployed as a weird model of sex-in-action and of sexual philosophy at once. The idea of sex between men as historically an act performed between one powerful male and the male he dominates is a confection Halperin claims to derive from a *History of Sexuality*, Volume 1. This image of impersonal sex between powerful and powerless males has loomed over all queer theory discussions. It is the primal scene of Foucauldian queer theory: the male citizen of antiquity penetrates and dominates the submissive and powerless male, devoid of rights. The usefulness of this image to Halperin's theory is its ability to challenge at every turn any presumptions about sex's meanings. Where some might wish to see love and tenderness or even erotic *frisson* in this coupling, there is only will and submission; where some might wish to offer alternatives to this model, the model maintains the might of its apparent historical accuracy.

Early Halperin writings such as the 1989 pieces "Sex before Sexuality: Pederasty, Politics, and Power in Classical Athens" and "Is There a History of Sexuality?" extended far beyond the field of Classics in their reach as position-statements regarding the Foucauldian view of sexual history. The views crystallize in Saint Foucault. "Ancient ethics, Foucault maintained, concerned itself less with the forbidden than with the voluntary: it was a practice of self-regulation with regard to pleasure," writes Halperin. He continues, "Principles of ethical conduct in such a system operated more like the rules of a bodybuilding regimen or a daily workout routine than like universal moral imperatives ... The ultimate goal of all this ethical work was mastery over self and others" (Halperin 1995: 69). I am quite out of field in discussing classical texts, so to be clear I am emphasizing the timbre of such statements and their transdisciplinary effect. Proceeding from this Foucauldian understanding of ancient ethics, the model of the gay male followed suit, conveying a sense of unflinching control over the self and discourse. Halperin was offering documentary evidence that the temple of self-control, of mastery over self and others was the gym, now enshrined as the definitive gay male-sanctuary and stronghold.

Halperin clarified the position further. "Unlike desire, which expresses the subject's individuality, history, and identity as a subject, pleasure is desubjectivating, impersonal: it shatters identity, subjectivity, and dissolves the subject, however fleetingly, into the sensorial continuum of the body, into the unconscious dreaming of the mind." Proceeding from this basis (though the echo of Freud is unmistakably present in "unconscious dreaming of the mind"), Halperin asseverates, "it is ultimately sexuality itself that will have to be resisted" (Halperin 1995: 95). Foucauldian queer theory's often misleading and myopic treatment of Freud and psychoanalytic theory demands discrete treatment. What concerns me here is the image of sex as more authentic and primally real than the artificialities and conformist capitulations of sexuality, not that Halperin would put it that way, of course.

One of the incoherencies at work here is the absence of passion, either erotic or sexual, in this model of what sex *was*—and therefore always already *is*—and in the emergent and widely propounded idea that postmodern, post-AIDS queer sex was utopian, "world-making," as Michael Warner proclaimed. This world-making sex, usually in group formation, jostled uneasily and also uncritically for dominance against the classical frieze of sex-as-*askēsis*. But more importantly, these two models merged, in their adamant de-emphasizing of any emotional dimension to sexual experience. Do not let sex degenerate into love; do not let sex degenerate into emotional meaning; fight for the right to be anti-relational.

Admittedly, many particulars of Halperin's argument in *Saint Foucault* would problematize my broader claims. For instance, Halperin is careful to distinguish the classical Greek understanding of *askēsis* as austerity from Foucault's use of it as "training":

> Foucault referred to the arduous activity of cultivating, fashioning, and styling the self in order to transform the self into source of self-sufficiency and pleasure—as ascesis (*askēsis* in Greek), ascetics, or ethical work. "Ascesis," then, as Foucault conceived it, does not signify self-denial, austerity, or abnegation; rather, it means something like "training," almost in an athletic sense.
> (Halperin 1995: 73)

For Foucault, both homosexuality and philosophy are modern forms of *askēsis* because they allow for self-transformation, or, more properly, they *should*. "Homosexuality for Foucault," Halperin parsed, "is not a psychological condition that we discover but a way of being that we practice in order to redefine the meaning of who we are and what we do, and in order to make ourselves and our world more gay; as such it constitutes a modern form of ascesis" (Halperin 1995: 73). A good deal of what follows is Halperin's precisely detailed articulation of all of the ways in which Foucault exhorts us to make use of our homosexuality not to discover the truth about ourselves but to form new ways of social relation. Indeed, homosexuality emerges as an unprecedented occasion for the development of entirely *new forms of relation*.

That this is a highly sentimentalized view of gay identity has been obscured by the tautness and precision of Halperin's tone. Yet it very much is an idealizing portrait of homosexuality, no less so than the famous-gays-in-history-approach was, though from an antithetical perspective. That one wishes to have sexual relations with members of one's own sex, to say nothing of loving them and wanting to pursue relationships with them, causes a certain amount of consternation, greater or lesser depending on where one happens to be, is demonstrable fact. But that these same feelings and desires cause one to seek out new forms of being and social relation is more dubious. That such pursuits naturally proceed from queerness is not at all a demonstrable fact, yet much Foucauldian queer theory has treated it as self-evident. Throughout works such as Michael Warner's *The Trouble with Normal* runs a reading of homo-desire as inherently political and politicizing, a kind of activist sexual fluid. Leo Bersani in *Homos* critiqued Warner on just such an idealizing view of homosexuality in 1995, but the same equivalence between queer identity and leftist political activism—for no other could ever possibly be sanctioned—continues to inform apprehensions of and attitudes toward queer people, especially in the academy.

Queer people used to be thought of as those who had better taste than everyone else, as Pauline Kael once put it. We were associated with our love for beauty, our connoisseurship, our aesthetics, our love for old movies and movie stars, our passion for art history, our devotion to the theater, and an entire range of other now quite archaic attributes. While I am not asking for a return to what were at best compensatory myths, it is quite remarkable the way *presumed* queer tastes have changed. At least in academia, queers are considered political animals first, political activism an inherent component. The transformation of gay aesthetic culture into political queerness, an erotics and an ethics of fiercely lived and maintained politics, is the ultimate achievement of Foucauldian queer theory, one that persists even as queer theory—as David Halperin's post-2000 work makes quite clear—has significantly revised its earlier orthodoxies.

Speaking from my own leftist, queer position, what I want to suggest is that queer theory in *this* Foucauldian cast has made the profound error of tethering sexual identity to political engagement. Desire, sexuality, and the work of art-making all have political aspects, but to claim that these aspects are indistinguishable from one another is a grievous error. One of the effects that this influential ideological position has had is the diminishment of the discussion of sexuality generally and queer sexuality specifically in literature and culture, especially before the late Victorian era. Instead of delving into the thorny questions of sexual history, most scholars simply ignore it altogether.

There remains a profound disjunction between this 1990s Foucauldian queer theory and that of more contemporary voices. Reading the blogs that feature testimonials from gay men especially to the power of Ang Lee's 2005 film *Brokeback Mountain* and D. A. Miller's scorching critique of the film in *Film Quarterly* is an instructive course in this disjunction. It is not that "popular" reactions should trump critical ones. Nor is it to suggest that if mainstream gays embrace a work, that acclaim is somehow more "real" than the critic's critique of it. Yet what is most troubling about Miller's treatment is its predictable conformity. One need not read the review to know exactly what it will say. If gay men, among other viewers, have found *Brokeback* to be an indelible and invaluable work, the arch-Foucauldian critic will take this as proof of its craftily engineered conformity. Miller says the same things about Lee's film that he did about Eliot's *Middlemarch* in *The Novel and the Police*. Every work of art is a case file of offenses, a network of regimes of surveillance, a determined system of enclosure and entrapment. In this queer theory, we are always the prisoner in Poe's "The Pit and the Pendulum," inexorably closer to the swinging, deepening cut of the pendulum, with no hope of reprieve.

A wider range of responses, more openness to the contours and diverse levels of art, some spontaneity, and, above all, some fresh thinking, are needed. As

LGBTQ+ populations become more integrated into the wider community, and as this integration itself poses an endless series of difficulties as it fills us with future hopes, we need a new set of critical principles to make sense of our place in nation, community, and representation. We need to develop an approach that melds our traditional joy with our ever-sharpening political awareness. Suspicion has its place, but so do spontaneity and excitement and pleasure. Pleasure can be found in a great work of art as well as in world-making anonymous sex. How did our critical rubric get so narrow? How do we reclaim the pleasures of the mind as well as the body? How can queer theory be of use to us in interpreting our joys as well as exposing our victimization? The word revolution seems apt.

Notes

Chapter 1

1. My gratitude to Allen Miller, Geoff Pfeifer, Paul Bruno, Sam Binkley, and especially to Penny Vlagopoulos. This chapter would not have been possible without their generosity and patience. Portions of this chapter have appeared in two previous articles: "The Role of the Dream in Descartes' *Meditations* and in the Historical Ontology of Ourselves," *Foucault Studies* Number 25, 86–9; "Dream and the Aesthetics of Existence: 'Foucault's Ethical Imagination' Revisited," *Philosophy & Social Criticism* 47 (8), 987–1000, 2021.
2. For a more complete account of these two trajectories and their relation to each other, see McGushin 2007.
3. See Foucault 1997a, Part Three, Chapters 1–2.
4. Foucault analyzes the formation of bio-politics and the concept of the population in a number of texts. Two sources for this paper are Foucault 2007 and Foucault 1990, Part V.
5. Foucault 1990: 59, and see Part 3, *Scientia Sexualis*.
6. Of course, for Freud the dream plays a central role in this hermeneutic process: "the interpretation of dreams is the royal road to knowledge of the unconscious activities of the mind" (Freud 1953: 608). Moreover, he claimed that the best way to become a psychoanalyst was to interpret one's own dreams (Freud 1961a: 33). See Derrida 1994 on the ambivalent place of Freud in Foucault's thought.
7. One can find several texts where Foucault argues that resistance is not necessarily the intentional or volitional act of a subject. For example: "The body . . . constructs resistances" (Foucault 1998: 380); "I think we need a history of the relations between the body and the mechanisms of power that invest it." (Foucault 1999a: 214).
8. Numerous texts attest to this aim. For example, Foucault 1988b, Foucault 1997b.
9. See especially Foucault 2005.
10. For the introduction of the term, *ethopoetic*, see Foucault 2005: 237. The arts of life were connected to this ethical fashioning of the relation to the self. Especially in Foucault 2005, Foucault focuses on this difference and the changing relationship between the two domains. For the purposes of simplification in this paper I will use them in a more general and almost synonymous way.

11 Foucault excavates and describes the Christianization of the care of the self and the formation of pastoral power in a number of texts for example, Foucault 2007 and Foucault 2012a.
12 In these lines Foucault contextualizes the reading of Artimedorus that is to follow. *The Interpretation of Dreams*, by Artimedorus holds a special place in Foucault's history of sexuality as well as his engagement with Freud. Here I do not intend to engage directly with Foucault's analysis of Artimedorus' book. Rather, I am interested in the context: the fundamental role of the dream in the history of subjectivity and truth.
13 In a way, the dream is more threatening to Descartes than is madness. Madness, according to Foucault, can be simply excluded by the deliberate, rational meditating subject. But the dream? Even the sane lose themselves in dreams. Of course, this issue returns to the Foucault–Derrida debate. See McGushin 2016 for my reading of this encounter.
14 We now know much more about Foucault's early engagement of phenomenology and psychology. See for example, Basso 2022 and Elden 2021 for excellent accounts of Foucault's early work.
15 Here I am thinking of the extraordinary passages in *The History of Sexuality 1* at the beginning of the chapter on Method that characterize power in terms of the self-organization of the field of force relations (Foucault 1990: 92–3).
16 See for example, Reid 2018, for a treatment of the politics of the imagination and the image.

Chapter 2

1 *alētheia*
2 [παντάπασι δή, ἦν δ᾽ ἐγώ, οἱ τοιοῦτοι οὐκ ἂν ἄλλο τι νομίζοιεν τὸ ἀληθὲς ἢ τὰς τῶν σκευαστῶν σκιάς (R 515c)]: But all in all, I was saying that the prisoners may not practice anything as *the* truth, other than the shadows of those artifacts.

Chapter 3

1 Translator's note: Where possible, quotations have been drawn from standard existing English translations. Citations refer first to these English versions, followed by the quotation's location in the French text. Dates given refer to the editions used by the author, not to the original dates of publication, which can be found in the References section. Where no translation is cited the translations are our own.

Author's note: I warmly thank Henri-Paul Fruchaud for his kind authorization to reproduce the facsimiles from the Foucault archives.
2 Translation slightly altered. "We must cease once and for all to describe the effects of power in negative terms: it 'excludes,' it 'represses,' it 'censors,' it 'abstracts,' it 'masks,' it 'conceals.' In fact, power produces; it produces reality; it produces domains of objects and rituals of truth. The individual and the knowledge that may be gained of him belong to this production."
3 "Not to pass universals through the grinder of history but to sift history through a way of thinking that refuses universals" (Non pas passer les universaux à la râpe de l'histoire mais faire passer l'histoire au fil d'une pensée qui refuse les universaux), Foucault 1994a: 56 (note of January 7, 1979).
4 Freud (1899) 1942: 612 n. 1. A few years later Friedrich Salomo Krauss, as founding editor of *Anthropophyteia: Jahrbücher für folkloristische Erhebungen und Forschungen zur Entwicklungsgeschichte der geschlechtlichen Moral* would publish there a translation by Hans Licht (the pseudonym of Peter Brandt) of the chapters Krauss himself had removed from his translation (Licht 1912).
5 A new translation, under the direction of Christophe Chandezon, is currently in preparation and will be published as a Budé edition by Belles Lettres.
6 See two letters edited by Vesperini 2020.
7 See also a very short chapter in Thonemann 2020 (71).
8 See the very interesting work of Chandezon and du Bouchet 2014.
9 The unpublished manuscript of this talk is forthcoming, edited by Daniele Lorenzini; I am very grateful to Niki Clements for making me aware of its existence and sharing her transcription with me. See Clements 2021a for a presentation of the context of this seminar, and the differences between the French drafts and the texts of the seminars as delivered in English.
10 Paul Veyne is referring to the page of his article where he defines what Foucault, and he himself, mean by "the 'discourse' of sexuality" (Veyne 1978: 52). These facsimiles are reproduced with the kind authorization of Henri-Paul Fruchaud.
11 Sometimes translated as "bisexuality of penetration." This does not quite convey the violence of Veyne's metaphor, which evokes the inflicting of a wound.
12 IV, 2 "*peri tôn hex stoicheiôn*" (concerning the six fundamental elements). About *stoicheia* in the *Oneirokritikon*, see Flamand 2014.
13 I, 78–80.
14 In this essay, all translations of Artemidorus that are quoted are those of Hammond 2020.
15 Foucault 1986b: 35; 1984b: 46.
16 See Boehringer 2021: 246, 325–30 for fuller discussion and bibliography.
17 V, 63. "It so happened that she unwittingly had sexual intercourse with her own son, and after that she took her own life and died a wretched death."

18 On this point, see du Bouchet 2016.
19 An influence underscored by Malosse 2014. On the stylistic proximity with the astrological writers, see Petit 2014.
20 See above for more on Festugière. For discussion of the intellectual exchanges between Veyne and Foucault about the subject of ancient sexuality, see Boehringer 2023.
21 Gros 2015 and 2018.
22 BNF, Box 21, 22, 24.
23 BNF, Box 40, Folder 6.5, transcription by Niki Clements.
24 For more on Foucault and Cassian, see Clements 2020.
25 Foucault 2021a: 185; 2018: 240. The preceding sentence reads, "[This is] so great a problem that Cassian will make the absence of erotic dreams or nocturnal pollutions the sign that one has arrived at the highest stage of chastity."

Chapter 4

1 For a more developmental account of Foucault's evolving views on the relation between rhetoric and *parrhēsia*, see Lorenzini (2023: 74–80).
2 It is unlikely that this lack of references is a product of ignorance. Foucault as a young man received a classical education, which would have included a healthy dose of Ciceronian Latin, as did most students bound to the universities and the Grandes Écoles in the forties and fifties. In addition, an examination of his notes in preparation for his unpublished book, *Le Gouvernement de soi et des autres* as well as the notes found in a dossier on his desk at the time of his death, both preserved in the Fonds Michel Foucault at the Bibliothèque Nationale de France, reveals references to the *Tusculan Disputations, Letters to Atticus, Letters to Friends, De Senectute*, as well as to other rhetorical writers such as Quintilian and Demetrius author of the *De Elocutione*. Paris, BNF, 28730, 71.5; Paris, BNF, 28730, 72.5.218, 227; Paris, BNF, 28730, 72.6.304–5; Paris, BNF, 28730, 72.7.209; Paris, BNF, 28730, 73.4.92–3; Paris, BNF, 28730, 73.7.195–6; Paris, BNF, 28730, 74.1.295. Foucault certainly knew Cicero and had a basic acquaintance with the rhetorical tradition. The lack of references in the lectures on *parrhēsia* and the modes of discourse during his final seminars at the Collège de France would appear to be a deliberate choice. Indeed, in all of Foucault's published work on antiquity, he by and large neglects the Roman Republic, so the reasons for this absence deserve further study.

I want to thank Niki Kasumi Clements for making me aware of the treasure trove of materials available in the archives.
3 In the drafts for *Le Gouvernement de soi et des autres*, there is a handwritten chapter that focuses squarely on the "traditional opposition" between rhetoric and

philosophy and the changes Foucault sees in this relationship in the early empire (he essentially ignores the Roman republic). Most interestingly, he has an extensive exposition on the way philosophy in this period develops practices of listening, which he defines as having not only a complementary relation with rhetoric but also an inverse relation, as philosophical listening guards the listener from being seduced by what is "contrary to reason and the truth." Paris, BNF, 28730, 72.5.219–44.

4 He would, of course, later use this same title for Volume 1 of the *History of Sexuality*.
5 The bibliography is vast. See among others, Heidegger (1982: 115, 129–31; 1998); Foucault (1988a: 12–13; 2011: 86–7, 94–5 n. 10); Defert (2011: 257, 272, 275); Zuckert (1996: 37, 49–50, 56); Brion and Harcourt (2012: 271); Miller (2020). See also Shokrisaravi's chapter in this volume.
6 I want to thank Emanuela Bianchi whose suggestions helped refine this paragraph.
7 The Latin is the same word for both ideas, *persona*. While there is not space in this chapter, one avenue to approach this phenomenon would be an examination of the orator's self-fashioning through what Foucault lists as the four activities of practical reason in the technologies of self: ethical substance; mode of subjectivation; askesis; and telos. See Clements (2021b) for a clear explanation of these technologies.

Chapter 5

1 Paris, Bibliothèque nationale de France, Département des Manuscrits, Fonds Foucault (henceforth BNF), NAF 28730, Box 40, Folder 1, page 1, handwritten:

> "And I had to wait several years before I became aware of a much more grand problem which is both a philosophical and an
> ethical problem
> both an institutional and
> an epistemological problem:
> Why are we obliged to tell the truth about ourselves? Which truth?
> In which forms? In which contexts and"

2 Dr. Leuret also opens the Louvain lectures; see Foucault 2014b. For more on Foucault on Leuret, see Clements 2022c.
3 BNF, 28730, 40.1.1.
4 For the construction of "true discourse" see McGushin 2007, for "truth as force" see Lorenzini 2023. For *parrhēsia* see Foucault 2019: xiii and 2016b: 11.
5 After completing this chapter, I learnt from Orazio Irrera and Gabriel Pochapski that Foucault even references "cette *parrhēsia*" in his intellectual journal from 1963–5 in relation to confession (BNF, 28730, 91.4); I thank them for this intriguing reference.

6 I follow Frédéric Gros's and Mark Kelly's insistence on Foucault's distinction between subjection and subjectivation (Gros 2005: 511; Kelly 2013: 513). Lynne Huffer stages these stakes poignantly, asking "What does it cost to tell the truth?" (Huffer 2020: 93).

7 My sincere thanks to Laurence Le Bras and her colleagues at the BNF, without whom I could not do this research. Ongoing thanks to the Foucault Estate for access to the Fonds Foucault, and Henri-Paul Fruchaud in particular for sharing his wisdom. Sandra Boehringer, Laurie Laufer, Allen Miller, and Federico Testa have my thanks for contributions to this work.

8 In the endnotes for *Discourse and Truth*, Henri-Paul Fruchaud and Daniele Lorenzini note of Foucault's May 18, 1982 lecture at the University of Grenoble: "Foucault had 'discovered' the notion of *parrhēsia* several months earlier. He mentions it for the first time during his lecture on January 27, 1982, for the course *The Hermeneutics of the Subject*" (Fruchaud and Lorenzini 2019: 2, 230fn9).

9 BNF, 28730, 40.1.1. "oct 80" indicates that Foucault had compiled these materials then, even if he had written them before.

10 BNF, 28730, 40.1.13.

11 Ibid. Foucault's French manuscript for this English treatment is in Box 76, Folder 1, in a section called "I L'aveu dans les rites de pénitence": "Et au point de jonction de cette amitié et de cette hiérarchie, il y avait l'obligation de la παρρησία, à laquelle Philodème a consacré tout un traité. La Parresia, c'est l'ouverture du cœur, c'est la franchise qui doit avoir cours non seulement entre le disciple et son maître, mais dans les rapports des membres du groupe entre eux." (BNF, 28730, 76.1.22).

12 BNF, 28730, 76.1.22. See also Testa 2023 for these dynamics.

13 For an analysis of these vertical and horizontal relationships, see Testa, forthcoming, and his treatment of Foucault and DeWitt 1936, 1954.

14 BNF, 28730, 62.4.57; in a folder archived as "Sans titre [sur l'aveu]; manuscrit autographe", the hand-written manuscript 62.4 shares many connections with the English typescript in 40.1.

15 BNF, 28730, 52.2.6. The folder begins with the title: "2ème partie / Chapitre III / Exercices".

16 BNF, 28730, 79.7.112 (paginated 25 by Foucault).

17 BNF, 28730, 79.7.114-115 (paginated 27-8 by Foucault).

18 BNF, 28730, Boxes 72–74 are grouped under the title "Le Gouvernement de soi et des autres" with the archival note: "Selon le témoignage de Daniel Defert, Michel Foucault aurait déclaré à la fin de sa vie que le manuscrit était terminé et prêt à être édité. Il envisageait de le faire publier aux éditions du Seuil, comme il se trouvait alors en conflit avec Gallimard depuis Pierre Rivière."

19 Using the title *Le Souci de soi* instead of *Le Gouvernement de soi et des autres* (as in archival folders 72, 73, and 74), Foucault describes this book in conversation with

Paul Rabinow (Foucault 1997b: 255). See also Eribon 2011: 471, 518–21 and Elden 2016: 191–2.

I am currently working out how Foucault drafts material for *Le Gouvernement de soi et des autres* on ancient ethics and incorporates sections into his published Volumes 2 and 3; note also Gros 2005, 515. A different collection in the archives at the BNF, NAF 28284, has transitional drafts between *Le Gouvernement de soi et des autres* and *L'Usage des plaisirs* (Volume 2) and *Le Souci de soi* (Volume 3) as published.

20 BNF, 28730, 72.6.197.
21 BNF, 28730, 73.5.122, section titled "II. Conversion à soi".
22 Dyrberg 2016: 217 notes "Foucault's studies of *parrhesia* (1981–1984)" but does not give evidence for 1981.
23 In the scholarly apparatus for Foucault's *Mal faire, dire vrai*, Fabienne Brion and Bernard Harcourt compellingly relate these lectures to *parrhēsia*, yet it is notable that Foucault does not use the term in these April to May 1981 lectures.
24 Foucault also declares the influence of Marcello Gigante's treatment of Philodemus, where *parrhēsia* is a *technē* and the guarantee of its frankness comes down to the presence of the person speaking (Foucault 2005: 387–405).
25 Miller is correct to identify this shift toward "a primarily political meaning" in 1983, although we can see how Foucault's use of *parrhēsia* in relation to a philosophical mentor is an earlier, instead of later, application (Miller 2021a: 131).
26 Foucault is particularly interested in Galen's construction of *parrhēsia* as the ability to "constitute himself as subject telling the truth about himself" (Foucault 2012a: 7).
27 Miller notes that for Diogenes, *parrhēsia* is the most precious thing (*to kalliston*) a man possesses (Miller 2021a: 178).
28 For important accounts of *parrhēsia* and early Christian usages, see Büttgen 2021a, Cremonesi 2015, Meunier 2021, and Senellart 2022.
29 Foucault's engagement with early Christian texts changes considerably between 1977 and 1984; see Chevallier 2011, 2022, Clements 2021a, and Colombo 2023.
30 I suspect that Foucault identifies the importance of *parrhēsia* in Nyssa through Camelot 1952.
31 Foucault describes these three theoretical movements in his 1983 lectures, but he does not directly note *parrhēsia* as central; see Foucault 2010: 42.
32 For chapters drafted for *La Croisade des enfants*, see BNF, NAF 28730, 51.4.1-66, 51.5.1-58 ; 64.5.43-83, 64.7.194-270, 64.8.275-330; for an example of a related chapter for this earliest version of Foucault's "Christian book" see BNF, NAF 28730, 64.9.333-372.
33 On Foucault and Epicureanism in a challenge to readings by Pierre Hadot, see Testa, forthcoming.
34 Archived reading notes show how Foucault fixates on the direction of conscience and the examination of conscience, both in the early Christians and then in Hellenistic philosophers. BNF, NAF 28730, includes a large box on 'Direction de

conscience' (27a and 27b) and archival folders on 'direction de conscience' (22.9), 'examen chrétien'(22.10), 'direction de conscience. Protestantisme' (20.5), 'direction spirituelle. XVIe–XVIIe' (20.19), 'direction chrétienne' (21.13), and 'confession du péché. église primitive' (24.10); see Box 23 for Greek and Roman philosophers.

35 For Foucault's research on *parrhēsia* and its relation to his historical analysis of *l'aveu*, see BNF, NAF 28730, 30, which includes many bibliographies and reading notes alongside Foucault's fall 1983 lectures at the University of California, Berkeley.

36 BNF, NAF 28730, boxes 72, 73, 74. *Le Souci de soi* (Box 71) has some elements as well.

37 Foucault takes important reading notes from Hadot 1969 and Rabbow 1914, 1954.

38 The influence of Ilsetraut Hadot has been eclipsed by that of her husband, Pierre Hadot, whose influence on Foucault is well known. Foucault indicates of *Peri parrhēsias*, "but I think that Monseiur Hadot intends to publish it with a commentary" (Foucault 2005: 387). Yet Foucault takes many reading notes on Ilsetraut Hadot's *Seneca und die griechisch-römische Tradition der Seelenleitung*; see, for example, BNF, NAF 28730, 23.10.441:

"I. Hadot
Seneca u. Seelenleitung
64–65

le Περί παρρησίας
de Philodème
"de la confession épicurienne"

39 BNF, NAF 28730, 30.8 "Parrhesia: notes bibliographiques" includes two sheets of references Foucault takes from Scarpat on *parrhēsia*. In Box 24.12, Foucault also kept a full photocopy of Marrow 1982.

40 BNF, NAF 28730, 71.3.1-2 has a bibliography corrected by Hélène Monsacré that includes references to 'Philodème/A. Olivieri Peri Parrhesias'.

41 Perhaps Foucault came across this concept in other research and then pursued it in parallel to his other work; for example, historian Peter Brown had shared his series of Hale lectures with Foucault in 1980 that engage *parrhēsia*; see Brown 1980 and Clements 2022b.

Chapter 6

1 Foucault 1990: 59, with Taylor 2009: 8–9, 13, 24, 53–5; Teti 2020: 216–17, 220–1; and Büttgen 2021a: 86–93; cf. Miller 2021a: 45.

2 See Foucault 2012: 266–75; 2014b: 165–71; 2021a: 87–96; 216–29; with Büttgen 2021a: 90–3; Clements 2021a: 13–14, 23–5; Zachhuber 2021: 54; cf. Miller 2021a: 45: "Ancient ethics sought to free the self. Christianity sought to dominate the self."

3   Foucault 1986a: 86–93, at 89, with Loesberg 2005: 112, 158–9; McGushin 2007: xvi–xviii, 103–4, 115–24, 134; Miller 2021a: 112–19.
4   Foucault 2012: 337–8, with Miller 2021a: 176–8.
5   Taylor 2009: 42–6; Büttgen 2021a: 93, 96–7; 2021b: 8–9.
6   Thus, alongside the two regimes of confession, confession of faith and of truth (Foucault 2012: 84, in Büttgen 2021b: 13–14), exists a third, confession of praise, a.k.a. epideictic, the "genre precursor of 'literature'" (Moretti 1983: 279). For some recognition of the salience of joy in the Jewish background, see Foucault 2012: 14–16, 29–30, via Zachhuber 2021: 56, with McGowan 2010: 68–78, 114–15.
7   Chevallier 2011: 133–44, with Carrette 2000: 38–9; Taylor 2009: 46–52; Zacchuber 2021: 61–3.
8   Elden 2016: 113: "[B]y the end of these courses, Foucault seems to have finished with this investigation into early Christian understandings of confession and subjectivity"; cf. Teti 2020: 226–8; Clements 2021a: 5–12.
9   On Foucault's foundational overreading of Christian sources in the late work, see Clements 2020: 139. For counter-conduct, see Foucault 2007: 194; 2012: 229–30, with Lorenzini 2016: 15–16; cf. Chevallier 2011: 78–91; Davidson 2011.
10 In all these cases, as Miller explains in this volume, "the point is not to detect a lacuna in Foucault's research," but to open spaces of possibility within an archive whose increasing closure Foucault rightly emphasized: "Foucault's position was perfectly orthodox"; Paulinus' model of joyful confession "is the outlier and undoubtedly strange"; cf. Zacchuber 2021: 60–1.
11 Lorenzini 2015: 264: "parrhesiastic utterance is rhetoric degree zero"; cf. Foucault 2012: 188; cf. Foucault 2007: 172–3; Chevallier 2011: 177–8; Zachhuber 2021: 60–1.
12 Brown 1981: 42–3; McGowan 2010: 132–3, 243–4, with Prudentius, *Peristephanon* 11.200–1, trans. Krisak 2019: 147): "Plebeian and patrician hosts ... [a]re one in worth."
13 Rancière 2009: 43 describes "capacities of feeling and speaking, thinking and acting, that do not belong to any particular class, but which belong to anyone and everyone."
14 Rancière 2009: 14–15 (cf. 55–9): "In the logic of emancipation ... there is always a third thing – a book or some other piece of writing – alien to both [artist and spectator] .... The same applies to performance .... It is a third thing that is owned by no one." See text at n. 37, below.
15 See Miller on rhetoric in this volume, and Escalle 2020.
16 See, e.g., Foucault 2014b: 15–17; 2016a: 72, 85, 91, with Teti 2020: 222.
17 In a 1978 interview, the Japanese leftist Takaaki Yoshimoto (Foucault 2001 [1978]: 609–10) distinguishes between class as a category of analysis and *the idea of class in social experience*; such an idea, such an image, may have social, strategic, and subjective value apart from its truth value.
18 For the "transcription in[to] comportment" of praise, and thus the positive form of confession, see Augustine, *Expositions on the Psalms* 34(2).15 (hereafter *Expositions*).

Throughout the following I use the Vulgate numeration of the Psalms and the translation from Augustine in Boulding et al. 2000. When Augustine offers multiple expositions of the same psalm, as here, I include the number of the exposition in parentheses beside the number of the psalm, and then provide, not the line of the psalm, but the section of Augustine's commentary.

19 On *commendat* in affective theories of communism in Roman philosophy, see Dressler 2016a: 3–4, 33, 49–50, 98–9, 189–91.
20 See Foucault 2014b: 111: "The true model to which this practice refers ... is ... the martyr"; more below.
21 Mattei 2021: 116–17. Contrast Foucault 2016a: 62: "Such a demonstration ... does not therefore have as its function the establishment of an identity," but note (61, underlining added): "self-revelation ... is, at the same time, self-destruction"; cf. 73–6.
22 If the synonymy of the Latin *confessio* assimilates public and private forms, even the monastic accounts, which Foucault discusses as exhaustively individualizing (but see Foucault 2021c: 378, n. 1), may provide evidence of collective aspects (Clements 2020: 148–53); cf. Augustine, *Expositions* 31(1).3–5, with McGowan 2010: 206: "The monks are praying ... as a collective self."
23 Foucault 2014b: 113 (cf. 108–10; 2016: 208–11), underlining added: *exagoreusis* would become "a continuous verbalization of oneself."
24 See, e.g., Psalms 29:10, along with Augustine, *Expositions* 44.33.
25 For biography, see Trout 1999, Chapters 1–4; Mratschek-Hafman 2002: 49–73, 209–41; Brown 2012, Chapters 12–13; and Dressler 2023, Introduction §§2–3.
26 Foucault 2016: 84, with Augustine, *Expositions* 39.16, for example, and Foucault 2012: 333; cf. Büttgen 2021a: 103–7, and the editors in Foucault 2016a: 82.
27 Contrast Foucault 2012: 333: "but from ... the fourth century ... you see the development of structures of authority in Christianity which ... embed individual asceticism in institutional structures, like those ... of ... collective monasticism, and ... of the pastorate."
28 Cf. Foucault 2007: 211–12: "Somewhat as asceticism had this aspect of almost ironic exaggeration in relation to the pure and simple rule of obedience, we could say that in some of these communities there was a counter-society aspect, a carnival aspect, overturning social relations and hierarchies." See Paulinus, *Poems* 27.118–26, with Brown 1981, Chapter 2; Markus 1990: 97–106.
29 Foucault 2021a: 134, 153–4, with Neamțu 2011: 127, McGowan 2010: 112, 121–2. See also Goldhill 2022: 354–6.
30 Foucault 2007: 212: "Pastoral power developed a system of truth that ... extracted ... a secret discovered in the depths of the[...] soul. Mysticism is a completely different system.... The soul is not offered to the other for examination, through a system of confessions (*aveux* [=*exagoreuseis*]). In mysticism the soul sees itself."
31 I.e., praise: *tui laus martyris et tua laus est*.
32 See text at n. 16, above. Cf. Augustine, *Expositions* 29(2).22, trans. Boulding et al. 2000.1, 315: "Confess now what you have done to God, and in the future you will

confess [*confiteberis*] what God has done for you ... so that hereafter you may confess his praises forever [*postea laudes ipsius confitens in aeternum*]," cf. *Expositions* 18(2).3; at *Expositions* 37.2, trans. Boulding et al. 2000.2, 147, the duality of confession is explicitly affective: "Yet a person who is miserable in this sense is truly happy [*felix est, qui sic miser est*]." *Expositions* 42.5 is more explicitly aesthetic theoretical: in cases of righteous action, ease expresses the praise of God as on a lyre, difficulty as on a psaltery, but "each of them is good" (Boulding et al. 2000.2, 260); cf. *Expositions* 42.7 (trans. Boulding et al. 2000.2, 263): "*Hope in the Lord because I will confess to him* [Psalm 42.5-6] ... This encouragement effects some healing at once, and the rest of the sins are purged by faithful confession." See Goldhill 2022: 96–8.

33 *Expositions* 37.6, trans. Boulding et al. 2000.2, 151: *sed nos in audiendo distinguimus; illa autem tamquam unus loquitur*; cf. *Expositions* 42.1 (*vocem ... notissimam ... tamquam nostrum*), with McGowan 2010: 123–4, 204–6.

34 Neamțu 2011: 122–3: "Psalmody, supported by the technique of murmuring and recitation *sotto voce*." On Augustine's related "prosopological exegesis," see McCarthy 2005: 234: "the reader of the psalm identifies what person [*prosopon*, viz. God, Christ, the Church] is speaking in a given verse."

35 On the liturgical context of Augustine's repetition, see McGowan 2010: 108–9. For other instances of repetition evincing prosopology (see prev.), see *Expositions* 18(2), 29(1).5, 29(2).8, 39.2. See Goldhill 2022: 39–40, 384–5.

36 Neamțu 2011: 128 describes "the recession of the indexical 'I', related to the sacred text, for the sake of the anaphoric 'I', through whom tradition can speak."

37 Note *communibus sensibus* in O'Gorman 2018: 146, with Dressler 2016a: 225–7.

38 On the populist potential of Roman rhetoric, see Miller in this volume; contrast Chevallier 2011: 178: "Foucault does not take into consideration the levels of language used by the ancients as a function of the state of progress of their interlocutor," which would include not only "laymen, postulants, novices, probationary monks," but also individuals of different class and status. Foucault can be excused for overlooking Paulinus' innovation, as the more orthodox example of Augustine, even in the use of poetry, illustrates the norm (see n. 10, above, with Wickham 2009: 54, underlining added): "[U]nderstanding the Christian calendar, through public enjoyment rather than (as Augustine proposed) psalm-singing in church, was pagan in the eyes of <u>most of our sources</u>, but doubtless fully Christian in the eyes of celebrants"—and Paulinus.

39 Perhaps not even when he made it: Chevallier 2011: 181–2.

Chapter 7

1 Throughout this chapter, I use the Standard Edition translation of Freud's works (cited in the form SE volume:pages) and standard English translations of Foucault. All other translations from Greek and German are my own.

2   In Whitebook's estimation, vol. 1 of *The History of Sexuality* represents "an end run around Freud, trying to trump psychoanalysis, as a theoretical and practical project, through an archaeological reduction of its significance." "Freud," he continues "isn't even granted the grandeur of a dangerous adversary—of the devil—who must be vanquished, but is reduced to a bit player in a much larger drama" (Whitebook 2006: 331).

3   I consistently use Freud's German title *Traumdeutung* for *The Interpretation of Dreams*, but also for the process of dream interpretation as practiced in early psychoanalysis. The German compound word erases any boundary between dreams and their interpretations, and this fusion is essential to Freud's approach.

4   For example, "To dream is not another way of experiencing another world, it is for the dreaming subject the radical way of experiencing its own world. This way of experiencing is so radical, because existence does not pronounce itself world." (Foucault 1984c: 59)

5   See Foucault 2017a: 167 note, 287 note.

6   See Freud's comment in the *Traumdeutung* where he calls the action of *Oedipus Tyrannus* "a process that can be likened to the work of a psychoanalysis" (SE 4.262).

7   See Freud's reference to the "misconceived secondary revision" of the core truth of Oedipus for "theological purposes" in the play (SE 4:264), and his later comments on Sophocles from *Introductory Lectures*, lecture 21 (SE 16:330-332).

8   On the popular dream books of Freud's day, see O'Donoghue 2009.

9   Freud refers to this dream as well in the *Introductory Lectures on Psychoanalysis* of 1916 (SE 15:86 and 236).

10 Letter of November 12, 1913; Ernst Freud 1992: 303.

11 This is explained at SE 5:350, fn. 1. Throughout this section, the Standard Edition editors put the date of the additions between square brackets, revealing the patchwork construction of this part of the book.

12 Over a decade later, Freud still seemed haunted by Stekel's virtuoso interpretations. He added a new introduction to the section on dream symbolism in the 1925 edition of the *Traumdeutung*, stating that Stekel "has perhaps damaged psychoanalysis as much as he has benefitted it" (SE 5:350). See also his comments the same year in the essay "The Limits to the Possibility of Dream Interpretation" (SE 19:127).

13 See in particular Brandt's large, illustrated history of sexuality, *Sittengeschichte Griechenlands* (1925).

14 See the paper "Dreams in Folklore," coauthored with David Oppenheim (SE 12:180-203), which cites the *Anthropophyteia* throughout. Freud also wrote a letter of support for Krauss (SE 11:233-235) and an introduction to a supplementary volume, both of which involved anal eroticism and scatalogical material. In 1913, Karl Abraham gave expert testimony in Berlin at Krauss's trial.

15 SE 16:335, "Mother-incest was one of the crimes of Oedipus, parricide was the other. It may be remarked in passing that they are also the two great crimes proscribed by totemism, the first socio-religious institution of mankind."
16 See letter to Fliess of October 15, 1897 (Masson 1885: 272–3), the first mention of the Oedipus complex. The first published mention comes two years later in the *Traumdeutung* (SE 4:261-266).

Chapter 8

1 Unless noted, all translations are my own.

Chapter 9

1 Laurie Laufer is a practicing psychoanalyst and professor in the department of Psychoanalytic Studies at the IHSS, CRPMS 3522, Université Paris Cité, and director of the UFR IHSS.
2 Dates in citations refer to the edition used, not to the date of original publication. The source of the English quotation is given first, followed by the French original.
3 Here, as whenever no translation is referenced, the translations is my own.
4 For an epistemological approach to the history sexuality applied to antiquity articulating Freudian psychoanalysis with Foucauldian methods, see Miller 2021b and Miller 2023.
5 His unpublished notes in the Bibliothèque nationale de France show that Foucault was working in the archives on material that goes back to the late sixteenth century. "In 1599, in Dole, Colas, until then considered to be a woman, is denounced: she is accused of being a hermaphrodite. Doctors visit her; conclude that in fact she bears features of both sexes; explain that this defect in bodily conformation is the result of sexual relations she supposedly had with Satan. Torture, confession; she is condemned to be burned alive. [...] The subject's 'anatomical "monstrousness' is explained as the immediate consequence of an illicit sexual relation. But in fact, to produce the tribunal's decision, a number of additional conditions had to be fulfilled. And first of all, the illicit and 'hermaphrodizing' relation had to be the act, not of the subject's parents but of the subject himself; what is inscribed on his body is his own sin." "[En 1599, à Dole, [ant ?] Colas, jusque-là considérée comme femme, est dénoncée : on l'accuse d'être hermaphrodite. Des médecins la visitent ; concluent qu'en effet elle est porteuse de l'un et l'autre sexe ; expliquent que ce défaut de conformation est dû à un rapport qu'elle aurait eu avec Satan. Question, aveu; elle est

condamnée à être brûlée vive. Affaire intéressante puisqu'on y voit le fait même de l'hermaphrodite servir de motif à une condamnation capitale. On reste dans la thématique traditionnelle puisque la '"monstruosité" anatomique' du sujet trouve son explication dans un rapport sexuel interdit dont elle serait la conséquence immédiate. Mais en fait pour provoquer la décision du tribunal, il a fallu un certain nombre de conditions supplémentaires. Et d'abord que la relation interdite et 'hermaphrodisante' soit le fait, non des parents mais du sujet lui-même; ce qui s'inscrit dans son corps, c'est sa faute personnelle.]"

(Sans titre. Manuscrit autographe d'un texte inédit, "'Les hermaphrodites'—ceux qu'on dit réunir en eux les deux sexes– ont été longtemps soumis à un régime disparate." ['Hermaphrodites'—those who are said to bring both sexes together in themselves—were for a long time subjected to a regime that varied). Paris, BNF, NAF 28730, 82.10.25-26.

I am very grateful to Niki Kasumi Clements for sharing her transcription with me.

6 For historical and juridical context, see the annotated edition made by Gabrielle Houbre (2020), a historian specializing on the nineteenth century and gender issues.
7 "Ambroise Tardieu was at that time medical consultant to Napoleon II (1860), Professor of Legal Medicine at the Faculty of Medicine of Paris (1861), President of the Academy of Medicine (1867), President of the Committee of Hygiene and Health (1867), President of the General Association of French Doctors (1868). A frequent expert witness in the law courts, he wrote nearly 5,200 medico-legal reports and produced more than 120 publications between 1839 and 1876" (Houbre 2014: 70). See also G. Vigarello's preface to the 1995 reprint of Tardieu's *Les Attentats aux mœurs*.
8 For the dating of this first edition, see Houbre 2020: 122 n. 5. Foucault gave the date as 1874, but the correct date of publication is 1872.
9 Tardieu published this manuscript in *Question médico-légale dans ses rapports avec les vices de conformation des organes sexuels* (1872). He did not publish the manuscript in its entirety. "First and foremost, a part of Alexina's recollections are missing. Auguste Tardieu seems to have received the complete manuscript from the hands of Dr. Régnier, who had reported the death and performed the autopsy. He kept it, publishing only the part that seemed important to him. He neglected the recollections of Alexina's final years – everything that in his opinion consisted only of laments, recriminations, and incoherencies. In spite of research, it has not been possible to rediscover the manuscript that Tardieu had in his possession." (Foucault [in Barbin 1980: 119] 2014c : 141).
10 [Tr. I have supplied the emphasis, which is missing from the English translation.] The original text of Herculine Barbin's memoirs includes passages underlined by the author her/himself, as the French edition indicates by italicizing those passages. The absence of any such indication from the English translation means that important information is lost: it is the *feminine* adjectives and past participles that Herculine

underlines in this way. For discussion of the many problems presented by the English translation of Herculine Barbin's text, see Gomolka (2012). I thank Meryl Altman for drawing my attention to this article.

11 "L'hermaphrodite n'est pas un être qui aurait simplement un sexe en trop, ou deux organes sexuels simultanés et différents, c'est un être double. Intrication, dans un même individu d'un garçon et d'une fille ? Jumeaux si fortement mêlés que leur dualité n'apparait que parce qu'ils sont de sexes différents ? – Explication qui n'est guère retenue par les naturalistes des ors qu'ils disposent de ce principe essentiel : que le sexe n'est pas tellement un ensemble d'organes destinés à assurer une fonction, mais qu'il est en lui-même une 'nature'. On n'a pas un sexe, on est d'un sexe, comme on est d'une nature : forte, chaude, sèche, hardie, vigoureuse, sanguine, prompte à la colère et au combat, apte à commander, etc. ; ou faible, froide, humide, timide, lymphatique, lente, faite pour se soumettre etc. L'opposition des sexes qui protège le genre humain, ne concerne le rôle dans la production que parmi bien d'autre traits, ni plus, ni moins essentiels ; elle marque l'existence de deux 'natures'. Et l'hermaphrodite, pour être un monstre, n'a pas besoin de combiner dans une même forme deux individus qui auraient dû être séparés ; il lui suffit de mêler dans un individu unique les deux 'natures' qui distinguent d'ordinaire les hommes et les femmes. L'hermaphrodite c'est le mélange indu de ces deux natures." ("Les hermaphrodites," transcription Clements, Paris, BNF, NAF 28730, 82.10.19-20). This is in a folder with unedited manuscript parts; the excerpt is from the first group of materials. Paris, BNF.

12 As Gabrielle Houbre (2014) points out, in 2013 "Germany became the first European country to offer an alternative to the sexual dichotomy imposed by the civil state at birth. Since then, it has indeed been possible not to specify 'masculine' or 'feminine' sex in the birth certificate of newborns who present an ambiguous genital or gonadic sex." This is not the case in France where the infant must by designated at birth as male or female, and the next step is often surgery.

13 The neologism combines *vérité* (truth) and *variété* (variety) [Tr.].

14 "Il faudrait voir s'ouvrir à la dimension de la vérité comme variable c'est-à-dire de c'que en condensant comme ça deux mots j'appellerai la varité avec un petit é avalé, la variété."

15 In his inaugural lecture at the Collège de France, Foucault announced his working method: "The fundamental notions which we now require are no longer those of consciousness and continuity (with their correlative problems of freedon and causality), nor any longer those of sign and structure. They are those of the event and the series, along with the play of the notions which are linked to them: regularity, dimension of chance (aléa), discontinuity, dependence, transformation" (Foucault 1981: 68; 1971: 58-9).

References

Afary, J., and K. Anderson. 2005. *Foucault and the Iranian Revolution*. Chicago: Chicago University Press.
Allen, Amy. 2016. "The History of Historicity: The Critique of Reason in Foucault (and Derrida)." In *Between Foucault and Derrida*. Ed. Yubraj Aryal. Edinburgh: Edinburgh University Press, 125–37.
Allouch, Jean. 1998. *La psychanalyse, une érotologie de passage*. Paris: EPEL.
Allouch, Jean. 2003. "Lacan et les minorités sexuelles." *Cités* 16: *Jacques Lacan, psychanalyse et politique*, 71–7.
Allouch, Jean. 2010. *L'amour Lacan*. Paris: EPEL.
Anderson, Quentin. 1970. "George Eliot in *Middlemarch*." In *George Eliot*. Ed. George Creeger. Englewood Cliffs: Prentice Hall, 141–60.
Armstrong, A. 2008. "Beyond resistance: a response to Zizek's critique of Foucault's subject of freedom." *Parrhesia* 5: 19–31.
Artemidorus. 1881. *Artemidoros aus Daldis: Symbolik der Träume*. Trans. Friedrich Salomo Krauss. Vienna and Leipzig: Hartleben.
Artemidorus. 1912. "Erotische Träume und ihre Symbolik." Trans. Hans Licht [Peter Brandt]. *Anthropophyteia* 9: 316–28.
Artemidorus. 1963. *Artemidori Daldiani Onirocriticon libri V*. Ed. R. A. Pack. Leipzig: Teubner.
Artemidorus. 1975. *Artémidore: La clef des songes*. Trans. A. J. Festugière. Paris: Vrin.
Artemidorus of Daldis. 1975. *The Interpretation of Dreams (Oneirocritica) by Artemidorus*. Trans. Robert J. White. Park Ridge, NJ: Noyes Press.
Artemidorus. 2012. *Artemidorus's Oneirocritica: Text, Translation, & Commentary*. Trans. D. E. Harris-McCoy. Oxford: Oxford University Press.
Artemidorus. 2020. *Artemidorus: The Interpretation of Dreams*. Trans. Martin Hammond, with introduction and notes by Peter Thonemann. Oxford: Oxford University Press.
Badiou, Alain. 2012. *Plato's Republic: A Dialogue in 16 Chapters*. Trans. Susan Spitzer. New York: Columbia University Press.
Barbin, Herculine. 2010. *Herculine Barbin: Being the Recently Discovered Memoirs of a Nineteenth Century French Hermaphrodite*, 2nd ed. Ed. M. Foucault. Trans. Richard McDougall. New York: Vintage Books. [see also Chesnet 2014.]
Barbin, Herculine. 2014. *Michel Foucault présente Herculine Barbin dite Alexina B.* Paris: Gallimard.
Barton, Carlin A. 2001. *Roman Honor: The Fire in the Bones*. Berkeley: University of California Press.

Basso, Elisabetta. 2022. *Young Foucault: The Lille Manuscripts on Psychopathology, Phenomenology, and Anthropology, 1952–1955*. Trans. Marie Satya McDonough. New York: Columbia University Press.

Bersani, Leo. 1995. *Homos*. Cambridge, MA: Harvard University Press.

Binswanger, Ludwig. 1984. "Dream and Existence." Trans. Forrest Williams. *Review of Existential Psychology and Psychiatry* 19 (1): 81–105.

Boehringer, Sandra. 2021. *Female Homosexuality in Ancient Greece and Rome*, with a new preface. Trans. Anna Preger. London: Routledge.

Boehringer, Sandra. 2023. "Paul Veyne, historien de la sexualité antique?" *Comment Paul Veyne écrit l'histoire: un roman vrai*. Ed. Paul Cournarie and Pascal Montaluc. Paris: PUF, 137–60.

Boehringer, Sandra and Daniele Lorenzini, ed. 2022a. *Foucault, Sexuality, Antiquity*. Trans. M. Altman. New York: Routledge.

Boehringer, Sandra and Daniele Lorenzini. 2022b. "Problematizing Sexuality: Foucault, the Ancients, and Us." In *Foucault, Sexuality, Antiquity*. Trans. M. Altman. New York: Routledge, 3–10.

Booth, Wayne C. 1983. *The Rhetoric of Fiction*. 2nd ed. Chicago: Chicago University Press.

Boulding, M., J. Rotelle, and M. Fiedrowicz. 2000. *The Works of Saint Augustine: Expositions of the Psalms*. Hyde Park: New York City Press. Six volumes.

Brandt, Paul [alias Hans Licht], trans. 1912. "Erotische Träume und ihre Symbolik." *Anthropophyteia* 9: 316–28.

Brandt, Paul [alias Hans Licht]. 1925. *Sittengeschichte Griechenlands in Zwei Bänden und Einem Ergänzungsband*. Dresden: Paul Aretz.

Braunstein, Nestor. 2020. *Jouissance: A Lacanian Concept*. Trans. Silvia Rosman. Albany: SUNY Press.

Brion, Fabienne and Bernard E. Harcourt. 2012. "Situation du Cours." In *Michel Foucault, Mal faire, dire vrai: Fonction de l'aveu en justice*. Eds. Fabienne Brion and Bernard E. Harcourt. Chicago: University of Chicago Press/Louvain: UCL Presses Universitaires de Louvain, 263–326.

Brion, Fabienne and Bernard Harcourt 2014. "Editors' Preface." Michel Foucault, *Wrong Doing, Truth Telling: The Function of Avowal in Justice*. Trans. S. Sawyer. Chicago: University of Chicago Press.

Bronner, Andrea. 2019. "The Three Histories of the Vienna Psychoanalytic Society." In *100 Years of IPA: The Centenary History of the International Psychoanalytic Association 1910–2010: Evolution and Change*. Eds. Nellie L. Thompson and Peter Loewenberg, London: Routledge, 9–24.

Brown, Peter. 1980. "Culture, Society, and Renunciation in Late Antiquity." *Hale Lectures*, Seabury-Western, now archived at Garrett Theological Seminary, BX5937.A1 H2 1980.

Brown, Peter. 1981. *The Cult of the Saints*. Chicago: Chicago University Press.

Brown, Peter. 2012. *The Eye of a Needle*. Princeton: Princeton University Press.

Burt, Raymond L. 1990. *Friedrich Salomo Krauss (1859-1938): Selbstzeugnisse und Materialien zur Biographie des Volkskundlers, Literaten, und Sexualforschers mit einem Nachlaßverzeichnis*. Vienna: Austrian Academy of Sciences Press.

Büttgen, P. 2021a. "Aveu et confession." In Büttgen, Chevallier, Colombo, and Sforzini 2021, 85–107.

Büttgen, P. 2021b. "Foucault's Concept of Confession." *Foucault Studies* 29: 6–21.

Büttgen, P., P. Chevallier, A. Colombo, and A. Sforzini, eds. 2021. *Foucault, les pères, le sexe*. Paris: Éditions de la Sorbonne.

Butler, Judith. 1990. *Gender Trouble: Feminism and the Subversion of Identity*. New York: Routledge.

Butler, Judith. 2006. *Gender Trouble: Feminism and the Subversion of Identity*. 2nd ed. New York: Routledge.

Byatt, A. S. 1991. *Passions of the Mind*. New York: Vintage.

Calcutt, Andrew. 2016. "The Surprising Origins of 'Post-Truth'—and How It Was Spawned by the Liberal Left." *The Conversation*. https://theconversation.com/the-surprising-origins-of-post-truth-and-how-it-was-spawned-by-the-liberal-left-68929.

Camelot, T. 1952. "Les traités 'de virginitate' au IVe siècle." *Mystique et continence: Travaux scientifiques du VIIe Congrès international d'Avon*. Études Carmélitaines 13. Bruges: Desclée de Brouwer, 273–92.

Canguilhem, Georges. 1962. "Monstrosity and the Monstrous." Trans. Therese Jaeger. *Diogenes* 10 (40): 27–42.

Canguilhem, Georges. 1984. "What is a Scientific Ideology?" Trans. Mike Shortland. *Radical Philosophy* 29: 20–5. https://www.radicalphilosophy.com/article/what-is-scientific-ideology.

Canguilhem, Georges. [1965] 2003. *La Connaissance de la vie*. Paris: Vrin.

Canguilhem, Georges. 2009. "Qu'est qu'une idéologie scientifique?" *Idéologie et Rationalité dans l'histoire des sciences de la vie*. Paris: Vrin, 39–55.

Carrette, Jeremy. 2000. *Foucault and Religion: Spiritual Corporality and Corporal Spritiuality*. London: Routledge.

Carroll, David. 1992. *George Eliot and the Conflict of Interpretations*. New York: Cambridge University Press.

Certeau, Michel de. 1984. *The Practice of Everyday Life*. Trans. Steven Rendall. Berkeley: California University Press.

Chandezon, Christophe and Julien du Bouchet, eds. 2014. *Artémidore de Daldis et l'interprétation des rêves: quatorze études*. Paris: Les Belles Lettres.

Chesnet, Hippolyte. [1860] 2014. "Question d'identité"; "Vice de conformation des organes génitaux externes"; "Hypospadias"; "Erreur sur le sexe." In *Herculine Barbin dite Alexina B.* Ed. Michel Foucault. Paris: Gallimard, 147–50.

Chevallier, P. 2011. *Foucault et le christianisme*. Lyon: Éditions École Normale Supérieure.

Chevallier, P. 2022. "The Birth of Confessions of the Flesh: A Journey through the Archives." Trans. Charles A. Piecyk. *Maynooth Philosophical Papers* 11: 55–73.

Clements, Niki Kasumi. 2020. *Sites of the Ascetic Self: John Cassian and Christian Ethical Formation*. South Bend, Indiana: University of Notre Dame Press.
Clements, Niki Kasumi. 2021a. "Foucault's Christianities." *Journal of the American Academy of Religion* 89 (1): 1–40.
Clements, Niki Kasumi. 2021b. "Afterword." *Gnosis: Journal of Gnostic Studies* 6: 233–9.
Clements, Niki Kasumi. 2022a. "The Decade of Foucault's 'Christian book.'" *Theology & Sexuality* 28 (1): 1–24.
Clements, Niki Kasumi. 2022b. "Foucault and Brown." *Foucault Studies* 32: 1–27.
Clements, Niki Kasumi. 2022c. "The Telos of Asceticism: Michel Foucault and John Cassian." In *Reaching for Perfection: Studies on the Means and Goals of Ascetical Practices*. Eds. J. Verheyden, G. Roskam, A. Heirman, and J. Leemans. Leuven: Peeters Publishers.
Cochrane, Donald and Jinjie Wang. 2020. "'Vision without action is merely a dream': A conversation with Li Yinhe." *Critical Asian Studies* 52 (3): 446–63.
Colombo, Agustín. 2023. *Christianisme et subjectivité chez Michel Foucault*. Paris: Les éditions Hermann.
Connolly, Joy. 2007. *The State of Speech: Rhetoric and Political Thought in Ancient Rome*. Princeton: Princeton University Press.
Connolly, Joy. 2017. *The Life of Roman Republicanism*. Princeton: Princeton University Press.
Cooper, John M. and Douglas S. Hutchinson, eds. 1997. *Plato: Complete Works*. Cambridge: Hackett Publishing.
Crary, Jonathan. 2014. *24/7: Late Capitalism and the Ends of Sleep*. New York: Verso.
Cremonesi, Laura. 2015. "La lecture foucaldienne de la *parrêsia* chrétienne." In *Michel Foucault et les religions*. Ed. J.-F. Bert. Paris: Le Manuscrit.
Davidson, Arnold. 1986. "Archaeology, Genealogy, Ethics." In *Foucault: A Critical Reader*. Ed. David Couzens Hoy. New York: Basil Blackwell, 221–33.
Davidson, Arnold. 2005. *L'Émergence de la sexualité: Epistémologie historique et formation des concepts*. Trans. Pierre-Emmanuel Dauzat. Paris: Albin Michel.
Davidson, Arnold. 2011. "In Praise of Counter-Conduct." *History of the Human Sciences* 24 (4): 25–41.
Defert, Daniel. 2011. "Situation du cours." In *Michel Foucault, Leçons sur la volonté de savoir: Cours au college de France, 1970–71. Suivi de "Le Savoir d'Oedipe."* Ed. Daniel Defert. Paris: Hautes Études/Gallimard/Seuil, 257–79.
Deleuze, Gilles. 1989. *Cinema 2: The time-image*. Trans. Hugh Tomlinson and Robert Galeta. Minneapolis: University of Minnesota Press.
Derrida, Jacques. 1973. *Speech and Phenomena and Other Essay's on Husserl's Theory of Signs*. Trans. David B. Allison. Evanston: Northwestern University Press.
Derrida, Jacques. 1978. "Cogito and the History of Madness." In *Writing and Difference*. Trans. Allan Bass. New York: University of Chicago Press, 29–61.
Derrida, Jacques. 1994. "'To Do Justice to Freud': The History of Madness in the Age of Psychoanalysis." Trans. Pascale-Anne Brault et al. *Critical Inquiry* 20: 227–65.
Detienne, Marcel. 1996. *The Masters of Truth in Archaic Greece*. Trans. Janet Lloyd. New York: Zone Books.

DeWitt, N. 1936. "Organisation and Procedure in Epicurean Groups." *Classical Philology* 21: 205–11.
DeWitt, N. 1954. *Epicurus and His Philosophy*. Minnesota: University of Minnesota Press.
Dover, Kenneth J. 1989. *Greek Homosexuality*. Cambridge, MA: Harvard University Press.
Doyle, Mary Ellen. 1981. *The Sympathetic Response*. East Brunswick: Associated University Press.
Dressler, Alex. 2016a. *Personification and the Feminine in Roman Philosophy*. Cambridge: Cambridge University Press.
Dressler, Alex. 2016b. "Plautus and the Poetics of Property: Reification, Recognition, and Utopia." *Materiali e Discussioni per l'analisi dei testi classici* 77: 9–57.
Dressler, Alex. 2023. *Selections from the Poems of Paulinus of Nola, Including the Correspondence with Ausonius*. London: Routledge.
Dreyfus, Hubert L. and Paul Rabinow. 1983. *Michel Foucault: Beyond Structuralism and Hermeneutics*. New York: University of Chicago Press.
du Bouchet, Julien. 2016. "Artémidore, homme de science." In *Clés des songes et sciences des rêves: De l'Antiquité à Freud*. Ed. Jacqueline Carroy and Juliette Lancel. Paris: Les Belles Lettres, 33–45.
Dyrberg, T. B. 2016. "Foucault on 'parrhesia': The Autonomy of Politics and Democracy." *Political Theory* 44 (2): 265–88.
Edelman, Lee. 2005. *No Future: Queer Theory and the Death Drive*. Durham, NC: Duke University Press.
Editorial Committee for *A Concise History of the Communist Party of China*. 2021. *A Concise History of the Communist Party of China*. Beijing: Central Compilation and Translation Press.
Elden, Stuart. 2016. *Foucault's Last Decade*. Malden, MA: Polity Press.
Elden, Stuart. 2021. *The Early Foucault*. Cambridge: Polity.
Eliot, George. 1965. *Middlemarch*. Ed. W. J. Harvey. New York: Penguin.
Eribon, Didier. 2011. *Michel Foucault*. Paris: Flammarion.
Escalle, Élise. 2020. "Notes Towards a Critical History of Musicalities: Philodemus on the Use of Musical Pleasures and the Care of the Self." In Faustino and Ferraro 2020, 89–100.
Fantham, Elaine. 2004. *The Roman World of Cicero's De Oratore*. Oxford: Oxford University Press.
Faustino, M. and G. Ferraro, eds. 2020. *The Late Foucault*. New York.
Flamand, Jean-Marie. 2014. "Recherche sur la causalité dans les *Oneirokritika* d'Artémidore: la 'théorie' des six *stoicheiai*." In *Artémidore de Daldis et l'interprétation des rêves: quatorze études*. Ed. Christophe Chandezon and Julien du Bouchet. Paris: Les Belles Lettres, 108–37.
"Foucault, Did He Blaze the Trail for the Post-Truth Era." 2021. *EUvsDisinfo*. https://euvsdisinfo.eu/foucault-did-he-blaze-a-trail-for-the-post-truth-era/#.
Foucault, Michel. 1963. *Naissance de la clinique*. Paris: PUF.
Foucault, Michel. 1971. *L'Ordre du discours*. Paris: Gallimard.

Foucault, Michel. 1972. *The Archeology of Knowledge*. Trans. Alan Sheridan. New York: Pantheon.
Foucault, Michel. 1975. *Surveiller et punir: Naissance de la prison*. Paris: Gallimard.
Foucault, Michel. 1976. *Histoire de la sexualité*, t. 1, *La Volonté de savoir*. Paris: Gallimard.
Foucault, Michel. 1979. "What is an Author?" In *Textual Strategies: Perspectives in Post-Structuralist Criticism*. Ed. and trans. Josué V. Harari. Ithaca, Cornell University Press, 141–60.
Foucault, Michel. 1980. Seminars delivered at New York Institute for Humanities. French and English manuscripts held by the BNF, Foucault archive, NAF 28730, dossier 40. "La généalogie du savoir moderne sur la sexualité" [working title], edited by Daniele Lorenzini and P-H. Fruchaud. Forthcoming 2022.
Foucault, Michel. 1981. "The Order of Discourse." In *Untying the Text*. Ed. Robert Young. Trans. Ian MacLeod. London: Routledge and Kegan Paul, 48–78.
Foucault, Michel. 1984a. *Histoire de la sexualité II: L'Usage des plaisirs*. Paris: Gallimard.
Foucault, Michel. 1984b. *Histoire de la sexualité III: Le Souci de soi*. Paris: Gallimard.
Foucault, Michel. 1984c. "Dream, Imagination, and Existence: An Introduction to Ludwig Binswanger's *Dream and Existence*." Trans. Forrest Williams. *Review of Existential Psychology and Psychiatry* 19 (1): 29–78.
Foucault, Michel. 1986a. *The Use of Pleasure: The History of Sexuality Volume Two*. Trans. Robert Hurley. New York: Vintage.
Foucault, Michel. 1986b. *The Care of the Self: Volume 3 of the History of Sexuality*. Trans. Robert Hurley. New York: Pantheon Books.
Foucault, Michel. 1998. "The Thought of the Outside." In *Essential Works of Foucault 1954–1984*, Vol. 2: *Aesthetics, Method, and Epistemology*. Ed. J. D. Faubion. New York: The New Press, 147–70.
Foucault, Michel. 1988a. "Technologies of the Self." In *Technologies of the Self: A Seminar with Michel Foucault*. Eds. Luther H. Martin, Huck Gutman, and Patrick H. Hutton. Amherst: University of Massachusetts, 16–49.
Foucault, Michel. 1988b. "The Ethic of Care for the Self as a Practice of Freedom." In *The Final Foucault*. Eds. James Bernauer and D. Rasmussen. Cambridge, MA: MIT Press.
Foucault, Michel. 1990. *History of Sexuality: Volume 1: Introduction*. Trans. Robert Hurley. New York: Vintage Books.
Foucault, Michel. 1993. *Archaeology of Knowledge and the Discourse on Language*. Trans. A. M. Sheridan Smith. New York: Pantheon Books.
Foucault, Michel. 1994a. "Note of January 7 1979." *Dits et Écrits* I. Ed. D. Defert and F. Ewald. Paris: Gallimard.
Foucault, Michel. 1994b. "L'extension social de la norme" (interview with P. Werner). *Politique Hebdo*, 212: *Délier la folie*, March 4–10, 1976, 14–16. *Dits et Écrits* III. no. 173. Eds. Daniel Defert and François Ewald. Paris: Gallimard.
Foucault, Michel. 1994c. "Sexualité et pouvoir." Conference paper, University of Tokyo, April 20, 1978. *Dits et Écrits* III: *1976–1979*. no. 233. Eds. Daniel Defert and François Ewald. Paris: Gallimard, 552–70.

Foucault, Michel. 1994d. "Rêver de ses plaisirs: Sur l'*Onirocritique* d'Artémidore (Conférence donnée au département de philosophie de l'université de Grenoble, le 18 mai 1982)." *Recherches sur la philosophie et le langage* 3, 1983. *Dits et Écrits* IV. Eds. Daniel Defert and François Ewald. Paris: Gallimard, 54–78.

Foucault, Michel. 1994e. "Sexual Choice, Sexual Act: Foucault and Homosexuality." In *Ethics: Subjectivity and Truth*. Ed. Paul Rabinow. Trans. Robert Hurley and Others, Volume 1. New York: The New Press, 141–56.

Foucault, Michel. 1994f. "Sex, Power, and the Politics of Identity." In *Ethics: Subjectivity and Truth*. Ed. Paul Rabinow. Trans Robert Hurley and Others, Volume 1. New York: The New Press, 163–73.

Foucault, Michel. 1994g. *The Order of Things*. Trans. Alan Sheridan. New York: Vintage Books.

Foucault, Michel. 1994h. "The Subject and Power." In *Power: The Essential Works of Michel Foucault 1954–1984: Volume 3*. Eds. Paul Rabinow and J. Faubion. New York: The New Press.

Foucault, Michel. 1995. *Discipline and Punish: The Birth of the Prison*. Trans. Alan Sheridan. New York: Vintage Books.

Foucault, Michel. 1996. "The Social Extension of the Norm." Trans. Lysa Hochroth. In *Foucault Live*. New York: Semiotext(e), 196–9.

Foucault, Michel. 1997a. *Discipline and Punish: The Birth of the Prison*. Trans. Alan Sheridan. New York: Vintage Books.

Foucault, Michel. 1997b. "On the Genealogy of Ethics: An Overview of Work in Progress." In *Ethics: Subjectivity and Truth: The Essential Works of Michel Foucault 1954–1984: Volume I*. Eds. Paul Rabinow and J. Faubion. New York: The New Press.

Foucault, Michel. 1997c. "Friendship as a Way of Life." Interview with R. de Ceccaty, J. Danet and J. Le Bitoux, *Gai Pied*, April 1981. In *Ethics: Subjectivity and Truth: The Essential Works of Michel Foucault 1954–1984: Volume I*. Ed. Paul Rabinow. Trans. John Johnston, amended. New York: The New Press, 135–41.

Foucault, Michel. 1997d. "The Ethics of the Concern for the Self as a Practice of Freedom." In *Ethics: Subjectivity, and Truth: The Essential Works of Michel Foucault 1954–1984: Volume 1*. Eds. Paul Rabinow and J. Faubion. New York: The New Press.

Foucault, Michel. 1998. "Nietzsche, Genealogy, History." In *Aesthetics, Method, and Epistemology: The Essential Works of Michel Foucault 1954–1984: Volume 2*. Eds. Paul Rabinow and J. Faubion. New York: The New Press.

Foucault, Michel. 1999. *Religion and Culture*. Ed. Jeremy Carrette. Trans. Richard Lynch. New York: Routledge.

Foucault, Michel. 1999a. *Abnormal: Lectures at the Collège de France, 1974–1975*. Ed. Valeerio Marchetti and Antonella Salomoni. Trans. Graham Burchell. New York: Picador.

Foucault, Michel. 2001 [1978]. "Méthodologie pour la connaissance du monde: comment se débarrasser du marxisme" *Dits et Écrits II, 1976–1988*. Eds. Daniel Defert and François Ewald. Paris: Jacques Lagrange, 302–28.

Foucault, Michel. 2001a. "Sexualité et pouvoir." Conference paper at the University of Tokyo, 20 April 1978. *Dits et Écrits* II. Paris: Gallimard, 552–70.
Foucault, Michel. 2001b. "Le vrai sexe." *Dits et Écrits* II. Paris: Gallimard, 934–42.
Foucault Michel. 2001c. "De l'amitié comme mode de vie." Interview with R. de Ceccaty, J. Danet and J. Le Bitoux, *Gai Pied*, April 1981. *Dits et Écrits* II. Paris: Gallimard, 982–6.
Foucault, Michel. 2003. *The Birth of the Clinic: An Archaeology of Medical Perception*. Trans. A. M. Sheridan. London: Routledge.
Foucault, Michel. 2005. *The Hermeneutics of the Subject: Lectures at the Collège de France, 1981–1982*. Ed. Frédéric Gros. Trans. Graham Burchell. New York: Palgrave Macmillan.
Foucault, Michel. 2005a. "Tehran: Faith aginst the Shah." In Afary and Anderson 2005, 198–203.
Foucault, Michel. 2005b. "The Revolt in Iran Spreads on Cassette Tapes." In Afary and Anderson 2005, 216–20.
Foucault, Michel. 2007. *Security, Territory, Population: Lectures at the Collège de France, 1977–1978*. Ed. Michel Senellart. Trans. Graham Burchell. New York: Palgrave Macmillan.
Foucault, Michel. 2008. *Le gouvernement de soi et des autres: Cours au Collège de France, 1982–83*. Ed. Frédéric Gros. Paris: Hautes Études/Gallimard/Seuil.
Foucault, Michel. 2008a. *The Birth of Biopolitics: Lectures at the Collège de France, 1978–1979*. Ed. Michel Senellart. Trans. Graham Burchell: New York: Palgrave Macmillan.
Foucault, Michel. 2009. *Le Courage de la vérité: Cours au Collège de France, 1984*. Ed. Frédéric Gros. Paris: EHESS-Gallimard-Seuil.
Foucault, Michel. 2010. *The Government of the Self and Others: Lectures at the Collège de France, 1983–84*. Ed. Frédéric Gros. Trans. Graham Burchell. New York: Palgrave Macmillan.
Foucault, Michel. 2011. *Leçons sur la volonté de savoir: Cours au Collège de France 19701971*. Ed. Daniel Defert. Paris: Seuil.
Foucault, Michel. 2012. *The Courage of the Truth: The Government of the Self and Others. Lectures at the Collège de France, 1984*. Ed. Frédéric Gros. Trans. Graham Burchell. New York: Palgrave Macmillan.
Foucault, Michel. 2012a. *On the Government of the Living: Lectures at the Collège de France, 1979–1980*. Ed. Michel Senellart. Trans. Graham Burchell: New York: Palgrave Macmillan.
Foucault, Michel. 2013. *Lectures on the Will to Know and Oedipal Knowledge: Lectures at the Collège de France 1970–71*. Ed. Daniel Defert. Trans. Graham Burchell. New York: Palgrave Macmillan.
Foucault, Michel. 2014a. *Subjectivité et vérité: Cours au Collège de France, 1980–1981*. Paris: Gallimard.
Foucault, Michel. 2014b. *Wrong-Doing, Truth Telling: The Function of Avowal in Justice*. Eds. F. Brion and B. Harcourt. Trans. S. Sawyer. Chicago: University of Chicago Press.

Foucault, Michel, ed. [1980] 2014c. *Herculine Barbin dite Alexina B.* Paris: Gallimard.
Foucault, Michel. 2015. *Le Souci de soi. Œuvres, Tome II.* Ed. Frédéric Gros with the collaboration of Philippe Chevallier, Daniel Defert, Bernard Harcourt, Martin Rueff, and Michel Senellart. Paris: Bibliothèque de la Pléiade.
Foucault, Michell. 2016. *On the Government of the Living: Lectures at the Collège de France, 1979–80.* Ed. Michel Senellart. Trans. Graham Burchell. New York: Picador.
Foucault, Michel. 2016a. *About the Beginning of the Hermeneutics of the Self: Lectures at Dartmouth College, 1980.* Eds. Henri-Paul Fruchaud and Daniele Lorenzini. Trans. Graham Burchell. Chicago: University of Chicago Press.
Foucault, Michel. 2016b. *Discours et vérité précédé de La parresia.* Eds. Henri-Paul Fruchaud and Daniele Lorenzini. Paris: Vrin.
Foucault, Michel. 2017a. *Subjectivity and Truth: Lectures at the College de France 1980–1981.* Ed. Frédéric Gros. Trans. Graham Burchell. New York: Picador.
Foucault, Michel. 2017b. *Dire vrai sur soi-même: Conférences prononcées à l'Université Victoria de Toronto.* Eds. Henri-Paul Fruchaud and Daniele Lorenzini. Paris: Vrin.
Foucault, Michel. 2018. *Histoire de la sexualité IV: Les Aveux de la chair.* Ed. Frédéric Gros. Paris: Gallimard.
Foucault, Michel. 2019. *Subjectivity and Truth: Lectures at the College de France 1980–1981.* Ed. Frédéric Gros. Trans. Graham Burchell. New York: Picador.
"Foucault, Did He Blaze the Trail for the Post. Truth Era." 2021. *EUvsDisinfo.* https://euvsdisinfo.eu/foucault-did-he-blaze-a-trail-for-the-post-truth-era/#.
Foucault, Michel. 2021a. *The Confessions of the Flesh: The History of Sexuality Volume Four.* Robert Hurley. New York: Pantheon Books.
Foucault, Michel. 2021b. "Nietzsche, genealogy, history." In *Language, Counter-Memory, Practice.* Trans. Donald F. Bouchard. New York: Cornell University Press, 139–64.
Foucault, Michel. 2021c. *Speaking the Truth about Oneself.* Ed. Daniel Wyche. Chicago: University of Chicago Press.
Foucault, Michel. Sans titre. Manuscrit autographe d'un texte inédit. "Les hermaphrodites – ceux qu'on dit réunir en eux les deux sexes – ont été longtemps soumis à un régime disparate. . . ." Handwritten manuscript sections of an unpublished text. Paris, BNF. NAF 28730, boîte 82, cahier 10 untitled. 116ff. Transcription by Niki Kasumi Clements, July 2022.
Foucault, Michel, Nicolae Morar, and Daniel W. Smith. 2011. "The Gay Science." *Critical Inquiry* 37 (3): 385–403.
Freud, Ernst, ed. 1992. *Letters of Sigmund Freud.* Trans. Tania and James Stern. New York: Dover Publications.
Freud, Sigmund. 1942. *Traumdeutung, Gesammelte Werke, II.* Eds. M. Bonaparte et al. London: Imago.
Freud, Sigmund. 1953. *The Interpretation of Dreams: The Standard Edition of the Complete Psychological Works of Sigmund Freud (= SE),* vols 4 and 5. Trans. James Strachey et al. London: Hogarth Press.

Freud, Sigmund. 1957. "Letter to Dr. Friedrich S. Krauss on *Anthropophyteia*." *SE* 11: 232–5. Trans. James Strachey et al. London: Hogarth Press.

Freud, Sigmund. 1955. *Totem and Taboo. SE* 13: ix–160. Trans. James Strachey et al. London: Hogarth Press.

Freud, Sigmund. 1958. "Preface to Bourke's *Scatalogic Rites of All Nations*." *SE* 12: 333–7. Trans. James Strachey et al. London: Hogarth Press.

Freud, Sigmund. 1961. "Some Additional Notes on Dream-Interpretation as a Whole." *SE* 19: 125–38. Trans. James Strachey et al. London: Hogarth Press.

Freud, Sigmund. 1961a. *Five Lectures on Psychoanalysis*. Trans. James Strachey. New York: W.W. Norton and Co.

Freud, Sigmund. 1963. *Introductory Lectures on Psychoanalysis. SE* 15–16. Trans. James Strachey et al. London: Hogarth Press.

Freud, Sigmund. 1999. *Conférences d'introduction à la psychanalyse*. Paris: Gallimard.

Freud, Sigmund and Ernst Oppenheim. 1958. "Dreams in Folklore." *SE* 12: 180–203. Trans. James Strachey et al. London: Hogarth Press.

Fruchaud, Henri-Paul and Daniele Lorenzini, eds. 2019. *Michel Foucault, Discourse and Truth*. English ed. trans. Nancy Luxon. Chicago. University of Chicago Press.

Gadamer, Hans-Georg. 2013. *Truth and Method*. Trans. Joel Weinsheimer and Donald G. Marshall. London: Bloomsbury Publishing.

Gan, Yang. 2011. "Zhongguo de dao lu: sans hi nian yu liu shi nian" 中国道路：三十年与六十年 [The Path of China: thirty years and sixty years]. In *Wen ming, guo jia, da xue* 文明・国家・大学 [*Civilization, Nation-State, and Universities*]. Beijing: Shenghuo, dushu, xinzhi, 33–44.

Genet, Jean. 1969. *Funeral Rites*. Trans. Bernard Frechtman. New York: Grove Press.

Gigante, M. 1970. "Philodème et la liberté de parole." *Association Guillaume Budé, Actes du VIIIe congrès, Paris 5–10 avril 1968*. Paris: Les Belles Lettres.

Goldhill, S. 2020. *Preposterous Poetics*. Cambridge: Cambridge University Press.

Goldhill, S. 2022. *The Christian Invention of Time*. Cambridge: Cambridge University.

Gomolka, Carl J. 2012. "Lost in (Trans)lation: The Misread Body of Herculine Barbin." *Synthesis* 4: 62–82.

Gomperz, Theodor. 1866. *Traumdeutung und Zauberei: Ein Blick auf das Wesen des Aberglaubens*. Vienna: Carl Gerold's Sohn.

Goujon, Étienne. [1869] 2014. "Étude d'un cas d'hermaphrodisme imparfait chez l'homme." In *Herculine Barbin dite Alexina B*. Ed. Michel Foucault. Paris: Gallimard (Collection Tel), 151–63.

Goujon, Étienne. [1869] 1980. "A Study of a Case of Incomplete Hermaphroditism in a Man." In *Herculine Barbin: Being the Recently Discovered Memoirs of a Nineteenth Century French Hermaphrodite*. New York: Random House, 128–44.

Graeber, David. 2011. *Debt: The First 5,000 Years*. Brooklyn: Melvin House.

Greven, David. 2016. *Gender Protest and Same-Sex Desire in Antebellum American Literature*. New York: Routledge.

Greven, David. 2017. *Intimate Violence: Hitchcock, Sex, and Queer Theory*. New York: Oxford University Press.
Gros, Frédéric. 2005. "Course Context." In M. Foucault, *The Hermeneutics of the Subject: Lectures at the Collège de France, 1981–1982*. Ed. Frédéric Gros. Trans. Graham Burchell. New York: Palgrave Macmillan.
Gros, Frédéric. 2010. "Course Context." In M. Foucault, *The Government of Self and Others: Lectures at the Collège de France, 1982–1983*. Ed. Frédéric Gros. Trans. Graham Burchell. New York: Palgrave Macmillan.
Gros, Frédéric. 2012. "La parrêsia chez Foucault (1982–1984)." *Foucault: Le courage de la verité*. 2nd ed. Paris: Presse Universitaire Francaise, 155–66.
Gros, Frédéric. 2015. "*Histoire de la sexualité* 2 et 3: Notice." *M. Foucault Œuvres*, v. II. Ed. Frédéric Gros. Paris: Gallimard, Bibliothèque de la Pléiade, 1529–42.
Gros, Frédéric. 2018. "Avertissement." In M. Foucault, *Les Aveux de la chair*. Paris: Gallimard, i–xi.
Gros, Frédéric. 2019. "Introduction." In M. Foucault, *Discourse and Truth*. Eds. Henri-Paul Fruchaud and Daniele Lorenzini. English ed. Nancy Luxon. Chicago: University of Chicago Press.
Hadot, Ilsetraut. 1969. *Seneca und die griechisch-römische Tradition der Seelenleitung*. Berlin: DeGruyter.
Haggerty, George. 2003. "Male Love and Friendship in the Eighteenth Century." In *Love, Sex, Intimacy, and Friendship Between Men, 1500–1800*. Eds. Katherine O'Donnell and Michael O'Rourke. New York: Palgrave Macmillan, 70–82.
Halperin, David M. 1989a. "Is There a History of Sexuality?" *History and Theory* 28 (3): 257–74.
Halperin, David M. 1989b. "Sex before Sexuality: Pederasty, Politics, and Power in Classical Athens." In *Hidden from History: Reclaiming the Gay and Lesbian Past*. Eds. Martin Bauml Duberman, Martha Vicinus, and George Chauncey, Jr. New York: New American Library, 1989, 37–53, 482–92.
Halperin, David M. 1990. *One Hundred Years of Homosexuality: and Other Essays on Greek Love*. New York: Routledge.
Halperin, David M. 1995. *Saint Foucault: Towards a Gay Hagiography*. New York: Oxford University Press.
Halperin, David M. 2002. *How to Do the History of Homosexuality*. Chicago: University of Chicago Press.
Halperin, David M. 2003. "Introduction: Among Men—History, Sexuality, and the Return of Affect." In *Love, Sex, Intimacy, and Friendship Between Men, 1550–1800*. Eds. Katherine O'Donnell and Michael O'Rourke. New York: Palgrave, 1–11.
Halperin, David M. 2012. *How To Be Gay*. Cambridge, MA: Belknap Press of Harvard University Press.
Halperin, David M., John J. Winkler, and Froma I. Zeitlin, eds. 1990. *Before Sexuality: The Construction of Erotic Experience in the Ancient Greek World*. Princeton: Princeton University Press.

Hammond, Martin. 2020. *Artemidorus: The Interpretation of Dreams*. Trans. Peter Thonemann. Oxford: Oxford University Press.
Harris, William V. 2009. *Dreams and Experience in Classical Antiquity*. Cambridge: Harvard University Press.
Harris-McCoy, Daniel, ed. and trans. 2012. *Artemidorus' Oneirocritica: Text, Translation, and Commentary*. Oxford: Oxford University Press.
Harvey, W. J. 1961. *The Art of George Eliot*. London: Chatto and Windus.
Heidegger, Martin. 1982. "The Age of the World Picture." In *The Question Concerning Technology and Other Essays*. Trans. William Lovitt. New York: Harper Torchbooks, 115–54.
Heidegger, Martin. 1998. "Plato's Doctrine of Truth." Trans. Thomas Sheehan. In *Pathmarks*. Ed. William McNeill. Cambridge: Cambridge University Press, 155–82.
Heidegger, Martin. 2013. *The Essence of Truth: On Plato's Cave Allegory and Theaetetus*. Trans. Ted Sadler. New York: Bloomsbury Publishing.
Houbre, Gabrielle. 2014. "Un 'sexe indéterminé'? l'identité civile des hermaphrodites entre droit et médecine au XIXe siècle." *Revue d'histoire du XIXe siècle* 48: 63–75.
Houbre, Gabrielle. 2020. *Les deux vies d'Abel Barbin, né Adélaïde Herculine (1838–1868): Édition annotée des Souvenirs d'Alexina Barbin*. Paris: PUF.
Huffer, Lynne. 2020. *Foucault's Strange Eros*. New York: Columbia University Press.
Iling, Sean. 2019. "The Post-Truth Prophets: Postmodernism Predicted our Post-Truth Hellscape. Everyone Still Hates It." *Vox*. https://www.vox.com/features/2019/11/11/18273141/postmodernism-donald-trump-lyotard-baudrillard.
James, Henry. 1986. "Middlemarch." In *The Art of Criticism: Henry James on the Theory and Practice of Fiction*. Eds. William Veeder and Susan M. Griffin. Chicago: Chicago University Press.
Kant, Immanuel. 2007. *Critique of the Power of Judgement*. Trans. Paul Guyer and Eric Matthews. New York: Cambridge University Press.
Kelly, M. G. E. 2013. "Foucault, subjectivity, and technologies of the self." In *A Companion to Foucault*. Eds. T. O'Leary, J. Sawicki and C. Falzon. New York: Wiley-Blackwell, 510–25.
Kindt, Julia. 2006. "Delphic Oracle Stories and the Beginning of Historiography: Herodotus' Croesus Logos." *Classical Philology* 101 (1): 34–51.
Klein, Melanie. 1957. *Envy and Gratitude*. London: Tavistock.
Krauss, Friedrich Salomo, trans. 1881. *Artemidoros aus Daldis: Symbolik der Träume*. Vienna: Hartleben.
Krisak, Len. 2019. *Prudentius' Crown of Martyrs: Liber Peristephanon*. London: Routledge.
Lacan, Jacques. 1974. "Déclaration à *France-Culture* à propos du 28e Congrès International de Psychanalyse." *Le coq-heron* 46/7: 3–8. https://freud2lacan.b-cdn.net/IPA-28th_Congress-TC.pdf.
Lacan, Jacques. 1976–7. *Séminaire XXIV: L'Insu que sait de l'Une-bévue s'aile à mourre*. Unpublished.
Lacan, Jacques. 1978. *Séminaire II: Le moi dans la théorie de Freud*. Paris: Le Seuil.

Lacan, Jacques. 1988. *The Seminar of Jacques Lacan Book II: The Ego in Freud's theory and in the Technique of Psychoanalysis: 1954–1955.* Ed. Jacques-Alain Miller. Trans. Sylvana Tomaselli. Cambridge: Cambridge University Press.

Lacan, Jacques. 2003–4. "L'insu que c'est de l'Une-bévue s'aile à mourre." Séance du 19 avril 1977. *L'Unebévue*, no. 21. Paris: L'Unebévue éditions.

Lacan, Jacques. No date. Seminar 24. Trans. Cormac Gallagher. https://lacanianworks.net/1976/11/seminar-xxiv-linsu-que-sait-de-lune-bevue-saile-a-mourre-1976-1977-begins-16th-november-1976-jacques-lacan/.

Lawlor, Leonard. 2016. *From Violence to Speaking Out: Apocalypse and Expression in Foucault, Derrida, and Deleuze.* Edinburgh: University of Edinburgh Press.

Lehmann-Haupt, Christopher. 1998. "English as a Useful Discipline, Not Hallowed Ground." *New York Times.* 9 March, natl. ed.: B8.

Le Mens, Magali and Jean-Luc Nancy. 2009. *L'hermaphrodite de Nadar.* Paris: Éditions Créaphis.

Le Saint, W. P. 1959. *Treatises on Penance: On Penitence and On Purity.* Westminster, MD: Newman Press.

Lévy, Carlos. 2014. "Parrêsia." *Michel Foucault: Un héritage critique.* Eds. Jean-François Bert and Jérôme Lamy. Paris: CNRS Éditions. 143–52.

Li, Yinhe. 2001. *Fuke yu xing: jie du Fuke xingshi* 福柯与性：解读福柯《性史》 [*Foucault and Sexuality: A Reading of Foucault's History of Sexuality*]. Jinan: Shandong ren min chu ban she.

Li, Yinhe. 2009. *Nue lian ya wen hua.* 虐恋亚文化 [*Subcultures of Sadomasochism*]. Huhehaote: Neimenggu University Press, 273–4.

Li, Yinhe. 2014. *Xin Zhongguo xing hua yu yan jiu* 新中国性话语研究 [*Discourses of Sexuality in the Post-1949 China*]. Shanghai: Shanghai she hui ke xue yuan chu ban she.

Li, Yinhe. 2015a. "*Fuke zhan shi de ren lei qian jing tai hui huang, cuo guo ta jiu cuo guo si xiang shi shang de qi ji*" 福柯展示的人类前景太辉煌，错过他就错过思想史上的奇迹. https://m.thepaper.cn/kuaibao_detail.jsp?contid=1285779&from=kuaibao (Last accessed on Dec. 13, 2022).

Li, Yinhe. 2015b. *Ren jian cai mi ji* 人间采蜜记 [*Honey-collecting Recording in the World: An Autobiography of Li Yinhe*]. Nanchang: Jiangxi ren min chu ban she.

Li, Yinhe. 2016. *Hei qi shi de wang guo* 黑骑士的王国 [*Dark Knight's Kingdom*]. Volumes 1–3. Hong Kong: Xianggang guo mai wen hua chuan mei gong si 香港果麦文化传媒有限公司.

Li, Yinhe. 2021. *Xing xue ru men* 性学入门 [*An Introduction to Sexology*]. Shanghai: Shanghai san lian shu dian.

Licht, Hans [Peter Brandt]. 1912. "Erotische Träume und ihre Symbolik." *Anthropophyteia* 9: 316–28.

Long, A. A. 1995. "Cicero's Plato and Aristotle." In *Cicero the Philosopher.* Ed. J. G. F. Powell. Oxford: Oxford University Press, 37–61.

Looby, Christopher. 2011. "Strange Sensations: Sex and Aesthetics in 'The Counterpane.'" In *Melville and Aesthetics*. Eds. Geoffrey Sanborn and Samuel Otter. New York: Palgrave Macmillan, 65–84.
Lorenzini, Daniele. 2015. "Performative, Passionate, and Parrhesiastic Utterance: On Cavell, Foucault, and Truth as an Ethical Force." *Critical Inquiry* 41 (2): 254–68.
Lorenzini, Daniele. 2016. "From Counter-Conduct to Critical Attitude: Michel Foucault and the Art of Not Being Governed Quite So Much." *Foucault Studies* 21: 7–21.
Lorenzini, Daniele. 2017. "La parrêsia et la force perlocutoire." In *Foucault(s)*. Eds. J.-F. Braunstein, D. Lorenzini, A. Revel, J. Revel, and A. Sforzini. Paris: Publications de la Sorbonne, 273–84.
Lorenzini, Daniele. 2022. "Desire as the 'Historical Transcendental' of the History of Sexuality." *Foucault, Sexuality, Antiquity*. Eds. Sandra Boehringer and Daniele Lorenzini. Trans. Meryl Altman. New York: Routledge, 103–11.
Lorenzini, Daniele. 2023. *The Force of Truth: Critique, Genealogy, and Truth-Telling in Michel Foucault*. Chicago: University of Chicago Press.
Lorenzini, Daniele, A. Revel, and A. Sforzini, eds. 2013. *Michel Foucault: éthique et vérité: 1980–1984*. Paris: Vrin.
Luzzatto, Maria Tanja. 2020. "Did Gorgias Coin *Rhētorikē*: A Rereading of Plato's *Gorgias*." *Lexis* 38 n.s.: 183–224.
Malosse, Pierre-Louis. 2014. "Oneiropolis." *Artémidore de Daldis et l'interprétation des rêves: quatorze études*. Eds. Christophe Chandezon and Julien du Bouchet. Paris: Les Belles Lettres, 140–60.
Mankin, David. 2011. *Cicero: De Oratore 3*. Cambridge: Cambridge University Press.
Marinelli, Lydia and Andreas Mayer. 2003. *Dreaming by the Book: Freud's* The Interpretation of Dreams *and the History of the Psychoanalytic Movement*. Trans. Susan Fairfield. New York: Other Press.
Markus, R. 1990. *The End of Ancient Christianity*. Cambridge: Cambridge University Press.
Marrow, S. B. 1982. "Parrhesia and the New Testament." *The Catholic Biblical Quarterly* 44 (3): 431–46.
Masson, Jeffrey, trans. 1985. *The Complete Letters of Sigmund Freud to Wilhelm Fliess, 1887–1904*. Cambridge, MA: Belknap Press.
Mattei, P. 2021. "Le Tertullien de Foucault: Entre *publicatio sui*, multiplication des œuvres et crainte de soi, quelle cohérence et quelle pertinence philologiques et historiques?" In Büttgen, Chevallier, Colombo, and Sforzini 2021, 111–22.
May, Todd. 2006. "Foucault's Relation to Phenomenology." In *The Cambridge Companion to Foucault*. 2nd ed. Ed. Gary Gutting. Cambridge: Cambridge University Press, 284–311.
Mayer, Andreas. 2018. "Conflicting Interpretations of Artemidorus's *Oneirocritica*: Freud, Theodor Gomperz, F. S. Krauss and the Symbolic Language of Dreams." *Psychoanalysis and History* 20 (1): 89–112.

McCall, C. 2017. "Parrhēsia." In *The Cambridge Foucault Lexicon*. Eds. L. Lawlor and J. Nale. Cambridge: Cambridge University Press.

McCarthy, M. 2005. "An Ecclesiology of Groaning: Augustine, the Psalms, and the Making of the Church." *Theological Studies* 66 (1): 23–48.

McGowan, A. 2010. *Ancient Christian Worship: Early Church Practices in Social, Historical, and Theological Perspective*. Grand Rapids: Baker Academic.

McGushin, Edward. 2007. *Foucault's Askēsis: An Introduction to the Philosophical Life*. Evanston, IL: Northwestern University Press.

McGushin, Edward. 2016. "Deconstruction, Care of the Self, Spirituality: Putting Foucault and Derrida to the Test." In *Between Derrida and Foucault*. Eds. Yubraj Aryal, Vernon W. Cisney, Nicolae Morar, and Christopher Penfield. Edinburgh: Edinburgh University Press, 104–22.

Meunier, Bernard. 2021. "Foucault et les évolutions de la pârresia chretienne." In Büttgen, Chevallier, Colombo, and Sforzini 2021, 159–71.

Michel, Alain. 1960. *Rhétorique et philosophie chez Cicéron: Essai sur les fondements philosophiques de l'art de persuader*. Paris: Presses Universitaires de France.

Miller, D. A. 1981. *Narrative and Its Discontents*. Princeton: Princeton University Press.

Miller, D. A. 1988. *The Novel and the Police*. Berkeley: California University Press.

Miller, D. A. 1991. "Anal *Rope*." In *Inside/Out: Lesbian Theories, Gay Theories*. Ed. Diana Fuss. New York: Routledge, 119–41.

Miller, D. A. 2007. "On the Universality of *Brokeback*." *Film Quarterly* 60 (3): 50–60. https://doi.org/10.1525/fq.2007.60.3.50.

Miller, J. Hillis. 1992. *Ariadne's Thread*. New Haven: Yale University Press.

Miller, Paul Allen. 2020. "Plato as World Literature." In *Philosophy as World Literature*. Ed. Jeffrey DiLeo. New York: Bloomsbury, 47–58.

Miller, Paul Allen. 2021a. *Foucault's Seminars on Antiquity: Learning to Speak the Truth*. London: Bloomsbury Academic.

Miller, Paul Allen. 2021b. "Unspeakable Enjoyment in Catullus (80, 16, 11, 63)." *Dictynna* [online], 18.

Miller, Paul Allen. 2022. "Plato's Seventh Letter or How to Fashion a Subject of Resistance." In *The Politics of Form in Greek Literature*. Ed. Phiroze Vasunia. London: Routledge, 125–44.

Miller, Paul Allen. 2023. "Beyond the Pleasure Principle: Antigone's 'No' and the Ethics of Psychoanalysis." In *The Bloomsbury Handbook of Literature and Psychoanalysis*. Ed. Jeremy Tambling. London: Bloomsbury, 137–48.

Mohr, Richard D. 1992. *Gay Ideas: Outing and Other Controversies*. Boston, MA: Beacon Press.

Moretti, Franco. 1983. *Signs Taken for Wonders: Essays in the Sociology of Literary Forms*. London: Verso.

Morrison, Paul. 2002. *The Explanation for Everything: Essays on Sexual Subjectivity*. New York: New York University Press.

Morstein-Marx, Robert. 2004. *Mass Oratory and Political Power in the Roman Republic.* Cambridge: Cambridge University Press.

Mrtaschek-Halfman, Sigrid. 2002. *Der Briefwechsel des Paulinus von Nola: Kommunikation und soziale Kontakte zwischen christlichen Intellektuellen.* Göttingen: Vandenhoeck & Ruprecht.

Muckelbauer, John. 2008. *The Future of Invention: Rhetoric, Postmodernism, and the Problem of Change.* Albany: SUNY Press.

Neamțu, M. 2011. "Psalmody, Confession, and Temporality." In *Meditations of the Heart: The Psalms in Early Christian Thought and Practice: Essays In Honour of Andrew Louth.* Eds. A. Andreopoulos, A. Casiday, and C. Harrison. Turnhout: Brepols, 119–40.

Nunberg, Herman and Ernst Federn, eds. 1967. *Minutes of the Vienna Psychoanalytic Society, vol II: 1908–1910.* Trans. M. Nunberg. New York: International Universities Press.

Nunberg, Herman and Ernst Federn, eds. 1974. *Minutes of the Vienna Psychoanalytic Society, vol III: 1910–1911.* Trans. M. Nunberg. New York: International Universities Press.

O'Donoghue, Diane. 2009. "The Magic of the Manifest: Freud's Egyptian Dream Book." *American Imago* 66 (2): 211–30.

O'Gorman, Ellen. 2018. "'The Noise, and the People': Popular *clamor* and Political Discourse in Latin Historiography." In *Complex Inferiorities.* Eds. S. Harrison and M. Matzner. Oxford: Oxford University Press, 129–48.

Paglia, Camille. 1992. *Sex, Art, and American Culture.* New York, Vintage.

Petit, Caroline. 2014. "Signes et présages: le discours prédictif et ses enjeux chez Galien, Artémidore et Ptolémée." In *Artémidore de Daldis et l'interprétation des rêves: quatorze études.* Eds. Christophe Chandezon and Julien du Bouchet. Paris: Les Belles Lettres, 161–90.

Porter, James. 2016. *The Sublime in Antiquity.* Cambridge: Cambridge University Press.

Price, Simon R. F. 1990. "The Future of Dreams: From Freud to Artemidorus." In *Before Sexuality: The Construction of Erotic Experience in the Ancient Greek World.* Eds. David M. Halperin, John J. Winkler, and Froma Zeitlin. Princeton: Princeton University Press, 365–87.

Rabbow, P. 1914. *Antike Schriften Uber Seelenheilung und Seelenleitung: Auf ihre Quellen Untersucht.* Berlin: Teubner.

Rabbow, P. 1954. *Seelenführung: Methodik der Exerzitien in der Antike.* Munich: Kösel-Verlag.

Rajchman, John. 1991. *Truth and Eros: Foucault, Lacan, and the Question of Ethics.* London: Routledge.

Rancière, Jacques. 2009. *The Emancipated Spectator.* Trans. Gregory Elliott. London: Verso.

Reid, Julian. 2018. "Foucault and the Imagination: the roles of images in regimes of power and subjectivity." *Subjectivity*: https://doi.org/10.1057/s41286-018-0052-3.

Remer, Gary A. 2017. *Ethics and the Orator: The Ciceronian Tradition of Morality.* Chicago: University of Chicago Press.

Robb, Graham. 2003. *Skrangers: Homosexual Love in the 19th Century*. New York: Picador.
Rojas, M. A. 2012. *Michel Foucault: la "parrêsia", une éthique de la vérité*. Thèse sous la Direction de Frédéric Gros, Université Paris-Est, Disponible sur HAL Id: tel-00856801.
Schiappa, Edward. 1990. "Did Plato Coin *Rhētorikē*?" *American Journal of Philology* 111: 457–70.
Sedgwick, Eve Kosofsky. 1997. "Paranoid Reading and Reparative Reading; or, You're So Paranoid, You Probably Think This Introduction Is About You." In *Novel Gazing: Queer Readings in Fiction*. Ed. Eve Kosofsky Sedgwick. Durham, NC: Duke University Press, 1–37.
Senellart, M. 2007. "Paradossi e attualità della soggesttivazione Cristiana." In *Dopo Foucault: Genealogie del Postmoderno*. Ed. Eleonora De Conciliis. Milan: Edizione Cartacea, 33–51.
Senellart, Michel. 2022. "Le concept chrétien de parrhèsia, de Peterson à Foucault." In *Liberté de parole*. Eds. M. Abbès and M.-C. Isaïa. Turnhout: Brepols, 9–24.
Sforzini, A. 2018. "L'autre modernité du sujet. Foucault et la confession de la chair: les pratiques de subjectivation à l'âge des Réformes." *Revue de l'histoire des religions* 3: 485–505.
Showalter, Elaine. 1990. *Sexual Anarchy*. New York: Penguin.
Sivan, Hagith. 1994. *Ausonius of Bordeaux: genesis of a Gallic aristocracy*. London: Routledge.
Staten, Henry. 2019. *Techne Theory: A New Language for Art*. London: Bloomsbury.
Stekel, Wilhelm. 1911. *Die Sprache des Traumes*. Wiesbaden: J. F. Bermann.
Tardieu, Ambroise. [1857] 1995. *Les Attentats aux mœurs*. Grenoble: Jérôme Millon.
Tardieu, Ambroise. [1872] 2014. "Question médico-légale de l'identité dans ses rapports avec les vices de conformation des organes sexuels." *Herculine Barbin dite Alexina B*. Ed. Michel Foucault. Paris: Gallimard, 145–6.
Taylor, Chloe. 2009. *The Culture of Confession from Foucault to Augustine*. New York: Routledge.
Tellis, Ashley. 2015. "Of Comrades and Cool Kids: Queer Women's Activism in China." In *The Global Trajectories of Queerness: Re-Thinking Same-Sex Politics in the Global South*. Eds. Ashley Tellis and Sruti Bala. Netherlands: Brill Rodopi, 137–44.
Testa, F. 2023. "Foucault's Epicureanism: Parrhēsia, Confession, and the Genealogy of the Self." *Arethusa* 56.3 (Fall 2023): 355–62.
Testa, F. 2024. "Between Care of the Other and Truth-Telling: The Place of Epicureanism in the Interrupted Dialogue Between Michel Foucault and Pierre Hadot." In *Hadot and Foucault on Ancient Philosophy: Critical Assessments*. Eds. M. Faustino and H. Telo. Leiden: Brill.
Teti, A. 2020. "Rethinking Confession." In Faustino and Ferraro 2020, 215–32.
Thonemann, Peter. 2020. *An Ancient Dream Manual: Artemidorus' The Interpretation of Dreams*. Oxford: Oxford University Press.
Trout, Dennis. 1999. *Paulinus of Nola: Life, Letters, and Poems*. Berkeley: University of California Press.

Vesperini, Pierre. 2020. "'Un gentil mécréant, avec qui l'on entre aussitôt dans le seul monde qui compte.' Cinq lettres du père Festugière à Michel Foucault (1956–1957)." *Anabases* 31: 125–30.

Vessey, D. 2009. "Gadamer and the Fusion of Horizons." *International Journal of Philosophical Studies* 17 (4): 531–42.

Veyne, Paul. 1978. "La famille et l'amour sous le Haut-Empire romain." *Annales, Économies, Sociétés, Civilisations* 33 (1): 35–63.

Veyne, Paul. 1982. "L'homosexualité à Rome." *Communications* 35. *Sexualités occidentales. Contribution à l'histoire et à la sociologie de la sexualité*: 26–33.

Veyne, Paul. 1997. "Homosexuality in Ancient Rome." In *Western Sexuality: Practice and Precept in Past and Present Times*. Ed. Philippe Ariès and André Béjin. Trans. Anthony Forster. New York: Barnes & Noble Books, 26–35.

Vigarello, Georges. 1995. "La violence sexuelle et l'œil du savant." In Amboise Tardieu, *Les Attentats aux mœurs*. Grenoble: Éditions Jérome Millon.

Vogel, L. Z. 1986. "The Case of Elise Gomperz." *American Journal of Psychoanalysis* 46 (3): 230–8.

Warner, Michael. 1999. *The Trouble with Normal: Sex, Politics, and the Ethics of Queer Life*. New York: The Free Press.

Weeks, Jeffrey. 1981. *Sex, Politics, and Society: The Regulation of Sexuality Since 1800*. London: Longman.

Weng, Leihua. 2015. "Revolution and Event: Mao in Alain Badiou's *Plato's Republic*." *Comparative Literature Studies* 52 (1): 47–64.

White, Robert, trans. 1975. *The Interpretation of Dreams*. Park Ridge, NJ: Noyse Pres.

Whitebook, Joel. 1999. "Freud, Foucault and the 'Dialogue with Unreason.'" *Philosophy and Social Criticism* 25 (6): 29–66.

Whitebook, Joel. 2006. "Against Interiority: Foucault's Struggle with Psychoanalysis." In *The Cambridge Companion to Foucault*. Ed. Gary Gutting. Cambridge: Cambridge University Press, 312–47.

Wickham, Chris. 2009. *The Inheritance of Rome: Illuminating the Dark Ages 400–1000*. New York: Penguin.

Wight, Colin. 2018. "Post-truth, Postmodernism, and Alternative Facts." *New Perspectives* 26: 17–30.

Winkler, John J. 1990. *Constraints of Desire: The Anthropology of Sex and Gender in Ancient Greece*. London: Routledge, 17–44.

Wisse, Jakob, Michael Winterbottom, and Elaine Fantham. 2008. *M. Tullius Cicero: De Oratore Libri III*. Band 5. Heidelberg: Carl Winter Universitätverlag.

Woolf, Virginia. 1975. *Granite and Rainbow: Essays*. New York: Harvest.

Zachhuber, J. 2021. "Intériorité de la conscience et extériorité des aveux: Le sujet chrétien selon Foucault." In Büttgen, Chevallier, Colombo, and Sforzini 2021, 53–65.

Zuckert, Catherine H. 1996. *Postmodern Platos: Nietzsche, Heidegger, Gadamer, Strauss, Derrida*. Chicago: University of Chicago Press.

Index

Adler, Alfred 126
AIDS 9, 172–3, 176, 181, 188
alētheia (*see* truth) 5, 18, 39, 72
Alexina 159–63, 165, 206n9
Allouch, Jean 167–9
anti-social thesis 176
Antonius, Marcus 76–7, 79
Antony, Mark (grandson of Marcus Antonius) 84
aphrodisia 6, 50, 53, 62, 64, 123, 139–40
Artemidorus 3–6, 8, 10, 51–62, 64–6, 121–3, 126–40
asceticism 12, 18, 43, 94, 105, 113, 187, 189, 202nn.27–8
attentats aux moeurs 160, 206n7
Augustine, Saint 103–4, 111, 115–16, 201–2, 203n38
Aurelius, Marcus 98

Bakhtin, Mikhail 182
Barbin, Herculine 8–9, 159–62, 164–5, 169
Bentham, Jeremy 13
Bersani, Leo 176–7, 189
Binswanger, Ludwig 3–5, 21, 123
Blanchot, Maurice 118–19
body 13, 19, 23–4, 62, 70, 76, 78, 82–3, 109, 113, 115, 152–3, 159–60, 162, 164–7, 171, 179, 181, 188, 191, 193n7, 205n5,
Buddhism 149
Butler, Judith 144, 158

Caesar, Gaius Julius 84
Calcutt, Andrew 1
Camus, Albert 1
Canguihelm, Georges 164,
capitalism 149
Cassian, John 65–6, 88, 97, 196nn24–5
Chevallier, Phillipe 50, 107, 199n29, 201, 203nn38–9
Christianity 7, 65–6, 68, 88, 94, 97–8, 100, 102, 104–19, 200n2, 202n27

Cicero, Marcus, Tullius 3, 6–7, 67, 69–70, 73, 75–6, 81–2, 84, 196n2
De Inventione 75
De Officiis 75
De Oratore 6, 67, 69–70, 73, 76, 84
Philippics 84
Clements, Niki Kasumi 2, 7, 50, 195n9, 196n2, 197n7, 206n5
communism 9, 131, 143, 146, 149–50
communism of the senses 7, 106, 111, 116, 202n19
Communist Party 150, 156
confession 6–9, 14, 19, 43, 85, 87–8, 93, 97, 100, 102, 103–18, 125, 140, 157–60, 186–7, 197n5, 200nn34 and 38, 201, 203nn30 and 32, 205n5
confessor 19, 96–7, 99, 103, 111–13
Connolly, Joy 80, 81
Crary, Jonathan 15–16, 22
Crassus, Lucius Licinius 6, 67, 69, 76–7, 79–82, 84
Cremonesi, Laura 91, 98, 199n28
Cultural Revolution (China) 8, 142–3, 145–50, 154–6
Cynics 94–5, 105, 113, 118–19

Davidson, Arnold 101, 157
democracy 74–5, 84, 95, 100
Democritus 79
Derrida, Jacques 1, 3, 44, 121–3, 140, 193n6, 194n13
Descartes, René 3, 19, 21, 193n1
Detienne, Marcel 72
Diogenes the Cynic 94–6, 199n27
Dionysius the Younger 73, 94
dreams 2–6, 8–9, 11–12, 15–16, 20–30, 33–6, 46, 50–62, 64–5, 70, 83, 122–3, 125–30, 132–40, 188, 193n6, 194nn12–13, 196n25, 204
Dressler, Alex 75

Edelman, Lee 176–7
effeminacy 177–8
Elden, Stuart 91, 194n14, 201n8
Eliot, George 182–4, 190
enjoyment (*jouissance*) 7–8, 69, 78, 80, 82–3, 150, 203n38,
Epictetus 54
Epicureans 87–8, 95, 98–9, 199n33
exagoreusis 7, 88, 97, 103, 105, 115, 202nn21 and 30
exomologesis 7, 103, 105, 107–10, 114–15, 117

Fantham, Elaine 81
feminism 156, 184
Festugière, André-Jean 51–2, 196n20
Firmicus Maternus 61
Fliess, Wilhelm 139, 205n6
Foucault, Michel
  aesthetics of existence (arts of life, *tekhnē tou biou*; see "technologies of the self" below) 5, 11–12, 16–20, 22, 25, 27–8, 104–7, 111, 113, 117–19, 142, 144, 151, 155, 169, 193n10
  alethurgy 11, 29, 31, 43–4, 83, 94
  archeology 7, 101
  bio-politics (bio-power) 13–16, 20, 22–3, 25, 28, 171, 193n4
  care of the self 12, 16–20, 22, 54, 89, 92, 95, 118–19, 151, 194n11
  counter-conduct 22, 105–6, 114–15, 201n9
  discipline 7, 9, 13–16, 20, 22–3, 25, 85, 87, 91, 98, 107–8, 111, 114, 171, 182, 185,
  ethics 2, 5, 7, 11–12, 15–17, 24–5, 65, 69, 85–7, 90–2, 95–6, 98, 100–2, 187–8, 190, 199n19, 200n2,
  genealogy 5, 8–9, 12, 15–16, 27, 31, 43–6, 65–6, 84, 100–2, 103–4, 113, 126, 131, 157–8, 169,
  governmentality 14–15, 23, 49, 96, 101,
  parrhēsia 6–7, 68–71, 73–5, 83–96, 99–102, 112–13, 125, 196nn1–2, 197nn4–5, 198n8, 199, 200
  power, *see below*
  spiritual practices 17–22, 33, 110
  technologies of the self 13–14, 17, 87, 105, 115, 197n7

Foucault, Michel (works)
  The Birth of Biopolitics 14–15
  Birth of the Clinic 159
  The Courage of Truth (Le courage de la vérité) 30, 68, 83, 104–7, 118
  Discipline and Punish 13
  The Government of the Self and Others (course) 6, 70, 74, 83, 99,
  The Government of the Self and Others (projected book) 2, 90
  Herculine Barbin, dite Alexina B. 157–69
  Hermeneutics of the Subject 11, 16–17, 90, 198n8
  History of Sexuality (series) 3, 6, 8–9, 54, 90, 96, 106, 122, 138, 144, 151
  History of Sexuality, Volume 1 (*La Volonté de savoir*) 12, 49, 121, 152, 157–9, 166, 174, 187, 194n15, 197n4, 204n2
  History of Sexuality, Volume 2 (*L'Usage des plaisirs*) 49–50, 70, 89, 139
  History of Sexuality, Volume 3 (*Le Souci de soi*) 49–51, 53, 66, 89, 118
  History of Sexuality, Volume 4 (*Les Aveux de la chair*), 6, 8, 50, 64–6, 96–7, 114, 157
  History of Madness 5, 12, 44
  Lectures on the Will to Know 71
  On the Government of the Living 11, 21, 29, 83, 106–7, 117
  Subjectivity and Truth 3, 5, 11, 17, 30, 54, 66–7
Freud, Sigmund 3–5, 8–10, 14, 51, 54, 57, 83, 121–40, 167–8, 188, 193n6, 194n12, 195n4, 204

Gadamer, Hans-Georg 4–5, 31, 35, 41, 44
Galen 89, 92, 94, 199n26
gay 9, 143, 171–3, 175–7, 181, 185, 188–90
  gay liberation 172, 176, 181
gender 83, 143, 146–7, 150, 155, 161–3, 173–4, 178–9, 182, 206n6,
Gomperz, Theodor 129–31
Gorgias 71, 81
Graeber, David 106, 117
Gros, Frédéric 50, 64, 90–4, 96, 198n6, 199n19

Hadot, Iseltraut 99, 200n38
Hadot, Pierre 199n33, 200nn37–8
Halperin, David 9, 43, 152, 171, 173–5, 177–81, 185–90
Hegel, Georg F. W. 35
Heidegger, Martin 5, 31, 34–5, 37–40, 72, 197n5
hermaphrodite 59, 159, 164–5, 205–6n5, 207n11
homophobia 172–3
homosexuality 56, 144, 150, 172, 174–81, 186, 189
Husserl, Edmund 123

Iling, Sean 1
Iran 110–11
isēgoria (free speech) 74, 93, 95
Isocrates 81

Jocasta 137–8
Jung, Carl 126

Kant, Immanuel 37, 100
kinaidos 178–80
Krauss, Friedrich 51, 132, 134–6, 138, 195n4, 204n4

Lacan, Jacques 4, 121, 167–9
lesbian 173
Levy, Carlos 91
liar's paradox 117–19
liberalism 1, 13–14, 15556, 181–2, 186–7
  neo-liberalism 14, 22–3, 25, 28
Li Yinhe 141–56
Looby, Christopher 180
Lorenzini, Daniele 50, 91, 195n9, 196n1, 197n3, 198n8, 201nn9 and 11
love 10, 27, 52, 54, 115, 135, 139, 146, 162, 168, 177–8, 180–1, 187–90
Lyotard, François 1
Lysias 73

Macrobius 128
Manetho 61
Mankin, David 81
Mao Zedong 143, 147
  Maoist 142–3, 146, 149–50, 154–6
Marx, Karl 83, 107, 124

McCall, Corey 91, 100
McGushin, Edward 91, 93, 193n2, 194n13, 197n4
medicine 159, 164–6, 183, 206n7
Meunier, Bernard 91, 199n28
Michel, Alain 81
Miller, D. A. 9, 171, 173, 177, 182–5, 190
Miller, Paul Allen 6, 50, 61, 92, 106, 118, 123, 186, 198n7, 199nn25 and 27, 200nn1–2, 201, 203n38, 205n4
monasticism (Christian) 7, 12, 18, 88, 94, 96–8, 104–5, 108–9, 114–15, 158, 202nn22 and 27, 203n38
Muckelbauer, John 70
Musonius Rufus 54, 89
mysticism 18, 94, 105–6, 115 119, 202n30

Oedipus 5, 29–30, 125–6, 128, 137–9, 204nn6–7
Oneirokritikon (Oneirokritika) 51–2, 56, 122, 126, 130, 132, 134–6, 139, 195n12
orator 6, 70, 76–84
Orwell, George 141–2

Pacuvius 78–9
Paulinus of Nola 7, 104, 111–18, 201n10, 202n28, 203n38
pederasty 178, 187
Pericles 81
Philodemus 7, 88–9, 91–6, 99–100, 199n24
philosophy 1–2, 6–7, 12, 16–17, 20, 22, 32–4, 53, 67–76, 79–84, 85–8, 91, 93, 95–6, 98–100, 102–6, 117–18, 121, 131, 141, 144, 150, 155, 165–6, 187, 189, 197, 199n25, 202n19
Plato 38–9, 67–75, 79–80, 94
  Apology 31–4, 73
  Gorgias 6, 69–73, 75, 81, 84
  Republic 4–6, 31, 34, 38–47, 72, 155
Platonism 5, 80
Plutarch 54, 94
postmodernism 1, 9, 188
power 72, 75–7, 80, 115, 143–4, 146–9, 151, 177–9, 185, 187
  power and narrative 182–3
  in Foucault 2, 4–5, 7, 9, 11–10, 22–8, 29–30, 43, 49, 70, 85–6, 93, 95–8, 100–2, 103–5, 108–9, 138, 144,

152, 157–9, 166, 169, 187, 193n7, 194nn11 and 15, 195n2, 202n30
Price, Simon 52
psychoanalysis 2, 4–6, 8–9, 51, 105, 121–6, 131–40, 157–9, 166, 168–9, 187–8, 193n6, 204, 205nn1 and 4

queer 9, 97, 144, 152, 171–81, 185–91
Queneau, Raymond 141–2

rhētor 69, 71, 81
rhetoric 4–7, 9, 56, 59, 67–84, 171–2, 175, 177, 180, 183, 186, 196–7, 201nn11 and 15, 203n38
Ricoeur, Paul 119
Rubin, Gayle 144

Sachs, Hans 132
sadomasochism 8, 141–56
same-sex relationships 172, 174, 177–8, 180–1
scientia sexualis 6, 9, 49, 157–9
Sedgwick, Eve 175, 185–6
Seneca 56, 68, 99, 152, 200n38
Senellart, Michel 91, 95 199n28
sex (sexual activity) 6, 8, 9, 49, 52, 57–9, 64, 66, 90, 96–7, 122, 127, 134–41, 152, 157–60, 169, 172, 175, 177, 181, 187–8
sex (versus gender) 49, 59, 160–9, 184, 189, 191, 205n5, 207nn11–12
sexuality 8–10, 14, 49–50, 52–3, 58, 60–1, 65–6, 83, 85, 97, 123, 135, 137, 142–4, 152–3, 157–60, 165–7, 169, 173–4, 177–81, 186–8, 190, 194n12, 195n10, 196n20, 204n13, 205n4
sin 68, 103–5, 107–8, 111, 113–16, 186, 203n32, 205n5
Socrates 6, 30, 32–4, 38–40, 45, 67, 69, 71–3, 75, 81–2, 84, 93–6, 113, 155

sophists 57, 67–8
Sophocles 4–5, 121, 126, 128, 204n7, 205nn15–16
Soranus 54
Stekel, Wilhelm 126, 131–4, 204n12
Stoics 7, 80, 98, 125
subjectivity 8–9, 11–13, 15–24, 27–8, 65–6, 86, 93, 95–8, 100–2, 103, 111, 114, 121, 144, 151, 154, 157, 160, 166, 172, 174–5, 178–9, 188, 194n12, 201n18

Tardieu, Ambroise 160–4, 206nn7 and 9
Tertullian 107–9, 125
Testa, Federico 88, 198, 199n33
Themistocles 81
Thrasymachus 81
Trump, Donald 1–2
truth 1–10, 11–12, 14–15, 17–22, 27–8, 29–47, 49, 51, 58, 61, 64–6, 67–84, 85–7, 90, 92–101, 104–7, 109–11, 113, 117–19, 121–8, 136–8, 140, 157–63, 165–9, 172, 189, 194, 195n2, 197, 198n6, 199n26, 201nn6 and 17, 202n30, 204n7, 207n13,
post-truth 1

varité 167–8, 207n14
verification 3
Vettius Valens 61
Veyne, Paul 6, 55–6, 59, 62, 64, 195nn10–11, 196n20

Wang Xiaobo 143, 156
Whitebrook, Joel 121–2, 204n2
Winkler, John 49, 52, 56, 178
women 56, 58–60, 97, 132, 143–4, 162, 165

Zeitlin, Froma 49

www.ingramcontent.com/pod-product-compliance
Lightning Source LLC
Chambersburg PA
CBHW071830300426
44116CB00009B/1495